ADDITIONAL PRAISE FOR *THE ORANGE CODE*

"ING is committed to constantly innovating the way we interact with our customers. The Orange Code wonderfully combines lessons in entrepreneurship, marketing, and leadership. A must read for everyone who is building a business and has a passion to stay ahead of the competition."
—*Michel Tilmant, CEO ING Group*

"A decade ago, Arkadi Kuhlmann and Bruce Philp started a kind of revolution in the way people think about banks, and now they've conspired to make their process and lessons accessible to all comers. The result is a handy compendium, a kind of handbook for the thoughtful revolutionist. Everyone from CEOs to marketing managers will find themselves scribbling notes in the margins, inspired in their own plotting by what this pair pulled off."
—*Erik Blachford, CEO of TerraPass, Inc., and former CEO of Expedia, Inc.*

"Life's business lessons better explained than I ever could at university."
—*Michiel R. Leenders, Richard Ivey School of Business*

The Orange Code

The Orange Code

How ING Direct Succeeded by Being a Rebel with a Cause

Arkadi Kuhlmann
Bruce Philp

*Tom,
Thank you for all your support and friendship!
Arkadi*

WILEY

John Wiley & Sons, Inc.

Published by John Wiley & Sons, Inc., Hoboken, New Jersey.
Published simultaneously in Canada.

For general information on our other products and services or for technical support, please
contact our Customer Care Department within the United States at (800) 762-2974,
outside the United States at (317) 572-3993 or fax (317) 572-4002.

Wiley also publishes its books in a variety of electronic formats. Some content that appears
in print may not be available in electronic books. For more information about Wiley
products, visit our web site at www.wiley.com.

This book is exclusively the work of the authors. The concepts and opinions expressed
herein originate with the authors, and do not necessarily represent those of ING Group, its
subsidiaries, associated companies, employees, of agents.

Library of Congress Cataloging-in-Publication Data

Kuhlmann, Arkadi
   The orange code : how ING Direct succeeded by being a rebel with a cause / Arkadi
   Kuhlmann and Bruce Philp.
       p.   cm.
   Includes index.
   ISBN 978-0-470-28723-1 (cloth)
       1. ING Direct.   2. Banks and banking—United States.   3. Internet banking—
   United States.   I. Philip, Bruce, 1958-   II. Title.
   HG2613.W724I545   2009
   332.1'202854678—dc22
                                                          2008026311

Printed in the United States of America

10   9   8   7   6   5   4   3   2   1

*This book is dedicated to all the ING Direct Associates
who are on the Orange Journey.*

Contents

Foreword   ix

Acknowledgments   xi

ING Direct Today: The Business Case for
   Being a Rebel with a Cause   xv

Introduction   1

Chapter 1   **The Guy in the Cape**   13
          Leading from the Front

Chapter 2   **Pixie Dust**   31
          Powered by Purpose

Chapter 3   **The Dirty Dozen**   49
          We Could Be Heroes

Chapter 4   **Clicking**   69
          The Conundrum of Advertising

Chapter 5   **You Say You Want a Revolution?**   87
                The Opposite of a Bank

Chapter 6   **Saving the Savers**   105
                Walking the Talk

Chapter 7   **It Takes a Village**   125
                Building the Orange Brand Nation

Chapter 8   **The Money on the Table**   147
                Winning the Battle, Losing the War

Chapter 9   **Steering by the Stars**   167
                Beyond Managing

Chapter 10 **Herding Cats**   185
                How to Snatch Defeat from the Jaws of Victory

Epilogue   **Peeling the Orange**   207
                A Guided Tour of the Orange Code, and
                What It Means to Us

Appendix A: Orange Milestones—An ING Direct Time Line   223
Appendix B: The Voice of Advocacy   235
About the Authors   241
Index   245

Foreword

Many people *talk* about leadership and about starting a business, building a business. These two authors have *demonstrated* all of it. They are proven leaders. They started a business, built it, and changed the whole game of the industry. Now they tell us the secrets of leadership, of starting and building a business, and changing the game.

Arkadi and his colleagues have identified an uncontested space in the marketplace, and their true passion and imagination has changed the financial services industry and, in particular, the consumer market space. As innovators, they set the standards against which others are being compared. The established players were caught unaware, and some of them are now trying to imitate this innovative model. There are important learnings of leadership, inventing a new business model and changing the modus operandi of the industry.

If you want to learn the lessons of these four major areas, this is the book to read. It is clear, it is authentic, and it is real. I personally have known the story of the Orange Code. I have visited the organization and know its leader Arkadi Kuhlmann. He leads from the front, comes to the point quickly, is an enormous energizer, and has incredible judgment in picking people and building teams.

Leadership has many facets. The ones that are especially critical to the Orange Code are commitment to its purpose, challenging the status quo in the industry, and relentless tenacity to pursue that which makes a difference.

Read this book carefully and judge for yourself how you rate in each of the ingredients of ING Direct—which ones appeal to you, and which you need to improve. Use it as a tool for your personal growth as a business leader.

RAM CHARAN

Coauthor of Execution, Confronting Reality,
and The Game-Changer
Dallas, Texas

Acknowledgments

From Arkadi Kuhlmann

There is a place and time for everything, and for this book to come to life now was pure serendipity. The Orange journey that Bruce and I embarked on in 1996 started like many others, yet it was extraordinary in the way it rippled out and the distance it covered. Who would have thought a statement like "What if we started over?" would create new ways to look at retail banking? The individuals who joined the journey and helped build ING Direct to what it is today are a unique and great list of characters and personalities. All are great actors on the stage of life. There is no question that, for me, Hans Verkoren, Dick Harryvan, and Michel Tilmant pulled all the pieces together and kept it going. Their professionalism and courage are seldom seen so clearly in business.

The support and perseverance of directors on the Canada and USA boards provided the glue for the unorthodox brand ideas and their translation among all the stakeholders. Eileen Mercier, Ross Walker, Michael Bell, and Michiel Leenders in Canada and Shannon Fairbanks, Jim Mills, Mike Shannon, and Steve Harlan in the United States have provided me with rubber shoes on a slippery rock.

A great deal of the ING Direct story is found in the passion, hard work, and commitment of the leaders who make it happen every day along with the dedicated associates. Jim Kelly, Rudy Wolfs, Peter Aceto, Brenda Ridout, Mark Kocaurek, John Mason, Deneen Stewart, Steve Stewart, and Brian Myres are but a few with whom I have the privilege to serve. This journey belongs to them.

The deep roots for the results and the success of the ING Direct brand are found at GWP Brand Engineering. Philippe Garneau kept sparking and Bruce, the thinker, provided the fuel. Even when the wind died down at times, the GWP team kept adding more wood to the fire. They kept the brand flame alive. It is remarkable that the thread between GWP and ING Direct is pure gold.

Sam Hiyate, thank you. You will make Bruce a famous writer and me a humble servant of the finer things in life. For Debra Englander and Kelly O'Connor at John Wiley & Sons, I hope to live up to the faith that they placed in this book.

An endeavor such as this Orange journey comes with personal turmoil and sacrifice. For all the times I have been away from family and loved ones, I hope this book will provide inspiration for Eric, Monika, Marcus, and Conrad, my children. Finally, Synthia, my wife, has been steadfast and true. Like the spouses and partners at ING Direct, she understood what ING Direct was all about and helped us get there.

There may be other books written about ING Direct someday, but surely none with more passion, truth, and, above all, love. So, Bruce, there is only one thing left to say: You are a good man.

A.K.

Wilmington, Delaware
June 2008

From Bruce Philp

There are no words to express my gratitude to ING Direct for allowing me to be part of this amazing story. Everyone who has touched this business has helped to write it, from the inspiring Associates who make it real for customers to the intrepid people of ING in Amsterdam, who let it all begin. It would be impossible on this page to thank them all by name, but two cannot go unmentioned here: Jim Kelly, who first discovered GWP Brand Engineering, who guided us and protected us from ourselves as we learned to be a partner to ING Direct, and who kept us going with humor, friendship, and unflagging belief in what we were all trying to do. And my co-author, friend, and hero, Arkadi Kuhlmann. His indispensability to this story is obvious. Less obvious to the reader might be his generosity, his willingness to be vulnerable and candid as we put it all together, his trust in me, and his utter authenticity. If there is anyone about whom it could be written, "None of this would have happened but for . . . ," it would be Arkadi.

My colleagues at GWP Brand Engineering, past and present, have also helped to write this story, from 1996 to today. I have been deeply gratified by their willingness to shed the emotional armor that usually goes with our job and become believers in ING Direct's cause. Again, it's impossible to acknowledge them all here, but a few special ones demand mention: My partner and friend, Philippe Garneau, for his role in the story, his support of this project, and his photographic memory. And Debra and Kristin, for covering for me while I worked on this and for loyally, cheerfully, instantly answering every random, impossible request and question I threw at them.

Our agent, Sam Hiyate of the Rights Factory, did so much more than represent us. He was a mentor to me, the first-time, part-time author, showing me the ropes and freely sharing his wonderfully wise, happy perspective on it all. To our team at John Wiley & Sons, heartfelt thanks for agreeing that this story was worth telling, and especially to Debra Englander and Kelly O'Connor for their patience and professionalism in helping to shape it.

My brilliant wife, Linda Courtemanche, was indispensable. She inspired me to see this story as a documentary adventure, read with sensitivity and insight, and soothed my Celtic soul in moments when

I wondered if I could do it justice. My children, too, were with me always: Lizzie, who has insisted I should write a book since she was six years old, Brendan, who taught me about "the hero's journey," and Rafael, who taught me to swear in Dutch. Your love and humor are the stars I steer by.

B.P.

Creemore, Ontario
June 2008

ING Direct Today

The Business Case for Being a Rebel with a Cause

If ING Direct hadn't succeeded as a business, there would have been nothing to learn from the experience, and this book would not have been worth writing. Here, by the numbers, is why we think it is worth reading.

After success in Canada, ING Bank fsb was chartered in the United States in August 2000, and launched as ING Direct the following month. Despite troubled financial markets and public distrust of dot-coms at the time, ING Direct welcomed its 100,000th customer and its first billion dollars in deposits within six months.

Today, ING Direct is the 21st largest bank in the United States, ranked by deposits.

It's the 10th largest direct mortgage originator in the country.

It's the No. 3 savings bank.

And the No. 1 direct bank.

Of the 9,600 banks operating in the United States today, ING Direct ranks 21st in electronic payment transfer volumes.

ING Direct serves 7 million customers in the United States, located within its actively supported 13 footprint markets and, thanks to the Internet, nationally. It takes care of more than $65 billion of Americans' savings.

Today, 70 percent of Americans recognize the ING Direct brand.

According to independent surveys, it is both the No. 1 most preferred financial services provider in the United States for deposit products and the one with the highest purchase intent among people who are not yet customers. It is also rated as having the highest customer satisfaction in the retail financial services industry.

Yet the cost of acquiring those customers and of keeping them has been amazingly low. ING Direct's marketing spending is far less than that of the country's major banks, and its expense ratio is just over one-fifth of the average for thrift institutions.

It accomplished this in just eight years.

It achieved sustainable profitability in less than two years.

ING Direct employs approximately 2,100 people in the United States, the majority of them in customer service roles. It operates its own call centers in Wilmington, Delaware; St. Cloud, Minnesota; Los Angeles, California; and Seattle, Washington.

Customer service, along with an excellent cup of coffee, is also available at ING Direct cafés in Wilmington, Los Angeles, New York City, Philadelphia, and Chicago.

On an average day . . .

ING Direct Associates will answer 14,789 customer phone calls.

They will welcome 5,192 new customers.

They will serve 2,456 cups of excellent coffee.

Customers will log on to our web site 263,143 times.

Customers will use their Electric Orange accounts to make purchases, get cash, and pay bills 49,642 times.

ING Direct ShareBuilder customers will make 10,419 trades.

ING Direct will receive $47,253,000 in net new deposits.

It will fund $29,670,000 in mortgages.

And it will pay $7,173,000 in interest on its customers' savings.

The reasonable man adapts himself to the world; the unreasonable one persists in trying to adapt the world to himself. Therefore, all progress depends on the unreasonable man.

—George Bernard Shaw

Introduction

It was a near miss that, fittingly, began and ended on Wall Street.

It happened so slowly—it took almost all of the 1990s—that the business world hardly seemed to notice, much less feel compelled to learn anything from it. But it left two unanswered questions so momentous that it might not be an exaggeration to say that the future of free market capitalism turns on them. And it has left much of that business world with its hands clapped on its ears, singing "Happy Days Are Here Again" at the top of its lungs so it doesn't have to pay any attention to these two sullen elephants in the room.

The first question echoes from April 2, 1993, a day that grizzled stock traders remember as "Marlboro Friday." Like most of history's train wrecks, it started innocently enough. Philip Morris, tired of having market share poached by generic cigarette competitors, unleashed its

---

* Throughout this book, coauthors Arkadi Kuhlmann and Bruce Philp will tell the story of ING Direct and provide insights in the first person.

Arkadi writes as ING Direct's founding CEO and the visionary leader who built the enterprise. His words appear in this font.

Bruce Philp writes as a strategic advisor to Arkadi and ING Direct from its beginning, and as an intimate observer of Arkadi's unique leadership philosophy at work. His words appear in this font.

1

nuclear option, cutting the price of Marlboro cigarettes by 20 percent. It would cost the company plenty, management must have reasoned, but it would teach those generics a lesson they would not soon forget. It might have worked; history doesn't record the business results of this tactic as thoroughly as it records its unintended consequences. Because, you see, Philip Morris' share price fell 26 percent immediately afterward, wiping out $10 billion worth of market capitalization, share value it would take the company two years to regain. And the trouble didn't end there. Iconic blue-chip consumer packaged goods companies like Heinz and Coca-Cola and RJR Nabisco saw value evaporate, too—so much so, in fact, that packaged goods companies drove the entire S&P 500 down nearly 2 percent in a single day after the announcement of the price cut. And all of this wreckage was the result of a simple loss of faith: If Marlboro, one of the most famous and studied brands in the history of marketing, couldn't justify a premium price anymore, then perhaps it was a canary in the coal mine, reasoned the ever-wise capital markets. Perhaps every future dollar of profit attributable to brands was at risk. Perhaps consumers just didn't care anymore. And in boardrooms across the world, with management consultants circling outside like jackals anticipating a kill, corporate leaders were asking themselves if they should care about brands, either. For all the millions and billions it takes to build one, what good is a brand?

The second question had its genesis barely three weeks after Marlboro Friday, in one of those ironic coincidences that make history so much fun: The world's first Web browser made its quiet debut, and the Internet age truly began. In short order, of course, it was a gold rush. By the end of the 1990s, the World Wide Web was fully commercialized. It had transformed into a kind of vast, omniscient Yellow Pages, and it was on its way to becoming the mall to end all malls. And building it all were not marketers, or at least not the marketers we'd grown up with. Instead, a new breed of businessperson roamed the earth. Flanked by programmers and more management consultants, they were more than happy to dance on the grave of traditional marketing. Business models were the new black. We don't need to persuade the mice to be captured, they proselytized. We just need a more elaborate trap, and they'll capture themselves. For countless entrepreneurs and investors, that trap was the Internet. Business models could be written in ones and zeros, and live on servers somewhere, printing money. The consumer, meanwhile, would be liberated from the shackles of dumb faith in how they buy things and instead be empowered by information.

Apparently, at least some of them were wrong. With the new millennium just a few months old, Wall Street was in chaos again, catastrophically this time. And the worst casualties were among these new economy start-ups, many of which simply vanished. By 2002, $5 trillion worth of supposed market value had disappeared, leaving recession in its wake. And back in those boardrooms, corporate leaders were asking themselves, what is value? Is sustainable profitability even possible anymore? If the consumer is empowered beyond faith, if business models are fallible, if the almighty Internet can commoditize anything it touches, what is the purpose of enterprise?

With two elephants that big stomping around, it was only a matter of time before they would meet.

The invitation came in the form of a modest letter of introduction, inkjet-printed on plain, gray paper from an office supply store. It was July of 1996 when it landed on my desk. GWP Brand Engineering, the company I'd co-founded with two partners to save branding and "invent what will replace the advertising agency" was about 10 weeks old. We were off to a good start, as these things go, with a blue-chip pedigree and a couple of high-profile clients already on the roster, when ING Direct's dry little note arrived in the mail inviting us to be a candidate in an ad agency search for its "new direct banking venture." We learned later that a number of the firms invited to participate in the search had not even bothered replying to the letter, because they'd never heard of ING Direct (which says something about the industry my partners and I had abandoned and why), but our little company had seized on the newfangled Internet thing pretty early: A 56k-quick search of the nascent World Wide Web, and we were able to verify that ING, at least, was a real, live, legitimate financial services company. Well, it had a web site that said so, anyway. And it was Dutch. Who didn't like the Dutch? So, naturally, we took the meeting.

Some lives changed that afternoon, though you couldn't tell at the time. The meeting went like this:

It was to be an initial get-together, the beginning of a process that we hoped would end with our pitching and winning the account. ING Direct, meanwhile, would decide if it liked the cut of our jib before committing to an invitation to the more formal competition that would follow. We showed up at the address ING Direct had given us, a respectable but anonymous location in downtown Toronto, not *in* but within sight of the smug towers of the city's financial district. So far, so good. Exiting the elevator, we found our way to the office suite and to the first clue that this wasn't going to be business as usual. Therein was a tiny sitting area, grimly furnished with the kind of chairs you'd expect to find in high school vice-principal's office and, where a receptionist might normally be, a telephone and phone list of nine names and extension numbers. Nine. Okay, sure, this was a start-up. But it was also a bank, a bank supposedly financed by a financial services giant. Where were the leather couch and wingback chairs? The Krieghoff paintings? The soapstone sculpture, the neatly fanned out copies of the day's papers, the officious, mahogany-fortified gatekeeper?

Or even a sign?

Undaunted, we dialed Jim Kelly's number, he being the author of the letter that got us here.

"Mr. Kelly? It's Bruce Philp, and I'm here with . . ."

"Yeah, okay." Click.

A minute or two passed, and then Jim shambled into the "reception area" and motioned us to follow him. Okay, we're thinking: No letterhead. No signage. No reception area. And now this man-of-few-words head of marketing, looking altogether too relaxed and unimpressed for the go-go 1990s, never mind the reinvention of banking. We are now officially down the rabbit hole, my partners and I thought. Nor was the office reassuring. It was much larger than nine people could possibly need, which was not surprising in itself. But the absence of furniture and the umbilical cables dangling from the ceiling made the place look, one of my partners observed, like a scene from *Die Hard*. Jim seated us in the little boardroom (at last, familiar territory, even if it, too, was a bit sparse). We busied ourselves hooking up the laptop computer and video projector while he went off in search of his boss, a man named Arkadi Kuhlmann.

I would love to tell you that we connected with these guys the minute we saw them. I would love to tell you that the chemistry was there instantly, and that the air was electric with a sense of impending, epoch-making adventure. But as I rose to begin my presentation, what looked back at me seemed to be two garden-variety executives wearing an all-too-familiar boardroom expression that always reminds me of the one you see on a cat sitting in a litter box.

One of the reasons we reckoned ING Direct was interested in our firm was that we had, in our previous agency lives, some pretty significant and well-regarded bank marketing experience. With this as our platform, our presentation that afternoon centered on the constellation of challenges this ING Direct thing was going to face getting off the ground. There were obvious ones, like the immense advertising budgets of Canada's big financial institutions, the fact that with half of Canadians invested in the booming stock market, a savings account was about the last thing on most people's minds, and how hard it might be to convince people to do business with an invisible bank. But the biggest one, the one we felt was far less obvious (and would therefore make us far more interesting) was the branding challenge. Like most of the world, North Americans, we said, have a love/hate relationship with their banks. As *consumers,* of course, they loathe them. Like most consumers dealing with oligopolies, people feel unimportant to their banks, and perceive these institutions to be arrogant, self-interested, and pretty much all alike. The symptoms of this arrogance are the usual suspects: branch closings, lousy service, arbitrary fees, badly dressed loan officers, little chains on the pens, and so on.

But ignore at your peril, we said, the fact that as *citizens* people feel differently. Big banks make a country matter on the world stage. Successful banks make people feel more secure about the economy they themselves depend on. Many, in fact, though they may not give it much thought, might actually be bank shareholders if they own mutual funds. And banks are very much wrapped up in the history of the nation ING Direct was planning to launch in: They built the railroads, they built the skylines of its cities, and, since the nineteenth century, the opening of a bank branch had signaled the legitimacy of countless rural communities. As a foreign brand, we admonished, ING Direct would do well to avoid attacking the country's financial institutions. Sure, attack their products and the abuses they embody, but institutional bank brands are like your dad: You can criticize him, but heaven help an outsider who tries to do the same. Make no mistake, there is an emotional dimension to the relationship between people and their banks, and it's not a simple one.

We were adamant, therefore, that people would judge the ING Direct concept not just on its merits, but on the apparent motives behind it. When consumers saw what ING Direct had to offer, their first thought wouldn't be about the value of the product; it would be to wonder what ING was up to. This, we said, is the job of your brand. Getting something like this off the ground was not going to be a matter of just selling to people, but of inspiring them: replacing the emotional tie they have to the status quo not with logic, but with a more potent emotion. Our closing flourish: "Don't make becoming an ING Direct customer a negative act of citizenship," we intoned. "Make it a positive act of consumerism."

Projector off, lights on. We expected a perfunctory Q&A from the litter box and then, maybe, to slink off to Starbucks for solace and latte. But no. Turning the lights on didn't mean the meeting was over. It just meant our turn was over.

From the moment Arkadi Kuhlmann opened his mouth, it was clear that he wasn't going to let the big banks off so easily, railroads or no. With the intensity of a campus revolutionary, he began to enumerate the outrages that these government-protected institutions perpetrated on their customers and on the society by whose grace they existed in the first place. With both rhetorical barrels blazing, he cited the paltry interest people got paid on their savings, while banks focused their marketing efforts on selling consumer debt. He railed against the usurious service charges people were forced to pay, the surly attention they received in return from their Soviet-esque bank branches (if the banks deigned to even keep them open), and the similarly totalitarian lack of alternatives. The way things were, he argued, consumerism was not possible. There was a handful of choices, but there was no real choice. The big banks were, by custom, by statute, by their own collective arrogance, all the same.

I girded myself to say something just about then, but without warning Arkadi leapt from his chair and stalked out of the room. My partners and I looked at each other wondering if this pitch was over, while Jim Kelly grinned knowingly and, pretending to look at his notes, said nothing. Seconds later, Arkadi stormed back into the room with a handful of competitive bank brochures and slapped them down on the table the way an angry father might do with the pornography he'd just found under his kid's bed.

"Look at all this fine print," he fumed, fanning the offending brochures out in front of him. "Who do you think they're in it for? You? Me? Their customers?"

We'd known these guys for only about 90 minutes by the time that meeting ended, but it was already clear that there was a lot more going on here than a "new direct banking venture." ING Direct was almost a year away from actually launching in Canada, its pilot market. There was a jungle of regulatory obstacles to overcome, technical pioneering to do, and sweaty debate to be had over its brand and its products and how to spend the precious, limited dollars invested by its parent, but Arkadi Kuhlmann was already trying to save the world.

And there it was: a cause. To Arkadi and Jim and their team, though they might not have used these words exactly at the time, this would be their answer to what enterprise is for. ING Direct was going to play Robin Hood to the big banks and empower the average guy to empower himself. It was on a mission to right a wrong, to make things fair, to advocate for people. This enterprise wanted to be a hero, a rebel with a cause. The direct banking thing was just the how of it. They were, to put it bluntly, going to do things backwards: Instead of inventing the business model and figuring out who it was for later, these guys knew who they were going to stand for months before they fully figured out how they were going to make a business out of it. It was irresistibly crazy. And from where GWP sat, the conventional definition of a brand was going to be inadequate and, frankly, paltry here. The brand they needed wasn't going to be the stooge of some marketing strategy. These guys wanted to start a revolution. Their brand was going to have to be its manifesto, and its constitution.

Crazy as it may have seemed, ING Direct would be in good company, if they could pull it off. When you think about it, the idea of enterprise-as-cause is actually a common denominator for many of the brands we admire most today, and the most successful ones of any era. If we could get Steve Jobs, Phil Knight, Richard Branson, Howard Schultz, and even Walt Disney or Henry Ford in a room, I seriously doubt that any of them would define his enterprise's success merely as the product of a clever business model. Ask Google's founders what propels them, and they probably won't say computing algorithms, not at first. Ask the creators of the MINI or Target or IKEA or Southwest Airlines or Coke or McDonald's, and they probably won't say it's a formula that got them where they are, despite the manifest importance of their systems of operation. We think of these businesses as smart schemes dressed in inspiring rhetoric, and yet closer study suggests the line between the two is not so clear, or so cynical. From the democratization of the automobile to the idea that computers should serve people rather than the other way around, the most successful businesses—not just the ones that made money, but the ones that made a difference—each built themselves around a higher sense of purpose, and then elevated their brand to sit at the right hand of leadership as its spiritual guide.

As answers to those two vexing elephant questions, these ones seem to hold promise, and they seem to be gaining traction in the business world. Look around, and you'll see a quiet convergence under way in which the wall between a company's consumer face and how that company is led and managed is disappearing for more and more of them. In organizations like this, leadership, corporate culture, customer experience, and the brand are blending together into a single, much bigger sense of purpose. And if you look closely at any of these companies, you're likely to see that the key lies in the relationship between its leaders and its brand. These leaders are inseparable from their brands, often create their brands, and sometimes *are* their brands, and they use them to give emotional power to what their organizations do rather than just to sell what they make. They use them the way a nation uses its flag: As something to inspire, to be loyal to, and to constitutionally guide the company's conduct, inside and out. They, the leaders, *use* their brands.

And when they do, everybody seems to win. As instruments of leadership, brands like this make companies stronger. They define, inspire, and help govern the organizations behind them. The people who work in organizations led this way, for their part, seem happier, more excited, and more productive. Meanwhile, from the marketer's point of view, such an approach to leadership keeps companies perpetually distinctive. Competitors can copy a product, after all, but trying to copy a mission simply looks foolish, and few dare. They also bring fantastic resiliency to those businesses, a stockpile of benefit of the doubt that lets a company try new things and even make the occasional mistake without lasting reputational damage. And, finally, for consumers, doing business with companies like this is, in an age of drearily predictable functional competence and browbeating salesmanship, a breath of fresh air: something to believe in and bond with in some small but satisfying way. Instead of the more typical adversarial seller-versus-buyer dynamic that marketing often devolves to, organizations that are led this way become one with their customers, in it together, out for the same thing.

Still, opinions about leadership and branding are like belly buttons these days. Everybody has them, and no two are the same. And neither leadership nor branding is an objective science just yet. Inasmuch as consumers and business leaders alike might agree on *who* today's business superstars are, debate among pundits will always rage about *why*, with history conveniently providing evidence to support almost any point of view you'd care to blog about. And that's what made the ING Direct opportunity so intoxicating and irresistible for all of us in that summer of 1996. This was its seminal moment. It was pure. There was nothing retrofit about it, no revisionist mythmaking, no "yeah, but's," no corporate nanny to take the edges off. There wasn't even a particularly favorable set of market conditions for it, given historically low interest rates and a booming stock market. It was the ultimate test of what we believed then—and with even greater conviction today—to be the noblest purpose for an enterprise: advocacy. And here, on the cusp of a new century, with economic chaos all around us, and seismic changes in media culture happening at the speed of light, we were going to be part of a vast experiment that might categorically prove it.

Which, of course, it did. By any rational measure, and certainly by comparison to the forgotten others who attempted to launch "virtual" banks of their own during those "irrationally exuberant" years, ING Direct made some history. At this writing, it is the continent's largest Internet bank and one of the largest savings banks in America, and it defied expert prediction by becoming profitable within a couple of years of its launch. It also created a product category where none existed before. It is studied at the world's most prestigious business schools, it is a model for what became a global brand with 20 million customers in nine countries, and it is the most successful online banking venture in history. And maybe these things alone make the ING Direct story worth telling. But they are not the only reason we want to tell it.

The Orange Code takes its name from a document that emerged very early in the history of ING Direct, one we'll talk about in depth later in this book. The original Orange Code was created to be a sort of ethical road map, a promise ING Direct made to itself about how it would do business. It has become very influential in this role—every Associate has a personal copy and many could probably recite it from memory—and it has come to reside very close to the soul of the company's culture.

But the Code isn't just important for the job it's meant to do; it has also mattered because it exists at all. Claiming to have a cause is not, by itself, a new idea in leadership or in marketing. Countless organizations have done it as a tactic, but usually rhetorically and without much conviction. ING Direct went two steps further: It attached this internal code of conduct to its mission so that every behavior of every member of its team would serve it every day, not just when it was time to address shareholders or write an ad. And then it made customers complicit in that promise by embedding the spirit of the Orange Code in the ING Direct brand, effectively transforming those customers into watchdogs who would keep the enterprise honest. If that sounds like a familiar formula, you don't need to look far for a role model: A sense of purpose for the common good, a set of rules about how that purpose should be pursued, and public transparency to ensure its integrity—these together resemble a formula for nation-building that most of us would probably agree is the best humanity has so far devised.

Of course, we realize that the idea of a business as a cause, with a brand as its constitution, might seem idealistic and even naive in theory. For ING Direct, being a bank of all things, it was certainly radical and risky besides. Yet here we are, more than a decade into it, and it has worked, and it continues to work, last year, last month, this morning. It is not theoretical anymore, and we think that its story might offer some lessons and some inspiration to a business world that could use a little of both right now.

These are, after all, pretty interesting times for leaders, their organizations, and their brands. You can hardly pick up a trade journal or a business publication, or stroll through your neighborhood bookstore, without seeing someone expounding on the perfect storm in which the marketplace finds itself: here, a cynical consumer whose credulity was squandered by corporate malfeasance and stupid advertising; there, a media industry fighting for its life as audiences shrivel and scatter and become impossible to reach with selling messages; over there, a global economy that threatens to commoditize each and every commercial idea almost as soon as it is hatched; and presiding over it all, a capital market that seems at a loss to figure out what *value* really means. The answers to those elephant questions might seem pretty discouraging. Maybe brands really do not have any power anymore. Maybe the purpose of enterprise really is, as a marketing professor once admonished me, only to make money by whatever legal means it can.

And yet people came to ING Direct. It has been hard to deny, living through this experience, that consumers still want to believe in what they buy, no matter what they tell you over sandwiches and soda in focus groups. It has been hard to deny that employees want their work to matter, to have a good purpose, no matter how grumpy they may seem on Monday mornings. And it has been hard to deny that there is more to enterprise than profit by any means, or that a brand's purpose, far from being diminished by all this consumer empowerment, is higher and more vital than it has ever been. It has been hard to deny these things when they have conspired to build a sustainably prosperous business, and especially when that business is a bank. Few industries suffer from such a deficit of consumer love as banks do; few industries are so systemically cynical. And yet people came.

That is the real reason we thought that this story needed to be told. Because if it can be done in banking, then maybe it can be done in any business.

The Orange Code is the story of ING Direct, told from two perspectives: that of Arkadi Kuhlmann, the visionary firebrand who conceived it and championed it by sheer force of will from day one, and of me, Bruce Philp, the cerebral one, the one who thinks too much, who was privileged to be a trusted adviser and to help give this brand its voice and its place in the world. What we share, besides friendship, is that we both left broken status quos—he, banking, and I, advertising—while we still had faith and energy for the idea that it is possible to prosper by standing for something.

We were not disappointed.

Chapter 1

The Guy in the Cape

Leading from the Front

I only have a quote to share with you today: "Your job as a leader isn't to keep people happy; it is to generate disequilibrium and keep them productively uncomfortable."

—AK, CEO Message #20

BP: Fast-forward eight years from our first meeting in that abandoned office space where ING Direct was born. Arkadi Kuhlmann and I are on a train leaving New York's Penn Station, bound for Wilmington, Delaware, headquarters of ING Direct USA. The Canadian experiment had been a historic success, and he'd been invited to the United States back in 2000 to do it all again, this time in the world's richest and most competitive financial services market. And just four years on, it was already happening, even bigger than the first time. Now, by any measure, he is a player: the CEO of the fourth largest deposit institution in the United States, a high-profile bank executive who made lightning strike twice. In most corporations, he could now write his own ticket. But, as the train clatters its way through the Northeast's gritty heartland, we aren't talking about golf or stock options or career strategies. He is telling me how difficult it is for economically marginal Americans to get a simple bank account. He's fulminating against the predatory lending practices of credit card companies in the United States, and their bait-and-switch marketing tactics. Seemingly with little left to prove, his evangelical fire is undimmed. Arkadi Kuhlmann is still trying to save the world.

In almost three decades of working with organizations to build their brands, I've met a lot of CEOs. They're a different breed, but they're by no means all the same. Some have been bureaucrats and professional managers. These are the bosses whose skill is operating the human machinery of an organization. Some have been technically superior practitioners of whatever it is their organizations sell. These are the bosses whose authority comes from being the best at what they do, and whose leadership is about setting a professional standard. And a few—the best of them, from a branding point of view, at least—have been charismatic leaders: the bosses whose authority comes from an inspiring and genuine sense of purpose, a purpose not served by the status quo as they see it. Where managers want continuous improvement, these leaders want to start over. Where an established order wants to evolve, these leaders want to revolt. They're the leaders who leave the world different than they found it, the ones who permanently change the game.

It's the most dangerous way to lead. A CEO like this is always a target for cynics, outside and inside the organization. A CEO like this has to depend on moral suasion, and not the more common Skinnerian carrot-and-stick approach, to make people show up in the morning and get the job done. And a CEO like this can never afford to have a single inauthentic moment. If they get caught out of character, their authority vanishes instantly. Think *philandering televangelist* or *gambling baseball hero,* and you get the idea of how hard and how fast they can fall. Yet, as thin as the ice of moral leadership always seems to be, it's always these bosses who make history. Whether it's nation building or selling lattes, personal computers, and cheap airline tickets, the chief executives who end up having the most lasting impacts are the ones who were on a mission to make people's lives better by turning the status quo upside down. Sure, they all spend their days in the management trenches as any boss must. But these people, as the Oscar Wilde cliché goes, always seem to be looking at the stars.

The ING Direct story simply couldn't be completely told without an honest look at the motivating role that leadership played. There probably wouldn't be a story at all, to be frank. ING Direct declared itself a rebel with a cause in an era when elaborate business models were more the fashion, when entrepreneurs spent more time with venture capitalists than they did with consumers, and when being clever got more attention than being authentic. Between this and the fact that nobody thought at first that consumers would even want what we had to sell, it was obvious that no mere manager was going to make this idea fly. And certainly the boss's job couldn't just go to the best banker. Bankers were, after all, the enemy. So the job went instead to this animated guy sitting across from me on a southbound commuter train, telling me how Americans prize freedom above all, and that the surest kind of freedom is to have some money of their own, quietly growing in a savings account.

Are success stories like ING Direct just cults of personality? Do stories like this happen only when fate decides to put the right person in the right place at the right time? Those leaders themselves might fear so, at least privately. But I'm not so sure it's just coincidence. Organizations don't decide to start revolutions; people do. And they begin with one person, a leader, someone at once bigger and more human than the cool, pinstriped alter ego they seem to show the world. For more than a decade, I've been in a unique position to both observe Arkadi's leadership firsthand and, just as important, observe the effect of his leadership on the way his organization behaves when he's not in the room. From this vantage point, it's not hard to deconstruct ING Direct's founding leader and find a template that neatly fits the most transformational leaders in modern corporate life, and certainly describes the man who led the charge at ING Direct. From this observation—and a certain amount of interrogation during the writing of this book—it seems to me there are five fundamental things that it takes to be a leader of a company that is a cause. They aren't all from the standard CEO playbook, and they aren't all easy or warm and fuzzy. But they are what it took to bring ING Direct to market and grow it profitably, against all odds.

A Calling

BP: Which of the following corporate vision statements would light you up? Which would make you most want to join the team?

Try this one: "ING Direct is a virtual bank that deploys technology to efficiently deliver retail financial services to its customers and passes the costs saved by that efficiency on to them in the form of superior interest rates without fees or service charges." It's an accurate description of the business model, but did it thrill you? Did it make you want to sign up as an employee, or go online and give ING Direct your nest egg? No, huh?

Then how about this one: "ING Direct wants to lead Americans back to saving."

That statement was seminal for ING Direct. In every sense, it was a spiritual beacon for the enterprise, a strategic true north as they built the bank, from day one to today. And it mattered not just because of the nature of the mission it described—inarguably a worthwhile thing to do—but because it *was* a mission. Inherent in the moment those words were scribbled down on a whiteboard somewhere, a decision was made that the idea behind this bank wasn't just a revolutionary business model, but a business model in the service of a revolution.

The truth is, though, it didn't start out that way—not exactly. During ING Direct's earliest days in Canada, its advocacy for consumers began and ended with its product, a high-interest savings account. In a market where there had never really been consumer choice before and where banks were paying next to nothing on the money savers were salting away, it seemed like enough: empowering choice, and a better product. But Arkadi is not a corner-office CEO. Then as now, he liked to take regular shifts in the ING Direct call center, staying close to the business, serving customers. And they, as it turns out, were the real inspiration. The revolution began not in a boardroom or in some mountaintop epiphany, but at a call center workstation.

AK: It's true—my emotional investment in the ING Direct brand came from working the phones in Canada. That's where I found our true purpose. I got to hear, firsthand, what people were dealing with when it came to their money, and I found myself identifying with that. I got converted by our customers. By the time we went to the United States, I knew what we had to do. Now, it just needed a battle cry: leading Americans back to savings.

In the summer of 2000, we were working on the advertising and marketing for the U.S. launch of ING Direct. Lots of creative ideas swirled around the room and with the advertising agency we were working with in the United States at the time. A number of shirtsleeve working meetings in a hotel conference room saw the discussions going around in circles. I had already drawn the ball icon on a napkin a few weeks earlier, but something was missing. We needed a point of reference. Someone said, "In Canada, we used 'Save your money.' Well, that is what we want Americans to do, too." But how would they see this approach? As preaching? As protesting? If it was really good for American consumers, then we should say it plain and clear. So let's . . . lead Americans back to saving! Right? Yes, they used to save. They were self-reliant. Families stuck together and taught their children about money around the family kitchen table. Okay. We would go after those same sentiments and support them in all our messaging and actions.

It then got really easy. Do good and make saving cool and smart for Americans just like you and me. This was a real democratization of money. And here was the next big thought: "Main Street." Now, I could picture the ideal customer. The story line and the products fit together, aligned to a consumer who had been misled or abandoned by so many financial institutions and now needed a positive message. There would be no bashing, only talk about good and helping everyday people by providing them with what they really needed and wanted—a simple way to make their money work for them.

For me, the day brought closure to the worries about how we would fit into this marketplace and why we should build a new type of bank. If Canadians were subdued in their response to a new approach to everyday banking, Americans would be a lot more vocal and exhibit stronger views. We certainly could not change messaging when so much marketing money would be spent on building a brand. The key was getting the message out and finding new ways to explain the same money values in a way Americans would understand.

Of course it did not stick from day one. There were a few weeks of back-and-forth over this vision. Do we need something better or is there a higher ideal to talk about? And if we were leading Americans back to savings, then how would we help accomplish this? That debate was even tougher. Good service, good prices? Everyone claims this, so we would just not be believable. So, instead, we would simplify. We would make our products simple, allowing customers to save time and money. I really believed that this would challenge us every day to be an enterprise of continuous improvement. It took many weeks to sell this to the staff and embed it into the staff orientation and the sales and service platforms.

Things were taking shape. Each of these steps to organizing the thoughts behind the business gave me energy. I felt that things were clicking, and this confidence was contagious. At times it felt like a party every day. Problems were sorted out, and the tests of will when new people joined us were manageable. I had always wanted to serve and to make a difference. For me, this direction was natural. I wanted to be on the side of the angels and did not worry when I was accused of being Pollyannaish. I felt confident in the vision and the mission, and it fit like a good glove. Another thought stayed with me: If we were to take on the big players in the United States, we needed to be a rebel with a cause—daring, brave—and be willing to gamble everything on it. The brand mission sure had these qualities. The first year was good.

BP: For Arkadi, a calling like "leading Americans back to saving" makes the leader's job description pretty simple.

AK: For a company that is built on a cause, shaped by and with its brand, the leader needs to carry the torch. Our credibility in the marketplace and the confidence of the people we employ can work and be sustained only if the leader can lead a company of people. We too often forget a company is fundamentally a company of people. The passion, the personal sacrifice, the belief that the cause, expressed by a vision, is real and can be actualized must come from the leader. Our personal as well as business experience is such that all people, including consumers, gravitate to a leader who will succeed—one who is on the right path and doing good.

My job is to take uncertainty out of all situations and remove doubt. You will follow someone only if you agree with them and are convinced by them, but most important if your belief is reaffirmed. I know good people can do great things if they can take risks that are worth taking, believing what they're doing is right and that it does good. It's the journey, the battle, that makes us human, but more than that it makes each of us count! I am privileged to serve, to earn my role in this venture and its cause every day. Win or lose, I know we have made a difference. I do not need the speeches, plaques, or awards. I know.

The Guts to Make It Personal

BP: When people judge the leaders of organizations like ING Direct, the difference between a cynical opportunist and the real thing resides in the character the leader came with. Yes, the leader's got to have a calling that motivates the enterprise, but it's just as essential that this calling comes from a real place. Otherwise, the "calling" can seem like a marketing invention, and the boss's moral authority can be pretty fragile and the leader two-dimensional. The boss can't be a creation of the mission or a shill for it; he has to be its author, and who he is as a person has to authenticate it.

Arkadi Kuhlmann probably wasn't born to start a bank, but those who know him well believe he was sure born to start something. His life and career have been a study in the power of positive disruption. ING Direct's chief information officer, Rudy Wolfs, on the team since 1999 and a man Arkadi calls "a true warrior," characterizes his boss as "a consistently optimistic contrarian"—never satisfied, yet never discouraged.

Lightning struck at ING Direct, but it had been looking for a place to land for a long time. Arkadi had been a career-long proponent and pioneer of using technology to reduce the cost of banking since the days of handwritten passbooks. And he has, for as long as anyone who knows him can remember, been a deep believer in the importance of what he used to call a personal "war chest"—a believer, in other words, in the duty everyone has to themselves to have savings. Consumers lit this fire for ING Direct, but the fuel came from a value system. This connection between what people needed and what Arkadi believed in, more than any other factor, defined for him the way he would have to lead ING Direct: It would be evangelical, and it would be from the heart.

AK: If this was the last day of my life, what would I do? I would think about those that I have had the privilege to mentor and coach. What shaped my leadership style? I started as a teacher. At university, I flourished in business school because of the interaction among the analysis, judgment, and people. Developing a business is a challenge of human nature. I have always believed that things get done only because someone wants them to get done. This, to me, was truer in business than anywhere else. As a boy, I delivered newspapers after school. I made money and had to deal with a wide range of good and bad customers. The money went to my mother, but I got something more valuable. The determination to persevere through all weather and obstacles imprinted on me a desire to win. A desire to belong was also a key driver; performance at work would be the ticket to success. With no connections, no legacy, my journey would be that of a typical immigrant: Work hard, promote ideas, and make something happen. For me, this became a way to make a difference.

To stand out, I did it by being creative, hardworking, and, above all, vulnerable in a very personal way. Along the way, as in all personal journeys, I was given a break, a chance by great people who allowed me to learn and to try things. My deep sense of gratitude for those opportunities left me with a great desire to give back. So I think, as a leader, I, in turn a mentor, give people a chance and look for their values and motivations. Giving back is the path to personal fulfillment. As a leader you must know who you are, what you stand for, and what you want to build. Above all, everyone needs to know this, too, consistently and clearly. It's tricky developing a reputation and not falling for your own PR. Only by being honest, vulnerable, and willing to deal with the good and the bad do you have a chance of beating the odds. So, a kid from Toronto ends up building a new bank that can be sustained because a lot of others said, "Yes, we want to be part of this vision. We agree and we are committed." And I simply said, "Let's do it. I will promise you a worthy battle. It will test you, but, most important, you and I together will earn our success."

BP: If there was any doubt about whether the opportunity shaped the leader or vice versa, Arkadi's history is matched by a personal ethos that he wears plainly on his sleeve. ING Direct has its own philosopher king.

AK: There is a lot of searching these days for different ways to look at business: business and the role of art; business as seen through the eyes of sports; business as entertainment! The headlines are everywhere, crowding the stage of everyday news and commentary. Maybe it's to explain the role of business or how it impacts the way people relate to business practices and ideas—what it means to how they see their lives. My view is that values and how they are continually born and reinterpreted are a necessary social function in which business plays a role. Today we are voting as much with our dollars as we are with the ballot box (the democratization of money!). The more things appear transient due to all the change in the world, and the more things are commercialized in everyday life, the more we as consumers yearn for meaning, solid values that reflect who we are and what we stand for. We say, save your money. Be self-reliant. These are watchwords for a stable foundation to manage the ups and downs of everyday life. Where is this going? To me, it means there has to be a spiritual element to what we do. A spiritual approach to business gives it a sense of purpose and stability that cannot be created in any other way. Business is not a religion per se, of course, but it still has to do good. To do good, you have to think of customers and their beliefs. A company with a cause that turns itself into a self-actualizing brand has a spiritual dimension. You can feel it, but you are always one step away from touching it or describing it. It's spiritual.

BP: And it's personal. It seems to me that when a leader is intellectual about his mission, it invites debate. ING Direct's leader made it instead about belief, and that really did make for a lot less doubt.

A Powerful Enemy

BP: There's a picture on the front page of the November 30, 2006, issue of the financial services industry journal *American Banker*. It accompanies an article about the publication's Banker of the Year awards dinner. Arkadi, to his own amazement, has been named Innovator of the Year, and has been invited to the celebratory banquet at New York's posh Pierre Hotel to accept the honor and address his colleagues in the banking business, the very people he's been pillorying since ING Direct's U.S. launch in 2000. The photograph is a posed affair, showing all of the honorees that night sporting forced-looking smiles and resplendent in black tie. Except for Arkadi. His tie is vivid orange. He's in the lion's den, and he knows it. If there were ever a situation in which he might be tempted to take the edge off his rhetoric, this would be it. And if there were ever a situation in which doing so would be a fatal mistake, this, also, would be it. Taking the podium, he says, grinning,

"I do feel honored—and threatened—getting an Innovator of the Year award from the competitors who have dismissed me over the years. Does this make me more likable, or have we risen above the fray?"

American Banker doesn't quote this in its story, instead blandly reporting the part where the CEO of ING Direct later said, "We have a great bunch of people . . . who have shown tremendous faith and signed up to an idea and a plan that looked really shaky, to put it mildly."

I think this is what's called irony.

It's pretty obvious that the ING Direct story wouldn't be the same without an enemy. With no wrong to right, there's no job for a white knight. But the fact of a broken status quo in retail banking does more than create a business opportunity or a strategic convenience. Having someone to blame for a broken status quo also creates a tremendously effective leadership tool. When a brand is a challenger, even an outsider, it doesn't need to think of its competitors in tactical terms anymore. Its competitors become a monolithic enemy, a dragon to be slain. For the people who work at ING Direct, that makes coming to work a bit heroic, and more of an adventure. It's also a critical ingredient in promoting employee loyalty. For most people, it's easy to exchange one job for another; for ING Direct employees, leaving the company would be like walking out of the theater in the middle of an action film. Meanwhile, for the people who market and sell ING Direct's products—including me—having an enemy's image taped to the wall focuses and simplifies the brand's message and offers a sort of compass for product development: If a bank would do it, it might be a bad idea. If a bank wouldn't dream of doing it, you might be onto something.

Less obvious is what having an enemy means to the leader himself. In choosing to lead the pirates rather than the navy, Arkadi has exiled himself from an industry that, for a successful CEO, is filled with plutocratic temptations. When your bank is a cause, nowhere more than at the top is it essential to remember that the status quo has a powerful gravity. Arkadi keeps his edge by constantly being aware of what a fragile target a cause like this is, and how it's not only competitors that might find it threatening. He has been quoted often as saying he feels like he's "leading a Southwest Airlines owned by an American Airlines." It's not comfortable, not for anybody. But there's nothing like it for preventing complacency.

AK: I have three enemies that follow me. Invented or real, the outcome is predictable. First, it's the corporate pragmatists. The money guys are in a sense trying to use me even while I in turn am trying to subvert them. In a way, their interests actually run counter to our cause, our vision to brand a blending of business with social consciousness. The financial services industry is full of traditionalists who say, "We can be innovative and cool. We can be cutting edge." They let money rule in the hopes of fame and good financial payback and they all follow the same pattern and same corporate approach.

Second, it's the Judas factor on the team. There is inevitably a wrong pick or a close, trusted person who has, does, and will betray us. In our "dirty dozen," there has often been one who didn't truly buy into what we were trying to do. I constantly test and watch for the signs that someone could turn, and if it happens, deal with the situation quickly and firmly.

BP: Strong language. But there's no room at ING Direct for doubters, or even for cynics, however benign they might seem to be. It would be devastating to the culture of the company to be seen tolerating someone senior who didn't have unflinching commitment. The whole organization is built on the belief that it's doing something important and good. Someone close to the top and visibly skeptical would make it all seem like a lie. For ING Direct's culture, its motivation, and its competitive energy, that would be shattering.

Still, even when someone has to walk the plank, it doesn't have to be a defeat for the cause. Arkadi sees it as just another chapter in the story.

AK: When you attack the status quo, when you ignore industry norms and conventional wisdom, and when you make yourself vulnerable as a leader, you're going to get stabbed in the back at some point. By definition, you're asking for it. It's inevitable, and you can't let the fear of it isolate you. What matters is not that it happens, but how you deal with it. The key way to deal with betrayal is to leverage it for the vision and the folklore of leadership. It's a trial that you and your team go through together, and it makes you strong. Getting stabbed in the back can be useful if you use it as a lesson in the value of trust and strength of character.

BP: And the third enemy? No surprise here.

AK: It's our competitors. They play hardball, or are just nasty.

BP: Which brings us back to the dining room at The Pierre. Arkadi gives as good as he gets when it comes to competitors, and never hints that the fight is anything but real and personal. The harder they play, the harder he comes out swinging. "The banking industry is a bust," he has said publicly. "The consumer always loses." Against them, Arkadi has a simple strategy.

AK: Stay in the ring with your enemies. There's no option of giving up. You can't back off your position; you can't get soft. You're in for the duration. If you're going to play the rebel card, there's no compromise.

The first rule is to convince them that your views are on the side of the angels and that you are not going away. Psychological pressure is important in waging a competitive battle. Stay objective; never publicly make it personal or single anyone out. Attack what those competitors stand for, but not who they are. The best battles, the ones that bring out the best in people, are the battles over ideas. Being good (which is all too often confused with being right) will prevail. You have to trust that. As the saying goes, the softest pillow is a clear conscience. But the best thing about a clear conscience is that you can win even in defeat. You preserve your moral authority, which is the most valuable asset you have. I believe that's what makes a great leader, and an effective one in leading people into battle.

An Inner Circle

BP: February 2007. Arkadi had just finished speaking to the Delaware State Chamber of Commerce, a home game, so to speak, that had taken months to schedule. A local newspaper, though, described his speech as "worth the wait," as he alternately shocked and charmed the audience, reportedly including eight bankers, with more scathing rhetoric about what's wrong with the banking system and how ING Direct goes about being different. One unusual theme turned up in this particular presentation, though: people. Picking a team, he declared, is one of a leader's most basic responsibilities, and is too important a task to rely on mere formal interviews and tidy curricula vitae (CVs) as the bases for making decisions, apparently, if his demonstrations of palm reading and numerology techniques were any indication. More than skill, he told the audience, motivation and character are the things that separate loyal, enthusiastic workers from paycheck-collecting journeymen. Don't hide behind the safety of a good-looking resume, he said. Hire people who have experienced rejection and have something to prove to the world.

Back at ING Direct, some staffers bristled a little at being described to the world as misfits looking for redemption. But they were selling themselves short. To Arkadi, they were the best because they had heart. Skills are easy. They can be learned if people don't have them already. But drive is in them or it's not. The hunger to be inspired is in them or it's not, and so is the need to make a difference. And nowhere is this more vital than in the people who are closest to the boss: the inner circle. These are the people who make the leader's vision visible and real to the people who touch the customer every day. They translate it into behaviors and processes. They endorse it by example. And they turn it into an unseen hand that guides the daily decisions that any business has to make, even when that business is a rebel with a cause. The inner circle turns one leader into an enterprise-wide force.

As a partner to ING Direct, I've seen the power and importance of this firsthand. Even in a company as high touch as this one is, the CEO is a busy guy. You don't see him often or for long. But you do see the people he has chosen to trust with the vision and, paraphrasing Emerson, you really can know a CEO by the company he keeps. And these people are much more than their resumes. Consider the first voice I heard when our relationship with ING Direct began: Jim Kelly. Spend some time with ING Direct's chief operating officer, and you'll learn two things about how important choosing that inner circle is.

First, for all his brusqueness and irreverence, Jim is plainly an exceptionally intelligent and instinctual manager. In more than a decade, I've rarely seen him hesitate or misstep on a matter of strategy. He's a strong and able leader in his own right, and more than capable of thinking and acting independently. So, when he represents a decision or a request from the top, you simply take it seriously. I've seen many senior and middle managers over the years curry the favor of their teams by presenting themselves as helpless pawns and victims of their masters, making the leader into a kind of common enemy. From people like these, you can only conclude that the boss is fearsome, but not much else. Far, far too many company cultures operate like this. But when someone of Jim's character and quality represents the boss, he also translates, makes operational, and endorses what the boss stands for. An inner circle made of people like this not only extends the will of the leader, it also adds value to it.

The second factor has to do with loyalty. No leader is perfect or omniscient. Every leader has moods and flaws, and the best ones are as emotional and mercurial as they are brilliant. In those imperfect moments, a leader's ability to lead is really in the hands of the inner circle. If a leader has an inner circle composed of people who are indiscrete, or who try to collect social or political capital by presenting themselves as smarter and cooler than the boss, then that leader's humanity becomes a liability. If that goes on long enough, eventually the boss can no longer lead effectively. But if a leader's inner circle gets the vision, if they are able to see the big picture and trust the boss's motives under any circumstances, then this gives the rest of the team confidence. And again, in all those years, through thick and thin, even in the heat of the most vigorous debates about the business, I've never witnessed a disloyal moment from Jim. That kind of respectful loyalty inspires the same. There are people on my team who have hardly been in the same room as Arkadi for five minutes, yet consider themselves loyal soldiers for the ING Direct cause. That's a tribute to the quality of the people he has around him, and to his focus on character and fit as essential companions to the skills that earned them the job. And it's maybe the best example I've seen of this one leadership skill that nobody seems to write books about: achieving genuine loyalty not by creating dependency in your team, but by connecting with them. In other words, it's not enough for you to need each other. You need to understand each other, too.

AK: A calling comes from a personal need for achievement. The motivations can vary, but the need to prove or achieve something is imprinted on one's personality. That's what I look for first. If you have it, you can readily see it in someone else. I think it's an instinct that we subconsciously recognize in one another. The body language changes and the energy level in a conversation goes up when you talk about a worthy vision or a goal. Leaders have always rallied others to join in the hunt. Man has always had a lot to prove, sometimes to others, sometimes to himself, but the best want to leave a mark that says, "We were here and it made a difference." Not everyone runs on this dynamo, but you can't make a lot happen without it.

Rudy Wolfs is a great example of this. When I met him, it was easy to see where he came from and what he wanted. He's resourceful and has a passion for ideas and how things work that's infectious. But what really made him different was that he needed to achieve something. Now, it will take a while to figure that out, but the hunger was clear from day one. That was enough for me. We needed people like Rudy, and he is as solid as they come. Solid, to me, means trust and a confidence that things will get done. It's like in the movies when the captain screams, "Give me all the engine power you have!" Rudy will get the last drop.

Building an inner circle is a matter of collecting characters and personalities. You need color and unique skills to manage the human side of any team. The idea that a pile of resumes makes a team is ineffective and stupid at best. To be clear, this is not politics or sports. It's business, and the stage is everyday life. So everything counts. My inner circle knows that they are there, and that loyalty and trust are not only central, but also the only real payoff for fighting alongside one another. Who are you going to stand with?

The Possibility of Failure

BP: It became known at GWP as The Friday Call. Sometime shortly before 5 PM at least every other Friday, my phone would ring and it would be Jim Kelly, then head of marketing at the fledgling ING Direct in Canada. Sometimes, he'd speak. Other times, he'd just groan. The conversation usually went something like this:

"Hi, Jim. What's up?"

"We are so screwed."

Sigh. "Fine, thanks, Jim. And you?"

"Oh, man . . ." You could almost see him at his desk, his free hand cradling his forehead like a character in an aspirin commercial. "Kuhlmann's on the warpath. (Insert impending and potentially fatal business crisis here.) You've gotta help me think of something, pal, or we're both going to be looking for a job."

It took some getting used to during those hectic first months. The odd bit of furniture at the office got kicked, there was some drywall damage, and telephone handsets never seemed to last as long as the phone company felt they should. But there was a kind of genius in it. The traditional rhythm of business had always been explained by business school professors and management gurus as "Make a plan; deploy the plan; wait for results; rinse and repeat." But this was different. This was happening in real time, every day. There was no "wait." If you felt too safe, even for a second, you would be playing the enemy's game.

If victory is certain, how could a cause be inspiring? If an idea has no mortality of its own, what would there be to fight for? Nothing is more fragile than an unproven idea, and ING Direct has been no different. But what has been different is the deft way that Arkadi's leadership never let anyone forget it completely, even in the moments when we seemed to be winning decisively. It kept our fighting edge, and it still does. As the Orange Code promises, "We will never be finished."

AK: It's true that if you do not move forward, you are sliding backwards. It's psychological. We have had a lot of steady success, but the team doesn't rest. There are stops and mental breaks, but that is all that they can be. If the business needs creative destruction to move forward, then so does the team. Only the best will last. I do create crises to focus on the issue of the day. It's necessary to get the best out of people, and maybe from myself, too.

Of course, there are always pressures to just get things done right and on time. Logistics is a mechanical process, and attention is always focused on markers to gauge the process you're making. Managers hold weekly progress meetings. It's like putting on one shoe after the other: automatic. But a company of people actually has a rhythm like a beating heart that rises and falls and varies its pace. Sensing this, I have always consciously made decisions to slow things down, speed them up, or somehow shift the pace. All human activity understands this concept, pace, yet in management we tend to ignore it and think activity is flatlined like the two-dimensional work calendars we look at every day. Connectedness and relevance come from involvement that is, in its pure form, emotional.

Keeping tension going, whether it's real or artificial, is like being in charge of the music at a party. One instinctively taps to the beat.

We operate on the concept that there can be no downtime, and you have to test everyone, all the time. I am clear that I see things on a number of levels and operate on that basis. It's always a change-up, always disequilibrium. It's positive one day, negative the next. But it's never, never indifferent or gray.

BP: This constant state of impending crisis and creative destruction is not for the faint of heart when it comes to being on a team like Arkadi's. It creates a continuing feeling in the enterprise, somehow, of being potential prey to some outside force. By itself, you'd imagine that this would be a tough corporate culture to have to function in. For some people, it has been. But, as ING Direct gets larger and more successful, it could run the risk of believing its own press. It could run the risk of becoming complacent and thinking that it knows all it needs to know. Its most dangerous predator could become its own corporate ego. Crisis is Arkadi's way of keeping the enterprise small in its own collective mind, as if it were a perpetual start-up that is just relieved and happy its doors are still open. Prey, after all, that doesn't learn to be tuned in to its environment, adaptable, quick, and smart, ends up as dinner. Prey that *is* all of these things stays alive and prospers. Prey feels safe only when it's awake, not when it's complacent. And its humility makes it stronger.

A former employee of mine once complained about ING Direct, "You just never win with these guys!" He doesn't work for us anymore because he never understood that this was exactly the point. If you win, that means the game is over.

One of the reasons you tell a story like this one is that you hope that other companies and managers might learn something from it. When you pioneer something, and you get more right than wrong along the way, you have a sort of moral duty to share what you know. When it comes to the role of leadership, what we know about the ING Direct story is three things: We know that charismatic leadership was a critical factor in its success. We know that the five strategies described in this chapter seem to describe that leadership. And we also know that, at the end of the day, it comes down to how authentic any leadership and its operating style are. This is not some oversimplified alternative playbook for CEOs. It's a reminder that the ones who make a difference operate from personal belief, know who they are, and stay true to both of those things. When your company is a cause, leadership can't be a science.

Back on the train, we're pulling into the station in Wilmington. Arkadi has been quiet for a while, making notes for something that is happening the next day. He doesn't mention what, but it has his full attention. That's how it is when you lead from the front. You see what is next before everybody else does, and you have to be ready. Ordinarily, the top executive of my largest client would expect and be entitled to a nice restaurant meal this evening, to celebrate the day's work. Instead, the CEO of ING Direct drops me off at my hotel and drives himself home. There is still so much work to do. The battle is far, far from over.

Chapter 2

Pixie Dust

Powered by Purpose

A company's brand really belongs to the customer. It is the customer who interprets it, talks about it, and defines it. Marketing can start the process, but like all living things the result is not precise . . . it's how people talk about it and act upon it. The final verdict on a brand is what people say about that brand when the company is not present!

—AK, CEO Message #96

BP: The cat was out of the bag.

In the late summer of 1996, Canada's financial newspapers were featuring headlines about yet another foreign corporation planning to invade a stronghold of domestic commerce. On this theme, emotions were easily stirred in Canada (a country with the same protectionist urges as Australia, but without the convenience of being surrounded by salt water), as one bastion of national identity after another fell to foreign ownership. In doughnut shops across the land, people shook their heads in resignation at the expatriation of everything from lumber to beer. Never mind that there hadn't been a successful large-scale launch of a new bank in that country in decades. Never mind that the category was tightly regulated. Never mind that Canadian banks were largely loathed by their customers

31

when it came to service and value, or that they had, as an industry, among the largest marketing budgets of any, save perhaps for beer, cars, and government. This was a story the press loved to tell again and again; and this time, to keep it interesting, the villain wouldn't be one of the usual suspects from the south or the Far East. It would come from, of all places, the Netherlands. "Dutch financial services giant," said the country's largest business paper ominously, "set to launch direct bank."

At GWP, we were, to tell the truth, a little bit nervous. ING Direct's launch date was still some time off and a bit uncertain. What's more, our competitors didn't know it, but ING Direct was not, in fact, wading ashore with bags of gold to finance a marketing invasion. It was going to be a bit more of a bootstrap thing. Having had some recent experience working closely with a major North American bank, my partners and I knew that the enemy had far, far deeper pockets than we did. And it was pretty obvious that the fear mongering behind those headlines was not entirely ingenuous on the part of the banking establishment. It was also a good way to make regulators jittery, slow us down from behind the scenes, stop us at the beach. You couldn't ignore the fact that these big banks were rich and had powerful friends.

Powerful though banks may be, however, they have a blind spot when it comes to their brands: They don't see any connection between what they do and the people they serve. Scratch a typical bank and you'll find that its real soul, its real sense of purpose, is its operations, not meeting the needs of customers. As often happens with airlines, for example, a bank's customers are all but taken for granted. By comparison with other consumer products businesses, banks don't usually have to fight all that hard to get customers or keep them; far from it, they actually operate as though customers are lucky to be there. All that matters to a bank, what determines profitability and even viability, is the structure and process by which business is transacted, not the people coming through the door with money in their pockets.

Even without ING Direct's imminent debut, it was already clear a revolution was coming in retail banking. It was already clear that the Internet would eventually change things. And, watching the buzz around the Midland Bank's First Direct success in the United Kingdom at the beginning of the 1990s, it was already clear that consumers could be persuaded to do business with a bank that had no branches. The sight of ING Direct's sails on the horizon galvanized all this for the industry in Canada. They woke up, but they didn't quite smell the coffee. True to their process-oriented nature, they leapt to the conclusion that we were going to be a "virtual" bank. They thought this was all about remote access: using ATMs more broadly, banking by phone, maybe even banking on the shiny new World Wide Web. And, naturally, they assumed that "virtual banking" was how we would position ourselves, because that's what *they* would do. So, they set about preempting our virtuality and, we can imagine, dreaming of the windfall profits that the resulting low customer service costs would bring them. They believed that they were fighting for their industry, not fighting for their customers' hearts, so beating ING Direct to the virtual bank punch would be a double win for them.

But it's never a good idea to assume that your enemy thinks the way you do. Down on Queen Street at ING Direct's prelaunch skunk works, being virtual was the last thing on anybody's mind. They were obsessing about, of all things, the consumer—not the sort of thing a bank normally concerns itself with, no. But then this wasn't going to be a normal bank.

AK: If you were to build a new bank, what would it look like? If you could start over, what would you do? From June 1996 to April 1997 we worked this question from a number of angles. In the summer of 1996 no one seriously thought of the Internet. There was no talk about the "new consumer." What we had was the telephone, and call centers were in full swing. The first pitches for telephone banking looked a lot like the last new banking wave—debit cards. Bank branches were more like traditional post offices, with high counters and tellers who were in the throes of changing their titles to "customer service representatives," yes, CSR for short. Debit cards and ATMs were in full swing, too, and the idea of bank kiosks in grocery stores was an ongoing debate in the industry. Call centers were popping up outside the country, too, as banks looked to trends that would help lower costs. The customers would swim in the waves of lowering costs and new ways to reach and do business with the bank, whether they liked it or not.

Well, with banks looking and sounding all the same, we knew we had to create a clear choice and not another bank that is just a little different; not just another alternative, so to speak. A clear choice that a consumer could easily recognize and be motivated by!

The business plan incorporated all the expected functions of a bank. Credit, human resources, finance, operations, and legal, but marketing would be key. The focus was on how important marketing's role was to be. If a "retail was detail" mentality was to take hold, then marketing and its various tasks should be organized differently and work in new ways. Advertising and the brand image would also need to be different from traditional bank thinking—not separate from the business, but an integrated part of it. It was to be an ongoing hard sell to all employees, regulators, and financial journalists who found it hard to believe that a bank could be organized and managed like a retailer. It was also clear to me that marketing would be a core competency that would change the face of the bank to one that customers would recognize and want to do business with. The talent for this marketing would need to be in-house, and we would find new thinkers and unorthodox ideas.

Those initial ideas had to be big and radical for the industry. The core of the concept was savings. Everyone could use savings, and the industry had long forgotten to focus on their value in the consumer's life. Rather than getting people to spend more, the idea would be to get people to save more—to return to the values of thrift, self-reliance, and building a nest egg. So we would start with savings and build a customer base there first. We would build a customer franchise and then work within the resulting financial and operational parameters. That in itself had never been tried before in banking. It put the challenge right up front. Would anybody notice? If savings were a dead issue, as they seemed to be, then the marketing challenge would be steep. Marketing would have to sell the story and convince all stakeholders that this could be more than a pilot and that it could work financially: a leap of faith. It would be one of many leaps of faith for building a new brand, building a new bank.

Classic marketing thinking would say to research your customers. Ask them what they want and study their purchase behavior. The trouble was, this approach has been used time and again. We would do it, too, as a discipline, but we'd remain highly skeptical of the information we got. Information was there for the taking. If this same information was not telling the other banks what to do to win more business, then what was missing? Something impossible? Okay, but everyone has done it the same way with research and testing ideas, so how do we get the insight for new way, a new idea? Doing some consumer research would tell us only so much. Research helps with a product or service details but not on the big picture questions. One thing was clear early on: What banks say in their advertising and what they say in their fine print at the bottom of product pamphlets are quite different, and are viewed with cynicism and not trusted by anyone. One way we could start being new was going to be to find a way to tell the truth and to make consumers believe that this time it would be different. This time, we were on their side.

BP: *Different.*

It's a simple word, used so often when businesses talk about marketing that it hardly gets noticed anymore. It's just assumed. This brand is different from that one, this product is different from that one, our corporate culture is different from theirs. Differentiation is a kind of shibboleth in the world of brands, the answer to a question by which admission is gained to the marketplace. And often—too often, I think—that answer is sought directly from the consumer rather than from the imagination of the entrepreneur. It's as if enterprises think their brands need help from customers to discover how they're unique, and then permission to say so. You can muddle along this way, I suppose, if what you have to sell is whiter socks or a quicker way to dust the dining room table. But, for ING Direct, it wasn't going to be quite that simple. *Different* and *bank* were not two words you had ever heard in the same sentence before now.

For one thing, banking has always had a lot of the characteristics of an oligopoly. There has never been that much consumer choice, at the community level. Consumers, while they don't use the word, know exactly what an oligopoly does. They know that an industry controlled by a few large companies will tend to behave as a herd. If one introduces something new, the others are sure to follow. And this is nowhere truer than in financial services, where the lack of meaningful differences tends to promote profound inertia in consumers' primary banking relationships as a result.

In focus groups we conducted in advance of ING Direct's launch (research is not entirely without its usefulness), consumers would come right out and say things like "They're all the same" or "If another bank offers something new, I'll stay where I am because I know that mine is sure to follow." And if you listened hard, you began to understand that somehow people actually preferred it this way. There was something comforting about your bank being almost like a public utility. That kind of unimaginative, predictable behavior was reassuring in an institution that was standing guard over your money. So they not only expected that their banks would soon match any innovation introduced by a competitor; they kind of hoped for it because it made life simpler. You didn't have to engage in banking as a consumer, apart from the social convention of complaining about banks. You didn't have to shop and discriminate. You could put the whole subject out of your mind and dedicate your attention to something more pressing, like choosing the fragrance that will have the most stupefying effect on the opposite sex.

And there was a thornier reason why consumers couldn't help us differentiate ING Direct: It was going to be something they had never seen before. How can consumers help distinguish this thing if they have nothing to which to compare it directly? They'll default, of course, to banks. And against that paradigm, we'd have a tough job: an unfamiliar brand, no history in the market, no physical presence in the community, no full-service relationship offering, and a lead product that consumers didn't even think they needed. If we were a bank, then all that would differentiate us would be our shortcomings. If we were going to get any traction when we launched, people were going to have to understand instantly what we were one of. It's a natural law of positioning. The problem was, the thing we'd be most naturally compared to would put us at a disadvantage.

"We are not a bank."

Our answer was found in those five innocuous words, a phrase that became a sort of ironic battle cry in the months leading up to the launch of ING Direct, and eventually even found its way into the script of its first television commercial: "We are not a bank." It was a perfect strategic sleight of hand. Being different doesn't have to mean only by comparison to known competitors in order for consumers to understand it. It can also mean being different from an entire category: a paradigm shift. Rather than talk our way around what we lacked as a bank—branches, for example—ING Direct could define itself by proudly declaring it wasn't one. Being different, for ING Direct, would come to mean something much more subversive than the orthodox view of differentiation most marketers have. This brand was not going to sit in the bushes, building a niche business by picking off weak competitors and restless consumers. It was going to run howling straight into the jaws of the status quo and expose it as a broken and unworthy basis for comparison. And by shattering those conventions, it would prosper. That was the idea, anyway. The proof would be in the pudding.

AK: To find these insights, it helped to look at other industries for examples to prove our ideas for a new way to tell the truth in words and in actions—industries where consumers already had a clear-cut choice, and where there were new challengers and traditional players in the industry. Retailing came quickly to mind. Companies like IKEA, Home Depot, Costco, and Canadian Tire are good examples. All are easily recognized and have distinctive brands with lots of business volume, and tight margins. In strategy terms, you can disintermediate a market with better value through lower prices, or you can come in with better value through new, improved products. But if you can do both in some combination, you increase your chances for success. Consumers understand everyday shopping and easily relate to a product or service offer, and they will try new methods of buying and even paying for a purchase. The choices in how and where to buy are also critical. Think of factory outlet malls, shopping centers, convenience stores, door-to-door selling, and TV shopping. We asked ourselves, what then stands out in retailing that we could use for everyday banking?

It was clear that a high-volume, low-margin banking business, with its 1 percent margins, looks a lot like retailing. We would create better value by lowering the costs of operating, paying higher rates, and improving the product to make it easier to use. We would offer lots of convenience in terms of customer access, with a friendly everyday feel. The question was, could a banking transaction be made to feel and work like an everyday retail product? Would anyone notice? Would customers perceive a difference?

We would have to help them perceive it, and that would begin with eliminating some traditional bank barriers. The offer to sell something has to be easily understood and contain no unpleasant surprises. The fine print at the bottom of the flyer or the advertising can't have a lot of typical bank rules and conditions. The attention span for a financial product is very short, and trust is limited. Yet, getting rid of all those bad reaction triggers was not going to be easy. Most were and are cloaked in "that's the way it's done" stuff. However, words like *simple, fast,* and *fair* kept coming to mind. To build credibility with consumers and build our reputation as a new kind of bank that is an advocate for the average consumer, we would have to get off to a good start and consistently tell the same simple story in our advertising and our sales effort. We would have to tell the truth: walk the talk. We'd have to commit ourselves to a direction from which we could not back away. Still, I worried, could this be done for a bank when there is so much cynicism in the market? And, not to be forgotten, could it be done when a bank is a regulated business that has deposit insurance and must follow regulations in all aspects of its business? Money for most people is a very personal antirisk kind of thing. The consumer sees all banks the same, believes that the truth is hard to find, and is slow to act when offered a better deal. Can a new kind of bank really break out, just by not acting like a bank?

BP: If you're a student of strategy, you'll appreciate this pivotal positioning decision—don't dominate the category, subvert it—and agree that it was smart, given the business model ING Direct had to support. But if you were a student of banking, you'd see something even more radical and brave in it: It meant that this banking enterprise was going to be driven not by the operational solutions upon which it would absolutely depend for survival, but by its brand and how it marketed its cause—things banks don't usually need to concern themselves with; things the enemy might be weakest at.

But, of course, you can't subvert just one thing when bringing a rebel bank to market. Every industry has its ecology, its natural laws. Disrupt one element, and your work has only just begun.

AK: The challenge on the IT side was just as daunting. If marketing was the first core competency, then information technology was second. We needed to use it to change and improve the customer experience and standardize the workflow. Productivity demands one-touch and beginning-to-end electronic processing. If a new bank were to act and sound like a retailer, then it would need this core competency in IT. It would need to use technology to standardize, to create easy access, and to provide transparency and information at the fingertips for customers to see and use. In banking, bringing technology to the customer front line was rarely done at all, or done very poorly. To build a brand that depends on marketing and IT as the key drivers was a leap of faith and required investments in what are traditionally viewed as support functions and, above all, not very well understood by bankers in this way. The payoff in business volume or profits was certainly in doubt. As a corporate experiment it looked okay, but for a thriving and sustainable business?

The business plan for ING Direct looked simple and straightforward. The projections were modest but upward trending in all aspects: profitability in three years, and all with old-fashioned savings and mortgage products. The look on a regulator's face could be summed up by the question, "Are you saying a bank that just wants to sell savings accounts and residential mortgages has a chance of succeeding in the marketplace? It will have no fancy financial tricks and no revolutionary products? You have capital, so it is okay if you wish to try it. We (the regulator) are okay with experimentation. Just don't get too big!" The banking regulators were not the only skeptical folks looking at our plans or listening to our story. The analysts covering the ING stock, not to mention the journalists in North America and Europe who cover the financial industry, had their eyebrows raised. They said everything from "It's a good test" to "Good idea but crazy approach"; the best of all was "New banking from the Netherlands has never been done." Mind you, there was some basis for this skepticism in Canada. After all, there had not been a successful, new retail bank launched by anyone in that country in the past 40 years.

BP: If there are deadly sins in business, pride has to be one of the deadliest. This lesson was learned dramatically and publicly by many of the technologically driven new economy start-ups of the past decade. The triumph of revolutionizing a business model creates irresistible temptations for marketers. The geeks who performed the technical feat want the world to bow down before what they have wrought. The marketers who are going to sell it turn cartwheels because they finally have something rationally superior to talk about, a promise made to them in business school but rarely kept in the real world. And the consumers are complicit, in their way: Get them into a focus group to talk about buying travel online, or groceries, or books, and they'll tell you they want to know what's behind the curtain. And companies fall for it. The ghost towns of the dot-com bust are littered with prideful claims of cheaper pricing, or miraculous technological empowerment, or some chimera made up of the two.

Banking was no different. During those years, ING Direct was far from alone in trying to leverage emerging technologies and the newly open-minded consumer to reinvent retail banking. In Canada, it was joined by Citizens Bank, Bank of Montreal's mbanx, and Ubiquity Financial, along with nonbanks like ManuLife and AmEx, who thought a high interest rate was all it took to build a deposit business on the side. In the United States, brands like Netbank, Telebank, Wingspan, Security First Network Bank, and others charged into the retail banking business thinking either like typical bankers—sell the operational solution dressed up as the convenience of online banking—or like typical marketers—sell the superior pricing that low-cost operations provide. Both strategies mostly failed, in some cases spectacularly. Brands like mbanx and Wingspan were quietly folded back into the traditional banks that had whelped them, while many of the others faded either into relative oblivion or into history. (In fact, across North America, it's generally true that the online banks that succeeded are almost all businesses that launched themselves in the wake of ING Direct.)

For ING Direct, the temptation to make the same mistakes was enormous. The savings product really was simple and convenient to use (once you were convinced you needed a savings account, that is). And the interest rate really was shocking, in most cases multiples of what traditional banks were offering on cash deposits. It's hard to hide that light under a bushel, no matter how inspiring the bushel might be. From the day we launched to this very moment, the debate has regularly been replayed with undiminished energy at ING Direct: Why don't we just tell and show people—tell them our rate, and show them how simple it is? The answer isn't always easy to accept for a product manager with quarterly commitments to meet, nor is it always wrong in every circumstance to think that way. But the fact remains that an operational innovation, no matter how beneficial to the consumer, is just code: ones and zeros. It can and will be duplicated. And a high interest rate, if it is presented as your only story, comes with the twin devils that it can be competitively matched and, when that happens, that the consumer will be trained to shop on price alone, ultimately resetting market pricing for everyone. And that, even in banking, is the beginning of the end of profitability.

For ING Direct, avoiding this trap entailed three things:

1. A heroic motive behind the enterprise, one that was about advocacy for the consumers and could inspire them.

2. A constellation of benefits rather than a single easily measurable and comparable one.

3. Just enough logical support in the proposition to make it believable without it being distracting or, worse, diminishing it to mere mechanics.

AK: In September 1997, I sat in the first newspaper interview following our launch in Toronto. ING Direct was four months old, evaluating its first results and getting in stride. The interviewer had read the press release and the story of who ING is and what this new bank, ING Bank of Canada operating as ING Direct, was all about. There was this pause and a moment of disbelief that hung in the air like a question. "So let me get this straight" was the unspoken challenge. "You are really going to start by marketing and selling savings accounts that pay high interest rates. That's it? No other story? Well, it's not the way a bank is built. You want deposits first—high-cost ones, as a matter of fact—and then later you're going to find loans and assets? How will you make money? It has never been tried before. It's not financially sound, but most of all it's not going to be accepted by customers, who want to know who they are banking with and, yes, entrusting their money to!"

As with all new ideas—especially new, rebellious, disruptive business models—the financial, commercial, and economic analysis will go only so far. The real test is customer behavior and the way society evolves to absorb new ideas and products and services, not to mention trends of taste and fashion. What becomes acceptable and, above all, in? To deal with this doubt, our thought was to go big. We would sell our savings offer with conviction, be an advocate on issues that would put us on the side of the customer when it came to values and principles, and align our whole marketing and advertising approach to the customer's point of view of the world: yes, how a customer would see it. Our mantra became "How would we build a bank if we could start over again today?" We would convince everyone to believe. To win in a small way by banking with us, starting with savings—that would be a token of fighting for a customer's right for "sunshine" . . . and it would click.

I smiled across the table with this reporter and said, "Yes, well, I have to admit we have a secret formula. We have this data IT system in a black box and it has a special program that we have developed and it's revolutionary. It cuts our costs more than any other bank can do, so we can offer higher rates and bring customers to do business with us. It's for real. It's a sort of 'pixie dust' that is the magic of the secret formula."

This mystical story was a much more interesting way to talk about our core business drivers—consumer advocacy, marketing, and IT. Beside the simple truth, there has to be a bit of mystery, a bit of the unexplained that makes it real, makes us want to believe. It creates room to imprint our own feelings as a customer into a brand that, in the end, makes it personal.

This reporter understood the pixie dust concept immediately, and conceded that he now knew that people would trust that this new bank would succeed! After all, we had created a belief that it would work and would be a smart move for consumers. So open your Orange Savings Account, we'd say, it's good, safe, and a way for you to beat the market out there. You will get what you deserve. It's for the folks on Main Street, not Wall Street. Everyday people can get value and move ahead. If everyone else in banking caters to customers with lots of money, then our best chance to build this new brand was to be on the side of the little guy and help him win in the everyday battle of living. Who doesn't want to be a smart customer? Who doesn't want to win?

Perception is as important as the reality when it comes to creating value and making a difference in people's lives. It's not that it should be a fantasy—it shouldn't—but I know that customers need a pinch of magic in a new proposition like this. It makes the outcome important and human. They can give themselves emotional permission to believe something that might seem too good to be true, otherwise. We all need some pixie dust in our everyday lives. It keeps our minds open.

Pixie dust is what it takes to make people willing to believe, but how do you know when they're convinced? It's simple: They tell you. Everyone has a different way to describe value, but the most straightforward proof that you have it figured out is when a customer says without thinking, "Thank you—you guys are great." When talking with customers on a telephone it's easy to see what they want. You focus on listening. A simple and easy experience confirms the confidence that the customer wants to have in their new bank, and confidence becomes conviction when they're asked, "So, do you like this ING Direct?" Answer: "Yes, they are great!" When I would ask a customer, "So they are great—why?" what I heard most often expressed in different ways was that we made it easy for them to save! It seems that building a brand is best done on a simple foundation of a concept that customers know is universally true. "Save your money." "Save your time." Our orange ball icon, the handcuffs icon, our color orange, the "guy in the commercials," and, yes, the Orange Savings Account itself are symbols that reinforce the customers' faith. And once they experience all this numerous times with repeat interactions as customers, they add their own stories to the brand.

They say, "They fight for the little guy." "They treat me like a real person." "They try to help me." "They are fun." And the best one of all is "This is my bank." The best place to see this happen in real time has always been in our cafés. Having a cup of coffee, asking a question, working on an e-mail, all could experience "this is my bank" in a simple, personal way. The word of mouth would continue, and it got to be powerful. As in most things dealing with emotions and how we live our daily lives, we are what we buy, and we tell the world this is who we are. Seldom do marketers see it in this context of what a customer is saying about them while they're living the product experience. It never stays constant, and it changes for everyone over time, but it becomes what your brand is. It gets personal. That's how you know.

Some services or products get so rooted and critical to who we are that they become a psychological fixture. We know that money and building a reserve of savings is a deep root that nourishes hope and other values that, for the most part, can't be described in words. As one customer told me when asked why he is saving his money, "It's for my grandson. I want him to have something to help him later for school." In the middle of this family value, and the trust that goes with it, is a powerful idea: We focus most on what we wish and hope for. When we tied together this truth and belief and added a little pixie dust, there was no guessing how far all this could go.

BP: The cold winter of 1996–1997 passed slowly and a bit anxiously for ING Direct and my team at GWP. While ING Direct burned the midnight oil turning its idea into a viable financial institution, we watched as our putative competitors, one by one, took their turns preempting our launch. The Canadian Imperial Bank of Commerce (CIBC) and the Royal Bank announced Internet and telephone banking services with lavish newspaper inserts, while Bank of Montreal launched a flanking brand on the First Direct model, called mbanx, and something calling itself Citizens Bank announced its arrival. In a matter of months, according to industry sources, mbanx alone outspent our planned advertising budget tenfold with a campaign that included bombastic television ads set to a lush remake of Bob Dylan's "The Times They Are A-Changin'." You could almost hear the self-satisfied chuckles from Bay Street in Toronto's financial district as some of the country's oldest, most trusted brands systematically stole our thunder and, as those darned oligopolies will do, commoditized what they believed would be our service offering—a virtual bank.

And if you had any sense, and you were ING Direct, you'd be worried. In fact, with only weeks to go before the scheduled launch in Canada, there were real questions being raised about whether our product was going to be inspiring enough to overcome the tidal wave of competitive pressure. In a memo entitled "Don't Blink," I wrote to Jim Kelly: "If we are going to challenge our assumptions, I believe we should do it because we have new insights, not because we're nervous." His questioning was meant to test our conviction, and we passed. He agreed, and we stayed the course. But we also kept listening for those new insights, just in case, and in doing so began to realize that something amazing was happening. With all of this hype about remote access banking, and so much of it coming from those old, trusted, conservative brands, the idea of banking by phone and online was very quickly becoming normalized and unremarkable before we even signed up our first customer. Our competitors were, in fact, commoditizing the very thing we didn't want to be forced to explain anyway: how it works. They were doing part of our job for us, and taking some of the perceived risk out of our proposition. That left us with just one thing to talk about, the thing they didn't see coming: our cause. In the end, the effort to preempt us produced only one change in our marketing plans: Our proposed slogan, "What if we started over?"—meant to inspire consumers to imagine a new kind of bank built for them—was scrapped. In its place something more modest and profound: a battle cry.

"Save your money."

The first advertising words this brand uttered to consumers when it officially launched in April of 1997 were, "Out here, you have real power. People compete for your business." But when it came to banking, the commercial hinted, that's never been the case. And then, "Our name is ING Direct. We're not a bank. . . . We're something different. A new way to save and borrow money that gives you real power." There wasn't a word about the telephone or the Internet, and just a passing mention of the astounding 4 percent interest rate, as if to simply validate the claim that we were here to give them a choice they had never really had before. We weren't there just to sell; we were there to help. Literally seconds after the first television commercial faded to black, the call center phones lit up, and they stayed that way. It soon became clear that something in that pixie dust had launched the most, and arguably the only, successful venture of its kind up to that time. Our competitors, acting out of fear, had paved the way; we, acting out of consumer advocacy, rolled right in. By the time Arkadi and his team headed south a few years later to take on the United States, this urge to advocate for the consumer had hardened into a crusade.

AK: "Save your money."

Every start-up company thinks about its values and the associated slogan it wants to represent it. Sometimes these get created in a marketing vacuum and just feel like slick ad copy. But a start-up that wants to change the way business works or the way customers buy has an opportunity to do more, to be proactive and leverage its employees' energy and commitment. The character and personality of the start-up team and the free flow of ideas and wishes created our vision authentically, almost organically. That's where these words really came from, as did our vision to "lead Americans back to saving," and indeed the Orange Code itself. Everyone could relate and test their own beliefs about what the business could achieve commercially in light of this idea. If all else failed, we would know that at least we did the right thing. New employee orientation classes, typically held on Monday mornings in Wilmington, would see 30 fresh faces, and the big, first question for them was "Why are you here?" This was the answer. We wanted them to feel it, to be emotionally committed. Doing this work has to matter. It must make a difference

BP: The pixie dust in ING Direct, you see, was never in how they did it. It was in *why* they did it. A heroic idea like this needs little explanation, once

people understand its purpose. Nobody ever stops to ask how Superman can fly, or where Batman gets all those gadgets. People don't question how you can be faster than a speeding bullet or able to leap tall buildings in a single bound when it's themselves you're rescuing. The pixie dust was our cause. It made ING Direct almost a category of one, highly resistant if not impervious to competitive assault. And it gave our product a context it could breathe in, one that would not just profitably attract customers. It would create believers.

ING Direct's Secret Formula for a Powerful Purpose

BP: ING Direct's pixie dust was its sense of purpose, its cause. The enterprise organized itself around consumer advocacy rather than a business model, and that has been critical to its success. But doesn't that sound a lot like a corporate mission statement, and don't lots of companies— even unsuccessful ones—have one of those?

The corporate mission statement is one of those things that went out of fashion too soon and for the wrong reasons. For a few years there, under the guidance of well-meaning consultants and B-level executives, squads of senior managers in companies around the world were whisked off to golf resorts, there to politely collaborate on writing a company mission statement everyone could agree on. These exercises became bonding experiences, the fruits of which were usually engraved on a plaque and hung in the reception area at the head office. They may have succeeded as bonding experiences, but they all too often failed at giving a company a real sense of purpose. It's hard to get adrenalized by a multiparagraph puddle of ambiguity, diluted by consensus until it is odorless, flavorless, and utterly unthreatening to the status quo. It's a bad sign when, at the end of the corporate retreat, handing out the Most Honest Golfer award elicits more applause than the declared purpose of the organization does.

And yet a mission—a cause—is one of the most effective leadership tools humans have ever devised. Groups with clear causes practically self-organize. They organically attract the right kinds of people and turn them into teams. They produce a more empowered employee who knows what's right, even without a policies and procedures manual. They naturally produce compelling and profitable brands, and direct the way companies behave in the marketplace so that everything is magnetically consistent. A team with a purpose is infinitely more formidable than a team with a process.

As an example, consider a particularly impressive statement of purpose millions are familiar with: The Declaration of Independence. That document, in its rational essence, is a list of social problems demanding solutions. But those problems and solutions aren't the heart of the document, or even all that relevant anymore. They're just the proof that the document was necessary. The heart is at the beginning of the second paragraph: "We hold these truths to be self-evident, that all men are created equal, that they are endowed by their Creator with certain unalienable Rights, that among these are Life, Liberty, and the pursuit of Happiness." The specific problems that spawned the American Revolution are essentially history now, and yet this core idea endures. The nation's purpose—to promote and defend life, liberty, and the pursuit of happiness for its citizens—is as relevant and inspiring as ever and, more important, continues to influence both the way the nation is governed and the expectations of its citizens. It's doubtful we could say this if the document had instead declared itself committed to a "fully integrated, customer-centric, end-to-end democracy solution."

Here's ING Direct's five-point formula for an enduring mission statement that makes things happen:

1. **Advocate for somebody.** Mission statements about how an organization works produce bureaucracies. Mission statements about those served by an organization produce armies.
2. **Make it next to impossible.** It's highly unlikely that the United States will ever believe it can stop standing guard over its liberty. It is equally unlikely that ING Direct will turn everyone on Earth into a saver anytime soon. It's the journey that inspires, and the horizon should always be just out of reach.
3. **Make it poetry.** Nobody talks about the wordcraft of a mission statement, but it matters. The great mission statements are music to hear and read, sticky, and difficult to walk away from. If it sounds like the instruction manual that came with your DVD player, keep working on it. And poetic doesn't just mean pretty; it also means pure and unnervingly simple. Arkadi calls this Kuhlmann's Law of Brand Value, and it applies just as much to the things we say to ourselves as

to the things we say to our customers: "The resistance to a brand message is directly proportional to the number of identifiable thoughts contained therein." Sound bites, he says, travel further and faster than lawyerly prose.

4. **Write it for you.** Of course, a company's purpose is something it should not fear having overheard by shareholders, the media, or consumers. But to include every stakeholder in the audience for your statement of purpose is to guarantee that your statement will devolve into being some sort of aspirational mirage. "We will be . . ."—that sort of thing. But if you write it just for the people who show up for work every day, you get the powerful advantage of making it into a command, a battle cry, a predicate instead of a subject. Instead of inviting them to be something, it can dare them to *do* something.

5. **Bring it down from the mountain.** Declaring a company's purpose is a leadership responsibility. Period. Collaborating on it or, worse, delegating it produces a perfect little storm of negative consequences for leadership: It shows weakness; leaders are supposed to be strong and to have ideas that foot soldiers don't. It invites a consensus process; a team will create what it can agree on, not what will challenge it. And it diminishes the importance of having a mission at all. Show us a leader who magnanimously gave rank-and-file managers the job of writing a mission statement, and we'll show you a dusty plaque in the reception area.

Chapter 3

The Dirty Dozen

We Could Be Heroes

Many people are sent to us; they are gifts in life's journey. Most of the time we don't want to see it. We want to be the one giving. But there are special people you work with if you look for them. The sign of a powerful manager is one who celebrates the nature of these gifts.

—AK, CEO Message # 101

BP: Akira Kurosawa doesn't come up often in business writing. I know. I checked.

But maybe he should. In the ING Direct story, at least, the iconic director of *Seven Samurai* has an influence that he could never have imagined. Why? Because that 1954 movie spawned a genre of films in which stories involve unlikely teams being assembled, and then achieving impossible things. From *The Dirty Dozen* and *The Guns of Navarone* to *Ocean's Eleven* and *The Italian Job,* stories like this portray a romantic and inspiring alternative to the industrial age management philosophy in which a fancy plan, technical competence, and blind obedience are what it takes to make an effective team. And we never tire of this heroic idea. Everybody who works for anybody clings to it. Who doesn't want to be part of a winning team without having to lose themselves in it?

Who doesn't want to believe that winning, rather than demanding the subordination of one's individuality, would be impossible without it? Certainly not the cast of the caper movie that is ING Direct.

"Casting" is exactly the right way to describe the building of the ING Direct team, and the process began with its very first employee. Arkadi Kuhlmann himself had been a dark-horse candidate for the job of founding CEO. The executive recruiters that had been retained to find employee number one had almost not presented Arkadi at all and, when they did, he had been offered as an unconventional alternative to an otherwise blandly competent and conventional talent pool: a maverick, notwithstanding his solid resume; a guy who might be tough to manage, but might also make magic. Hans Verkoren, executive sponsor of the ING Direct project at ING Group in Amsterdam, had been curious enough to meet this maverick and then had guts enough to hire him, Verkoren himself being an entrepreneur at heart. With a start like that, ING Direct was bound to be anything but a bank, and Arkadi was certainly not going to settle for a team of off-the-rack bankers.

AK: I've always believed a leader's first job is to remove doubt from any situation. His second is to pick the right team. That first job takes talent, but the second is art.

The movie *The Dirty Dozen*, with Lee Marvin, brings clear images to mind that are classical: a big objective, dangerous and calling for something unusual and outside the normal course of operation, and the Dirty Dozen, all prisoners and unusual types, coming together to win against impossible odds. Now, ING Direct is not World War II, and "leading Americans back to savings" is not taking out the enemy's command headquarters. But it comes close. There are many ways to describe missions and the people who make them up, and it takes the right leadership to suit each mission. For our mission, the recruitment and the leadership style are best thought of as a posse. In fact, early on, the leadership was called "The Canadian Posse," but this term became divisive and started to hurt more than it helped. It wouldn't have been smart to keep an inner and outer circle going at the same time, isolating ourselves too much from our corporate parent. The mission and the number of people involved eventually got way too big, and we couldn't act as if we were totally on our own. In the United States alone, at this writing, ING Direct is 2,000 strong and counting. Still, the Dirty Dozen folklore remains, and riding my

Harley on our ING Direct Independence Rides only keeps the image alive and makes everyone else wonder: Can a bank, especially a big bank, really be run like a posse and led by a motorcycle-riding guy like me? For real?

Why do I think of this as a posse? Maybe it's the way we came together. Different types of people have always come in and out of my journey at work. Some have been students, some neighbors, some friends of friends. I would meet them at a car dealership, a shop, or an airport, and the question would be, who are you and what are you up to? Maybe it was my intense look, but usually we would be in a counseling session within the hour. Next step: Why not take a shot and join me on this next adventure? I can't promise you much, but it's a ride worth taking, and besides, what have you got to lose? For me, ours was a collection of talents that were not the normal kind you pull out of a resume folder. Maybe we attract people who are like us or maybe we look for differences. I have always gravitated to who's different, maybe because everyone always treated me as the outsider. That point of view came naturally to me. The start for any journey was the collection of talents and personalities that would make it click.

My own view has always been that real heart and commitment only come from someone who has tasted failure and injustice. Life is not a straight line. So, if you're to motivate someone and make a success out of an audacious goal, to realize a bold vision, well, then, you have to work with raw talent that has something to prove. If you have someone who was blessed with a great resume, good looks, a good upbringing, and an established family, what is the best you can hope for? Often, people who haven't fought for their success only need to preserve what they've got. My experience said, for a lot of people to whom things have come easily, you can only help them maintain their stature and career path. That's not even close to the motivation opportunity of giving someone who is down a chance to prove to himself and to the world that he can be a success and wants it really badly. The stakes are higher. "Fail me this time and I will kill you" is the deal, so to speak. This comment always got a smile and a handshake that was clearly understood.

Writing about the team is difficult to do, because most of us are still riding on this ING Direct journey. It's hard not to love them for their loyalty, talents, and strengths. To work with them is energizing, challenging, and sometimes downright ugly. A posse, by definition, is bit like a floating raft. It's hard to steer and it's never pretty. I got and continue to get lots of distracting chatter about this and that along the way, but forcing order and logic is a bit like throwing more wood on a fire. It might burn brighter for a while but it won't get you anywhere. So I work hard to earn my role with the team. I take nothing for granted and on a regular basis bring up the subject of leadership. "Am I doing a good job in representing you?" "Here's where we are going and I want you in on this." It's not to say every decision is made with a town hall debate and a vote. It's not. But it's good to have it out there.

BP: As Arkadi points out, a team like this can't be a democracy. Consensus management isn't very compatible with a young organization on a mission. And yet, he argues, you can't have an organization with any real strength or drive if you populate it with conventional people who will just do as they're told. In building a core ING Direct team, that meant searching for a combination of the two qualities that could reconcile the dilemma: a strong-minded internal sense of purpose, and a genuine belief in what ING Direct was trying to do. For Arkadi, that made every new member of the team a real discovery, and not just one less empty box on the org chart.

So, who were the Dirty Dozen? Well, to all outward appearances, they weren't Lee Marvin's ragtag collection of antiheros. In fact, they looked very much like financial, operations, and marketing professionals. Fortunately, employee number one could see past all that.

AK: Who do you pick for a job and what role should they play? It is easy to sort through data and practically decide what is needed in terms of skills and experience. Somehow, though, this does not get you beyond good. We see this often in sports teams, where the supposed talent and the resulting score just do not match up. Why? There is chemistry, an interaction of sorts that makes a team as unique as an individual. Seeing this and making it happen is important. Successful ventures get this right.

In June of 1996, in walks Johanne Brossard. I had known her from Guardian Trust, a firm that sold foreign currencies and precious metals and a competitor to Deak International, where I had previously worked. She was petite, dark-haired, and very French-Canadian: straightforward, energetic, and emotional. You just knew she was an operator, the person who could make the machinery work. You sensed that she was dependable, worked on principle, and would fight for what was right. She would get commitment, loyalty, and results mixed up at times, but who didn't? She was a great fit, but she had to be convinced to join. After asking a lot of questions (and often looking skeptical), she finally said, "I'll give it a try." Always quick with decisions, I knew she was already on board. Johanne worried a lot. Maybe she did the worrying for all of us. That seemed to be her role. Intensely private, she was honest and true. We could see ourselves in the way she thought about right and wrong, and understood the constant temptation to "give it up because of the craziness."

Not far behind was Jim Kelly, or more precisely James John Kelly. Outgoing, friendly, and gregarious, Jim understood family, loved people, and was a troublemaker. He was the type that created bedlam, but you knew he was just mischievous. He never made a big deal of joining the posse; he just showed up and rode. With the corporate guys, he tried to put on that manager-style stuff. It was okay, but if you knew him you had to bite your tongue to stop from laughing. He is a character, and those of us who have the pleasure to ride with him know that it's a privilege. Street-smart Jim loved to beat the competition and had lots of passion for the business. He lived the vision to its very core. Having worked with me at North American Trust in product development and marketing with small banks and trust companies, he had seen all aspects of the financial services world. Jim knew how to make a buck. His straightforward approach made you think and challenged you, but we had confidence in his passion and his ideas. You always felt that his Irish eyes had a twinkle that said he knew something you didn't. But that was okay. He was in the posse. Jim would take our success in stride and agonize over any small setback. He loved the fight and held little back. In any debate he was near the center of the flame.

BP: Arkadi's description of Jim Kelly is apt, but it doesn't tell the whole story. Jim's presence on this team is testimony to Arkadi's ability to cast. Whatever his various formal roles in the company have been and whatever his own formidable skills, Jim has always been in some sense Arkadi's most trusted lieutenant. Look again at Arkadi's description: Jim brings humor to Arkadi's intensity, common sense to his visionary zeal, measuredness to his passion. To ride beside him, Arkadi didn't choose a copy of himself, but a counterweight: yin to his yang.

AK: Tall and straight, Peter Aceto is our boy wonder. A Canadian pickup hockey player, on a pair of skates he looks the part. It's hard not to like Peter. I met him through a crazy set of circumstances that started with a broken Porsche and ended up at Engineered Automotive, a high-end performance car tuning shop owned by a mutual friend. Peter was a graduate law student looking to get his teeth into something with more meaning than racking up billable hours at a Bay Street legal firm. He started with us as general counsel at ING Direct Canada and learned and studied and was a dedicated apprentice. One always knew that Peter could be counted on.

When we moved to the United States, Peter wanted to come, but having a U.S. passport was not enough. We needed local legal talent, which we would find in Deneen Stewart, another out-of-the-box choice that paid off hugely for ING Direct. Undeterred, Peter eventually showed up in Wilmington, having resigned his position with ING Direct in Canada, and said he wanted a job. Well, it was not your typical corporate move, but Peter wanted to be with the posse and make things happen. Canada was going into maintenance mode, but we were just getting started in the United States. I had taken some of my original team with me. Of the posse members left behind, a few stayed and the rest left. Peter moved to Wilmington and started in credit, determined to work his way up. Wherever Peter was, the focus was business and he operated as a natural facilitator. Lots of associates like to follow Peter because you get what you see—a rare quality in the corporate world, and one that would result in Peter being a pillar of this team. Like many of us, Peter became a husband and a dad while we were on this journey. We attended Peter's wedding, and he is now a proud father of three, building his future while he helps us build ours.

It seemed like we all got married, had children, and moved around in those first years. There never was any shortage of excitement and challenge, even on the personal side. Deneen got married while with us, and looked very happy. Jim got married and adopted two great boys. He does look more tired these days! I got married, too, and was blessed with more children, this time two boys. It was a time of beginnings!

Rudy Wolfs has a list of interests that includes cars, boats, and planes—strange for a tech guy running the CIO function for a bank. You'd think he would be playing PlayStation 3. There isn't a hobby that he won't try or take a shot at. He started in the painting business with his father and brothers but soon got into data processing. An entrepreneur, he had experienced all the knocks of running a business day to day. Rudy, more than anything, is helpful and logical. He solves problems and doesn't play politics. I think that a key thread that runs through the posse is a "get it done and get it right" attitude, and Rudy personifies this. Rudy started in a consulting role with us in Wilmington, but it never felt like that. He was on the team and everyone trusted his commitment and talents. He prefers variety, does not like to be pinned down, and is up for anything. You sense that he likes to live life large and make some money along the way. Longtime married with the greatest gal around, Veronica, he has three girls who will try any one of his hobby ideas. One thing is for sure: Like the rest of the posse, he will only work for a good cause and stay as long as it's getting done right. Holding a tight rein on this posse does not work. Few see and understand this dimension of our Orange culture, but it's all part of being in the posse.

Hudson White was a student of mine at the Thunderbird School of Global Management in Phoenix. A true Texan, he was larger than life and an all-around good guy. Not unusual in the posse, he also knew where he came from and where he belonged. But he was on his journey to see and conquer the world. Yes, he got married, too, and had two girls. Straight-shooting Hudson added lots of color to our buildup in Wilmington. He had worked with me in Toronto at North American Trust and then tried a few other things, looking for a place that suited him. His faith, family, and passions were straightforward. He also likes to hunt, and his time in the Guard only deepened his conservative values and upbringing. When he joined the posse in 2000, he said, "I'll take whatever role you need me for." Well, we needed a CFO and Hudson stepped up to the task. He really wanted to lead, maybe needed something to lead, since it was in his character and in his blood to be on the front line. His time with the posse would end, and a few years ago he struck out on his own, going home to Texas and into water, oil, and—what else?—banking. He is too creative to get the Orange off his sleeves, though. I think he'll be back with the posse again one day.

As time passed and we grew, more joined the ride.

There is Marie Rueda, our current CFO, with a smile that would melt any difficult moment. Tough and resourceful, she, too, can get it done. Relatively new to the bank, she is earning her place with quiet, consistent work. Marie is married to a Parisian film producer, and you just know there is more going on than meets the eye. John Mason, our treasurer, hangs out in Wilmington but has a home in Ohio. John just knows his stuff. As a finance guy, it's amazing that he thinks finance but works commercial, a rare combination. John is liked by all and inspires a lot of confidence in the team.

In marketing, it's John Owens and Todd Sandler. With classical marketing training, they have earned their place here and are anxious to carry our brand torch. It's a huge challenge that gets bigger by the day, and they continue to fight the setbacks that go with tough competition. Then there is Kjel Hegstad, who works with Jurie Pieterse, our resourceful South African Web guy. He's mainstream, but in the Web world, working to pull us up by our bootstraps. Kjel joined us, left us for a while, and now is back. He's half tech guy, half start-up guy, and now on the "I want to build something good" kick. He finds it hard to wear socks and loves to ride a Harley. Kjel is going to kill the Web challenge for us.

John Bone, who also served as CFO, used to hold court as our wise voice of experience. His desk was covered with the papers he could not get in his briefcase and the ones he did not want to read. John walked his own path in many ways. When was court in session? It just happened between 5 and 8 PM when all were going home unless John said, "How are things?" or you stopped by his desk to ask a question. Before you knew it he was your sounding board and you were explaining your line of thinking about some issue of the day. John offered common sense and a lifetime of experience, and wisdom was served up generously. It was good stuff, and everyone loved John for it.

No story about the posse would work without Brian Myres. To us, he is known as Mr. St. Cloud. A great outdoorsman, Brian makes our brand fly in Minnesota. Operations and call volumes, all banging on the door in St. Cloud, are managed by Brian. It's his court and he runs it clean. Brian came from a community bank, and odds were that he could not operate this new type of bank, but he carries the torch and sets the pace. There are many of us who feel that Brian is covering our flank.

The leadership team counts 24, and it's a good team. Overall, I would say the posse is about 30 strong. It's loose and in different places, but I have a clear connection with each and every one of them. It's important to see how the posse evolves and changes and influences what ING Direct is. Guided by our Orange Code, these personalities make an impact that far outstrips their formal job responsibilities. This is why my partnership with Rick Perles, who heads up human resources, is so vital to us. He is very clear on who is committed and who is not. A commuter from Pennsylvania, Rick works the short tactics with personnel issues. Acting more like a sales guy, Rick makes moves that always consider our cause first. He is as much a manager of our brand as anyone here.

Without support from its community, a posse is just a bunch of outlaws. It's important to acknowledge here that this posse had support where we needed it. A year into the ING Direct project, my monthly trips to Amsterdam had fallen into place as a predictable routine. Then, ING Group made a significant acquisition in Belgium, and along with it came Michel Tilmant, CEO and later the vice chairman of ING Group. His duties were Europe and banking, all very corporate except that when you met the man the conversation became very classical. He does pride himself on being a good banker and, above all, a gentleman. He loves a cigar and genuinely likes people. You can talk to the man. This aspect of his character was so important to our story because he listened and saw the potential in the ING Direct idea. He knew that growth for ING Group required new directions, and he backed our fledgling ING Direct project. More important, he has consistently supported the building of the business for the past 11 years. In corporate terms, that's unusual.

While the building of ING Direct always served a corporate reality at the ING Group level, it had its challenges and, as Michel often remarked, "You need the capital and the protection of a large group to get to meaningful size." When Michel became the chairman in 2004, he did not abandon the project; he continued to promote it, although at times it felt like the expectations attached to that commitment were pushing us out onto a ledge. He and Cees Maas, the CFO there at the time, sold the story to the investors and analysts who study and follow ING. This in turn helped slowly turn ING Group to a more retail focus worldwide, and the business of ING Direct and the cachet of the brand did its part to help in this, returning the favor.

Maybe the best way to think about the posse and our brand is that everyone plays his or her specific role with the common vision of "leading Americans back to savings" firmly in mind. It's about the cause, not about rules or structures. It's the open floors, the lack of titles, the understanding and importance of our message to the marketplace. Certainly, neither money nor work itself would move things forward in this way unless the mission was huge and mattered. When I do town hall meetings, CEO messages, CEO Corner e-mails, job swaps, and Saving Summits, or connect with associates and customers, who we are and how we work together is noticeable. It's in the air.

BP: Now, hearing Arkadi talk about his unique art of team building and looking back at how we've worked together, it's pretty clear that my team at GWP were riding along with the Dirty Dozen from the start whether we realized it or not. It couldn't have been any other way. This thing we called ING Direct's brand, the thing that we were there to help them create, was really the flag for their revolution. There to help them bring the cause to life, we had to be more than a competent, obedient supplier. We couldn't be just a sushi-munching, black-turtleneck-wearing bunch of mercenary esthetes hired to exchange creativity for cash. We, too, had to be independent-minded and be believers. And we, too, had to be restless antiheros with something to prove.

AK: Some companies are like families, led by leaders who act as parents. Some companies are like armies, led by generals. Some are like teams, led by coaches. GWP has always been more like a rock band, led by whoever is writing the songs. For much of the time we've worked with them, the strategy guy was usually Bruce. And he had a cause of his own. By the time he and his partners started GWP Brand Engineering in 1996, Bruce had decided that marketers and their ad agencies were in a dangerous state of denial about the changing consumer and the media revolution that was happening around them. They founded GWP Brand Engineering to wake them up.

BP: As broken as Arkadi thought the banking business was, so we thought the brand-building business was. And, as with banking, nobody seemed to be paying attention. To heat up our own rhetoric, we thought of this stuck-in-the-past attitude as marketing's two lies:

The first lie is that a marketer sells things. Traditional marketers arrogantly assume that consumers part with their money in a spontaneous moment in which the bait is just right and the fish reflexively takes it. Besides disrespecting consumers, this assumption is comically inaccurate. Nobody sees a television commercial or clicks on a Web banner and is suddenly moved to act on it without any forethought. Buying something isn't a spontaneous event; it's the end of a process and, if you're lucky, the start of a relationship.

The second lie is that you can tell a consumer what to think about your product. The ad business clings to an unconscious nostalgia for the 1950s, when you could speak to half of America's adults by buying a commercial spot on *The Ed Sullivan Show.* Advertising was powerful then. You could say what you wanted to say about your brand in ads and, if you said it often enough and with enough conviction, people would just accept it. But that fairy tale has been over for a long time. Consumers don't just learn what you tell them. They figure you out by observing everything you say and do as a brand, and draw their own conclusions. They trust their own eyes and ears and instincts. They aren't dupes, and they are always paying attention.

When you think about these two commonsense ideas—that consumers aren't sold things (they buy them at the end of a process they control) and that they don't learn about brands from ads (they draw their own conclusions about them from everything they observe)—doesn't the concept of an advertising agency suddenly seem a little naive? We certainly thought so. And I guess that's what *we* had to prove.

AK: What a unique idea this would be in financial services: to earn a reputation and a relationship with a consumer—*earn it*—with each interaction! This was unusual thinking for retail banking, since it's viewed by most as a distribution business. What better way to redefine the market than to think differently, and you cannot do this in any meaningful way unless you're a posse and have a rebellious way about you. The key, of course, is focusing your rebellion on things that the stakeholders can tolerate (think of it as like saying you can wear your hair long, but you can't sleep with your father's new girlfriend!). These were values and a philosophy that we shared. Instinctively, I knew that the chemistry with GWP was going to be right. But most fascinating was the passion, the jumping of creative ideas and the genuine commitment to work together. Best of all, these characters were just as interesting as the members of my own posse.

BP: My original partners, Philippe Garneau and Michael Wurstlin, reunited with me to start GWP Brand Engineering in 1996 after we'd worked together at a big, mainstream advertising agency. Three things had drawn us together: One was a passion for brands. Each of us had our own way of looking at them, but we all shared this fascination with the idea of branding as a kind of virtual nation building. The second thing that brought us together was the power of our collaboration. As a team, it had seemed like everything we touched turned to some kind of gold. Our work was provocative, and it was productive. People talked about it, and it got results. Who wouldn't want to take that show on the road? And the third was simply that we enjoyed working together. It sounds like a platitude, but work is a big part of your life. If you can make it important and make it enjoyable, that's a big step toward living well.

By trade, Michael Wurstlin is a designer and art director. By the time we met, his resume was fantastically eclectic, careening from designing the game board for Trivial Pursuit to making auteur art films to collecting awards for his quirky take on advertising. He was one of the most brilliantly creative people I'd ever worked with, but he was also a wild, restless spirit. I don't know whether he'd confess to this himself, but I always believed that he was an artist at heart, and this was his cultural role at GWP: to promote chaos and subversion as a way to find unexpected solutions to creative problems. It was unpredictable and electric, and it often produced work you couldn't take your eyes off. But—and this is sometimes the price of having a company that's a cause—this put his true nature on a collision course with the strategic discipline that defined what GWP did and does. Nobody can work in a place where the values of the organization conflict with their own in some basic way, not for long and not for any amount of money. In 2002, probably inevitably, Michael left our company to pursue his own interests—proof again that it's not enough to be good. You also have to believe.

My first sight of Philippe Garneau was from the audience at an advertising awards show. He was wearing a yellow silk blazer that flapped like a cape as all six feet five inches of him swooped down on the podium to claim his trophy. He looked like an immense tropical bird of prey, if a charismatic and talented one. A couple of months later, he joined the agency at which I was creative director, my star hire and a big statement to the advertising community that the agency would be one to watch.

Unlike Michael, Philippe had very much been a creature of advertising's mainstream. He had worked with a succession of high-profile creative partners over the years, and had his name on some significant campaigns. Between that and his flamboyant personal style, it would have been easy to write him off as another ad-biz esthete. But there was and is much more to him, qualities that made it as inevitable that he would stay with our cause as that Michael would abandon it. For one thing, he is a pretty erudite fellow. An avid reader, he has an intellectual appetite for chewy new ideas that keep the piles of magazines and books in his office waist deep. Being a mere copywriter might eventually bore him, but giving voices to brands would not. For another, he is the son of a soldier. He understands duty and perseverance. These things, alloyed with creativity, make for a formidable brand engineer.

I'm the idealist in the band.

I, too, had come from the mainstream advertising world, and I had a comfortable place there. I had a blue-chip resume that featured famous multinational brands. I was the executive creative director at a major agency in which I had equity. It was actively looking for a buyer, and I stood to do pretty well with my stake when the right one came along. Meanwhile, being a strategy guy, my appointment to the top creative job had been an industry first and got me a lot of profile. And I did pretty well as a creative director, if you measure success in awards. But I had this Jerry Maguire moment at the height of it all. I felt like nobody was talking enough about the people we were trying to sell for or to. And I felt like we were the last dinosaurs to show up at the tar pit.

So I walked. I didn't want to be the kind of guy that advertising turns you into by the time it's finished with you. And I really wanted to do work that mattered, work that built important brands. An ad can't be a legacy, but a great brand can. It's the marketing equivalent of architecture. Make it strong and beautiful, and it will last and matter.

As we were writing this book, Arkadi asked me slyly if I'd started GWP for fame and fortune. I told him that I had not. I'd done it for freedom. Advertising legend Bill Bernbach once famously said, "A principle isn't a principle until it costs you money." I hoped for fame and fortune when we opened our doors in 1996, but I was willing to take whatever came.

AK: As a business model, I think a rock band must be impossible to manage. You can't corral independent creative talents with processes and structures, and you can't do it by handing out orders and formal job descriptions. The critical thing for an organization like that is to never lose sight of what it's sound is. That, for Bruce, was the key to trying to lead. He figured if he just kept playing and trying to get better without fundamentally changing his tune, his example would generate a gravitational pull on the rest of the team. It's his variation on "leading from the front." From day one to today, Bruce has been a practitioner first, not a boss. He never wanted or was able to hand the product reins over to someone else so that he could focus just on leading. It's just not who he is, even if it might have been a wiser move. When it came to his company's mission, he wanted to prove it by doing it. Bruce, the idealist, was to meet me, the pragmatist, and it seemed like the right bullet for the right rifle at the right time. We were both far enough along in life to know who we were and why we were looking for something important.

BP: So this was the cast. In one of those twists of fate that Arkadi likes to call serendipity, a bunch of people who wanted to rescue consumers from banks crossed paths with a few guys who wanted to rescue brands from ad agencies. The result truly was a Dirty Dozen, in spirit if not precisely in number.

In the final analysis, I think the collection of characters assembled by Arkadi to take on the ING Direct mission—and their ultimate success—challenges more than just banking orthodoxy. This has not been only about reinventing banking; it has been about inventing a new way to create any product, constitute an organization to deliver it, and then take it to market. It is proof of what a purpose-driven enterprise, a company that is for some*one*, rather than some*thing*, can do. ING Direct's Dirty Dozen shows that an organization with a sense of purpose is more likely to happen if it is built by aligning people who have their own individual senses of purpose, just as a great story in film is more likely to happen if it is populated with deep, human characters whose paths in life collide at the perfect moment.

Team Building the Orange Way

BP: The case Arkadi makes when he describes his posse is that building a high-performance team isn't a mechanical process. Our reference to Hollywood's great caper movies is really meant to illustrate the power that character and motivation bring to the mix, the way that these things amplify skills and aptitude. An enterprise like this isn't a machine; it's an unfolding story. Here are three principles we think any leader can use to make theirs a great one.

Don't Just Hire—Assemble a Cast

Competence is a commodity. Sure, you need everyone in an organization to be able to do his or her job reliably and efficiently. But competence is table stakes for any employable candidate, and that means that it's equally available to your competitors. Worse yet, if team building depends only on competence, then the price of competence in the marketplace will inflate without any concomitant increase in its real value. Companies will look at resumes and decide that the more years you've gone without screwing up, the more valuable you must be. But there's no profit in that. Not losing isn't the same as winning.

Demand competence, but look for character. Who are these people as people? What drives them? What are they looking for, or what hole are they trying to fill in their own lives? Much has been made in the press of Arkadi's palm reading performances, his fascination with personality typologies like DISC (dominance, influence, steadiness, and conscientiousness), and his penchant for asking startling personal questions. He will tell you, though, that there is no pat formula for this, no single tool. Instead, he uses every interaction as what he calls a "data point," even something as seemingly benign as watching someone react to having their palm read. It's the collection of data points that reveals the candidate in three dimensions, with every bit of genius, every flaw, quirk, and hang-up, and most important, his or her true motivation. Nobody is perfect, so casting an organizational team really becomes a matter of selecting the right kinds of imperfect. Only when that is understood can the decision be made to give an actor the part. It takes courage to hire people this way. It is much safer and easier to fall back on a tidy resume. But there is more to business than just not making mistakes. Competence can do what's possible. It takes character to do what's not.

Manage Your Business's Culture, and That Culture Will Manage Your Business

Like every management strategy, the decision to hire individuals for their individuality comes with a built-in risk. In this case, the risk is that you could end up with an organization of free agents, making decisions that are more likely to be driven by their own agendas than by the company's sense of purpose. The fix for this is to have leadership spend as much time thinking about culture as it does strategies and processes. In Chapter 7, we'll talk in some depth about the power of marketing to your own people, and that's a big part of this. But it starts earlier, and in a more fundamental way, with the core team.

To the outside observer, ING Direct's operating style can seem chaotic. Decisions seem provisional, and they're often made in a way that goes far beyond consultation. I've been part of meetings there in which not only are there participants with no direct functional connection to the issue at hand, but the participants don't even seem to be peers in a hierarchical sense. Yet they all seem to have a voice, and they all seem to get heard. On the surface, this might seem like some kind of forced collegiality, but it's not. It's a way of making sure that everyone's input is heard publicly. That, in turn, forces the team to consider and care about the team. It eliminates silos not only functionally, but also culturally. And it promotes accountability to one another as well as to the cause.

AK: With the posse, it's about creative ideas, innovations, and looking for new answers to big questions. To handle the frustration of the process, you have to be oriented a certain way. I imagine it's not much different in a creative ad shop or a movie production house. ING Direct's core competencies are marketing and information technology. But the value comes mostly from art and ideas, sifted through quantitative methods to harvest them.

BP: Bonding plays a role, too. In many organizations, promoting team bonding is aimed at minimizing conflict and enhancing the quality of working life. At ING Direct, it has taken on a lot more meaning in the context of that open decision-making process we just described. They know that people can feel vulnerable in this kind of setting, and that might make them pull their punches or be political. The solution is to give them chances to get to know each other as intimately as the leadership got to know them when they were being hired.

AK: One thing a posse likes to do is hang out. Playing baseball, soccer, hockey, you name it, and the ING Direct guys are out there. Trapshooting, sailing, running marathons and joining walks for causes, we just get out there. Employee annual events are always tied into music, food, and activities that force people to be themselves. Sometimes, you'd think it is an extension of college. And the best thing to do when we're together is debate, argue, and discuss the vision, mission, and what customers think. There isn't a boundary between work and play; they're just two different contexts for us to pursue our cause and make it real.

BP: Build a team of individuals, give them a collective cause, and then make them care about each other, and you get an organization that organically does the right things.

Make Everybody a Hero

Any revolution, even a business revolution, relies on mythmaking to keep it alive and inspired. Remembering heroic acts and defining moments seems to be essential to keeping the energy in a revolution and making it something to live up to. Whether it's George Washington crossing the Delaware or Arkadi Kuhlmann and his posse riding Harley-Davidsons across the Golden Gate Bridge, successful revolutionaries know a mythic moment when they see it, and make it part of the story.

The fact this chapter was written at all makes the point about what an important organizational tool mythmaking is. Look at the colorful language, words like *posse* and references like *The Dirty Dozen*. This is a genuine and deliberate effort to give the team a sense that what they're doing is important and heroic and that it can create a legacy for each of them, if they play their cards right. Consider as Exhibit A the script from a video that was shown to the handful of employees who were at ING Direct on the first anniversary of its U.S. launch. Barely a year into the enterprise, you would expect Arkadi and his team to be immersed in organizing the product, placating the shareholders or the regulators, or hiring madly to fill seats as the company grew at warp speed. And they were. But they also had time to make a home movie for the people who had been working their hearts out from day one.

You had to be there. The auditorium was filled with salespeople, and this was the climax of a motivational and training experience that already had spirits high. Still, this was a one-year-old start-up bank. The future must have seemed colossally uncertain, especially with the market littered with the still-smoking wreckage of failed dot-com start-ups. The lights went out and the screen lit up. And what did they see? Was it a high-energy call to arms with a snappy sports motif or martial theme? Or was it something more Hollywood, all bombast and adrenaline and Vegas dancers?

Nope.

It was a Robert Frost quote:

Two roads diverged in a wood, and I—
I took the one less traveled by,
And that has made all the difference.
—*Robert Frost, "The Road Not Taken," 1915*

The words faded from the screen, but there were still no fireworks—no wailing guitar or throbbing drums. Instead, there was a quiet meditation. Over music that first soothed and then swelled emotionally, and stock footage scenes of humans challenging themselves to do courageous things, a voice said to the now slightly confused audience:

What brought us here?

Any one of us could make a living a hundred ways—a hundred easier ways.

Why did we choose this "road not taken"?

Maybe it's because we each, for our own reasons, wanted to make a stand.

Instead of inheriting someone else's vision, someone else's mountain, we wanted to climb our own, so that when we're done, we can look back at the trip and say, "I did this."

No asterisks. No footnotes. Just the simple fact that all you see around you would simply not be here but for you.

And here we are.

And we realize . . . the thing about making our own road is that we can never coast, or we'll just stop.

This place is our mountain.

We have a good idea, something that will help people.

But it's new.

So we have to inspire them. Every day. Relentlessly.

And that is what makes this road so steep, and why at the end of the day it is one that not everyone is meant to take.

But they say the view is best closest to the edge.

Today, we'll stop and look. And it *will* be beautiful.

And tomorrow will be another mountain.

There wasn't a dry eye in the house, and people stood cheering in the aisles. Why? Because the leadership of ING Direct had just told them that their work was indispensable to the cause. That they had done something that mattered in the world, and given themselves some immortality in the process. They told them they were heroes.

Still today, the "Road Less Traveled" video is a bit of a sacred rune around ING Direct, which I think tells you something about how real it was for them. There is something amazingly disarming and motivating about this kind of authentic emotion. Combine it with the promise that your people will not just make a living, but they can also make history, and, well, there aren't enough management-by-objectives handbooks in the world to beat that for lighting a team up and making it want to win.

Who, after all, doesn't want to be a hero?

AK: A loose number of names and characters have drifted in and out of the ING Direct journey. Rebels are restless by nature, and some stayed while some moved on to other ventures—maybe a new tech start-up or to a family business or even to start another bank. But when the sense was it's time to take a break, I encouraged it. We were not, and I am not, a traditionalist. We had no uniforms, hand signs, company song, or team motto. We were not the Marines or the Boy Scouts. We are, in today's world, a posse of odd lots with a very big desire to kick butt. We are on a mission, clear and simple, tolerant of other agendas and side issues but clear on why we are together. The Orange Code, developed over time, set forth our values and focused the orientation on "why you and I are here"

and why it should matter. In that motivational video GWP put together for us, they called this "The Road Less Traveled." It brings tears to your eyes because it says the words you have trouble finding but you know they are there. Still, that's the best thing about a posse. You don't need to say much. It's all in the eyes. Let's get this done.

Chapter 4

Clicking

The Conundrum of Advertising

Many companies fall into the classic trap of advertising their brand and not their product. The credibility gained by delivering what you say you are going to deliver and making your product remarkable from a customer's perspective is what creates the buzz. The role of advertising is to deliver a message to consumers, but it's the selling process that defines what a brand is all about.

—AK, CEO Message # 82

AK: Well, they sure were different!

It was the fall of 1996, a crisp autumn day in Toronto, and at 9 AM in a sterile conference room at the dull Ramada Inn in the suburb of Don Mills, there we were: Hans Verkoren, Dick Harryvan, Jim Kelly, and I were to meet the GWP team again and see what they could really do. They were the third advertising agency we were seeing, and it was time to hear their pitch and see if we should hire them. In walk three guys from a new, unknown firm called GWP Brand Engineering.

This was high-risk stuff: three partners just starting out, having given up the sanity and comfort of big accounts and a brass nameplate. The chances that they would stay in business and stay the course to help us launch our new bank seemed slight. Mind you, liking the personalities and what they had to say was the key, but the "buts" would get debated, especially with our ING colleagues, Hans and Dick. Sounding good and smart was not always a winner in business. Tried and true counts, too. So, who was going to help launch whom? This firm, GWP, was basically three guys who sounded very straight and passionate that morning, but oh so different from anybody else we had seen. Who was their leader and how was it going to work? Sorting out the partnership and the formula for our ad team was my practical worry at that moment.

We'd met these guys once before, informally, and they had lost none of their energy: Philippe Garneau, tall, cultured, and creative, still fluttered and danced, a true creative director inside and out who wore everything on his sleeve. My only question about him was, would he bend and would he compromise if needed for the campaign? And there was Michael Wurstlin with his trademark crew cut, operator look, and funny smile, always wound up but it was never sure where he was emotionally. If three was ever to be a crowd, he was it. And then there was Bruce Philp, the low-key one. You immediately felt that he was the thinker. If he was quiet, you knew he wasn't absent-minded. He was thinking and you sensed it was going to be productive when he finally let you in on it. He had a strong grasp of the objective and just oozed insights. I felt that if we wanted to work out an idea, then Bruce would be the go-to guy. You could also sense he had something to prove. I connected with this immediately, and looking back now I think it's because Bruce was at a turning point on a personal as well as professional level.

Timing is everything in life. I was at the same crossroad. I was on my way to San Francisco when this ING Direct project showed up and made me pause and take a hard look. It didn't take long before I started digging in, pushing the energy and thinking of the possibilities. I was going to give this project a go. I wanted to be part of a new bank pilot in Canada, prove it, and then take the proof statement with me to the United States, the big market. Working the program for a few years and shaping the message would be time well spent. I needed to get my concepts and ideas together in a way that made sense and that could be logically stitched into a business that worked. I had always believed that talk is cheap, and I only had faith in what was real. This led to a more a personal view of people, and it affected my view of business practices. Where is the proof statement that makes our effort and our plan relevant

to consumers? That was my question for us, and for these three guys at
the front of the room.

No more bullshit. If there was a chance to see how the players would
work together, this was it. I liked Philippe, was easy with Michael, and
found Bruce engaging. I knew I could spar with him and that boundaries
would not be a problem.

BP: Clearly, trust was going to be an issue here.

We knew this because the night before that pitch to ING Direct's
agency selection committee, Hans Verkoren had been accosted by a
woman of dubious morals in the elevator of his very respectable hotel
while on his way to send a late-night fax to Amsterdam. He assumed that
one of the ad agencies competing for the account had put her up to it.
And, because we had decorated that selfsame elevator with a sticker bear-
ing our company's logo in a modest, if misguided, act of entrepreneurial
showmanship, he further assumed it was us. We were blissfully unaware
of this until after we stood up to make our case the next morning, but
that didn't mean that the road to this moment had been an easy one.
Between trying to make a four-and-a-half-month-old company of five
people look reassuringly competent, and marshalling resources that our
bigger competitors could take for granted, and dealing with the calamity of having my laptop computer stolen two days before the pitch, the
whole thing had taken on a plucky sort of "My uncle's got a barn, let's
put on a show!" vibe at GWP's little King Street office. We had nothing
to lose, and we had plenty to say. "Three chords and the truth," as one of
my partners melodramatically put it while we sat in an anteroom waiting
our turn. If this was meant to be, it was meant to be.

As is GWP's way, our first pitch to them (it took two before everyone
on that committee was convinced) was rooted in core strategic principles
rather than the typical shiny creative confections upon which ad agencies
usually rely to seduce new clients. We began by forcefully making the point
that ING Direct's brand was not going to live only in advertising, but would
have to speak through every experience, every transaction, every exposure
customers had. Without history, without buildings and tellers, without a
soul in the country who could say, "I opened my first savings account there
with money I made delivering newspapers," ING Direct was going to have

to colonize hearts and minds with every single thing it did and said, from day one.

Next, we said they should build their brand strategy on three principles that must have seemed a little radical—okay, strange—at the time: First, don't attack banks, we said. It's too risky, and it invites consumers to compare the wrong things. Attack their products, sure, but not the institutions. Second, don't have a target group. The people who belong at ING Direct will find us, but they can't be allowed to define who we are. We have to be for everybody and be defined by our own purpose. And third, don't build a brand at all. Build a culture that people can join.

Don't attack your competition, don't have a target group, and don't build a brand. So far, so good. Nobody was laughing yet (not out loud, anyway).

Next came the creative work, the climactic moment in any pitch. And what we showed them that day was nothing if not a thorough response to those three strategic principles, and most likely nothing like anything they'd seen before. Using a variety of media and promotional and publicity tactics, our creative team (who happened to be my business partners, not to mention 40 percent of our company's staff) painted an elaborate vision for the postmodern, consumer-advocate brand-as-cultural-phenomenon. The central character was a vaguely alien spokesperson in Devo-esque coveralls, and the central theme was subversive activism. Frank critique of the status quo was delivered with the kind of innocence that only an alien could carry off, brash billboards would spring up everywhere almost as proxies for bank branches, and what could only be described as performance art would erupt in the nation's streets. It was all designed to provoke and inspire a consumerist revolution in retail banking, the thing we knew we needed before we could convince people to give us their money. And over the lot of it, gobs and gobs of vivid, spasm-inducing orange, a color called Pantone 165. We'd plucked it from the little lion in their logo, and it was everywhere in this campaign: on billboards, on the street, on the coveralls of the spokesperson. Blue, we said, is the color of a bank. Orange is not. Orange is the color of optimism, and bright colors, just as for IKEA and Target and Southwest Airlines, are a signal of value.

Orange is also, of course, a color of great cultural significance to the Dutch. We didn't think that would hurt our case, either.

Throughout all of this, our jury sat expressionless. Jim and Arkadi were completely poker-faced. The contingent from Amsterdam were polite and attentive, but pointedly neutral about it. This included the group's apparent mandarin, Mr. Verkoren, who seemed to have taken in the proceedings with his eyes closed, making it slightly unsettling that it was he who spoke first after I'd triumphantly dealt with the last Power-Point slide and closed by inviting questions. Opening his eyes, he leaned across the table, leveled a predatory glare in our direction, and rumbled,

"Where's the beef?"

He didn't mean it as a flattering reference to the iconic 1984 Wendy's ad campaign, either. He meant it more the way Walter Mondale meant it while excoriating Gary Hart. He was telling us that he was unimpressed by anything but a substantial presentation of their product on its merits, and that he'd not seen quite enough of that in the preceding two hours. We had invested most of our thinking for this pitch into the idea that without a brand, this product, however attractively priced, was going nowhere in this market. That nothing short of sheer inspiration was going to make consumers challenge such a monolithic status quo, not to mention their own inertia. He and his colleagues, by contrast, just wanted to sell their savings account.

It might seem in the retelling that we were about to have a typical ad-agency-versus-client creative debate, but with the clarity of hindsight it was actually a defining moment for ING Direct and its complicated relationship with advertising. Why? Because the fact was that we were both right. ING Direct, as a brand, had no future if it couldn't light consumers up with some kind of inspirational fire. And ING Direct, as a business, had no future if consumers were going to be even a little bit confused about what we had to sell. If this enterprise was determined to ignore banking convention and be an authentic consumer advocate, then conventional advertising of either kind on its own would betray it. Inspiration alone would make ING Direct seem inauthentic; product information alone would make it seem ordinary.

Reconciling the essentially vain, self-important nature of advertising with Arkadi's vision of ING Direct would prove to be tortured work for years to come. And this tortured work was going to start with the kind of agency ING Direct would choose to work with. An un-bank needed an un-agency. That, after all, was its only real hope of getting un-advertising.

AK: When Hans, Dick, Jim, and I sat and discussed the pitch from GWP afterward, we were positive but worried. As we drove back to the office, the conversation turned to the risks and one recurring theme: Does ING use recognized brand names elsewhere in the world for things like back-office systems, ad agencies, and headhunters? Yes, of course. It's safer to choose IBM because they're proven, so there's less personal and corporate risk. And then there was ING Insurance behind us who would provide cover if decisions like this went wrong. The thought of Dutch institutional money and all it represented was never far from our minds. Taking a big chance on something like this would not be a victory if it meant that we couldn't count on their support later if things didn't work out.

GWP Brand Engineering, however, was about as far from a name-brand ad agency as you could get. Though we liked their independence, their strong point of view, and their unusual approach, we also realized that GWP was only a few months old, and very small. They had the creative line and they saw our marketing opportunity the way we saw it, but did they have the bench strength and financial resources to execute the advertising and production work we needed? Would they stay together long enough and grow their own business alongside ours? Those questions lingered. Yet the thing I liked best was that Bruce gave you a feeling that they were interested more in the work than the money. God knows, the team I was hiring was not motivated by the money! This was no free-spending dot-com. This attitude fit right in with my original Canadian team, the Dirty Dozen with things to prove, working for an institution that was unique in its own right. For all its risks, GWP fit.

As a contrast, the other two agencies we got pitches from were big, famous multinational firms. Their pitches went like this: "Here is our work, and we would be honored to do this project for you. Let us tell you how we operate. First, this is the market and we have confidence that we can steer you through it. We're experts, and it's our creative brilliance that has helped every other big name in your field. You will recognize these names. . . ." Throughout their presentations, I was either on my way to falling asleep or totally pissed and ready to argue or criticize their pitch line. What held me back? These multinational agencies had back channels to my new Dutch colleagues through the expats ING had put on our Canadian team. Their back-channel message was, "This guy Kuhlmann doesn't get it and is really your biggest liability." I was having enough trouble fitting into Amsterdam's wavelength and building their confidence. A multinational ad agency with uncertain loyalties was not going to help my case with the Dutch.

In the end, it's still business. Time would reveal that "if you're not Dutch you're not much," and loyalty only went as long as the numbers came in, just as in most corporations. You had to be entrepreneurial and creative, but at the same time look and act institutional enough to make them comfortable. So we suffered through the advertising agency review process, despite those conflicting agendas. Fortunately, Hans Verkoren was a bit of an unorthodox Dutchman when it came to people and business. He worked on instinct and trusted his comfort zone. In this sense, he was the complete opposite of the rational and careful Dick Harryvan, so the three of us made a complex—but actually effective—unit. The amount of tension could be horrendous sometimes, and the power play among us always kept us one step away from quitting on each other. In many ways it was this salt-and-pepper relationship aspect that produced the most fascinating results. From a Dutch cultural perspective it was good to have this kind of tension, because they tend to trust conflict and unhappiness in a relationship. These things are, at least, honest. I, on the other hand, was determined to get what I wanted, and that was a project and a bank that would make a difference. I had very deep passions about what I was doing. I could put up with the politics. You see, I'd been abandoned by two insurance institutions on similar projects before this. I already had my hard knocks badge. My eyes were open. This thing would get built even if it had to mean different things to the different players. For Dick and Hans, their professional and social standing in the Netherlands would be enhanced a great deal if they led a successful greenfield venture. For me, it would be a proof statement that would affirm my mark.

I sensed that the same type of dynamic was going on with GWP, that they were putting up with the process because they had something to prove. In many ways, ING Direct got built, its launch got shaped, and our climb began with none of us looking back. It was pure serendipity. I felt then and still do today that great ventures are achieved because someone wants them to be. Without GWP and the unique chemistry of Hans, Dick, and me, ING Direct would not have succeeded. Why is this critical? Serendipity happens all the time. If you can sense it early on, you've got to go with it and push like hell.

BP: I have to admit that it did seem fated somehow. Here was a new bank challenging itself to act like anything but, and here was a branding firm whose stated mission was "to invent what will replace the advertising agency." We were both running away from broken status quos, and we both had something to prove.

Pitching a prospective client is usually a bit of an out-of-body experience. Any agency, never mind a start-up with strong opinions and no track record, obviously depends on winning new assignments all the time. And then, for GWP, there was this extra ingredient: the chance to validate the beliefs that made us leave the advertising industry behind and start a branding company from nothing. A pitch is an alchemy of proof: that you are passionate, that you know something about the business your prospective client is in, that you have a point of view that's different and compelling to them, and that you can create a brand experience out of that point of view that will actually build their business. Get each of those things in the right proportion, and the alchemy produces gold. The fact is, though, that when you're up there talking, you can't hear much besides the ringing in your ears and the sound of your own voice. You are focused on making sure that you don't miss anything, thereby giving someone in the room an excuse to strike you off the list. You don't rejoin the world until you sit back down again, at least not usually. But there was one moment in that meeting when I could sense the energy change. Something . . . clicked.

It happened when we paused our slide presentation and played 90 seconds of videotape that we had produced for this occasion. Its purpose was simple enough: I believed (and still do) that before you can convince a company of how it should sell its brand to a consumer, you first have to sell that brand to the company. Show them who they are, as if in a mirror, burnished with the semiotic and rhetorical power of cinema. Show them that you not only understand their enterprise, but you're also inspired by it. And show them that a brand is not just a marketing tool; it's something to live up to. This policy, that a client is the first consumer, was central to our belief system at GWP and, as it turned out, very much so for the people of ING Direct, too. I believed that this next 90 seconds was, to be frank, the most important part of our pitch that day. The analytical stuff, the nuts and bolts of strategy, all those pages of charts and elegant logic risked being abstract, or easily duplicated by any of our competitors, or moot because they were based on speculation and incomplete information; such are the risks in a pitch. But this was our cri de coeur. We were going to offer them a manifesto that came straight from the heart of what made them and us alike. It went like this:

We are new here.

There has never been a time like this before.

Our name is ING Direct.

Our mission is to help people take care of the wealth they make for themselves in ways that fit this new time.

We will be fair.

We will constantly learn.

We will change and adapt and dwell only in the present and in the future.

We will listen.

We will invent.

We will simplify.

We will never stop asking why, or why not.

We will create wealth for ourselves, too. But we will do this by creating value.

We will tell the truth.

We will be for everyone, except those who are truly served by the old way.

Because we aren't conquerors. We are pioneers.

We are not here to destroy. We are here to create.

We will never be finished.

We are not a bank. We will never be a bank.

But we will be what a bank would be if it began tomorrow and asked simply,

"What if we started over?"

"What if we started over?" These words were lifted directly from the title page of GWP's own seminal business plan, written a year before on my kitchen table as my partners and I dreamed about whether it was possible to create something better than an ad agency. And here we were, quite deliberately, offering this sacred text of ours to these guys who claimed to be dreaming about creating something better than a bank. I shut the VCR off and turned to face the room just in time to catch Jim looking at Arkadi with one eyebrow raised. Yeah, it was fated. The Orange Code had been born. And it was probably the last and only piece of uncontroversial advertising we would ever write for ING Direct.

AK: Well, that first creative campaign pitch was not quite right.

It was professional and demonstrated the theme, but it was missing a broad, easy-to-follow product story line. The orange color, the spokesman in the street, and the stunts that invited the consumer to be curious—these were novel and interesting. To my way of thinking, though, it was too deep. It required too much thinking, and the "aha" moment was too long in coming. Yet I was still certain these were our guys, and there was something there. What now? Would the GWP team take another run at it? If I got them another chance, would they be willing to try? They understood what ING Direct was trying to do, but it is universally known that creative directors, however brilliant, never really did a second act. I was nervous. I wanted GWP and I believed the other agencies would put the whole project at risk.

My new Dutch colleagues, however, felt safer with the big-name advertising firms. Arguing their case, they even pointed out that they had, after all, used a big-name headhunter to find me. The institutional wheels would turn for us here as well, they insisted. As with most issues like this—from IT systems to operating procedures—everything would get debated in big bank terms, when what we really needed was fresh thinking and new ideas. Again, it was Hans's unorthodox style and my salesmanship that tipped the scales in the end. It was razor close. The previous August, in one of our many debates over people, systems, and marketing, I had been confronted with Hans's sleepless night's worries. Two months and 12 days into the project, he had said to me, "Maybe, Arkadi, you are too entrepreneurial a guy and you're not sure you can make it work the way we want it." This decision was a test of my own conviction.

Dick was somewhat reserved through all this, though he was clearly ready to push the direction Hans wanted. He would not weigh in on the creative side of the process. Hans had brought him on board. Hans was the one I had to persuade. I started selling both Dick and Hans and convinced them that I had the right ideas, the ones that would get them the results they wanted, and I needed this team. My back was to the wall. The Dickens novel *Great Expectations* comes to mind. This debate would mark the start of a long string of moments over the next 10 years when

I would have to spend political capital, so to speak, to keep the game going. I could not afford to be mercurial or shortsighted if I wanted the financial capital, the support, and the opportunity to build this new kind of bank. But I also couldn't afford to compromise on the things that really mattered.

Two weeks later, in the end, a moment of calm came. Feelings were positive and the second campaign pitch from GWP was presented. They had stepped up and shown that they were flexible, and they'd hung in there. I'd managed to get Hans's support, although it would come at a price later on when we debated the choice of a direct marketing consultant (Hans is a horse trader, an entrepreneurial quality I like about him). I was thrilled and never doubted the advertising direction we were now taking. Jim Kelly liked the GWP guys, too, and I trusted his intuition. If there ever was a guy to go to the wall with it was Jim. He was Canadian through and through, but with an Irish soul that made him tick a lot like me in this complex, Dutch-supported project. He understood. Together, we would play the game. Later, when we got to decisions on the style of our commercials and our pitchman, Frederik, it was always easy and a pleasure. But the best was yet to come. For now, we had our agency, and the political price hadn't been too high.

BP: Remember the sock puppet?

When all of the foregoing drama was unfolding, Pets.com's notorious advertising mascot was still a couple of years in the future, but that puppet stands as a monument to why so much political capital was bet on ING Direct's choice of an advertising agency. Today, the sock puppet, along with the now-defunct business it represented, is an icon for the arrogant marketing excesses of the dot-com bubble. Everyone has their own take on that new economy tale of woe but, as it relates to ours, I think the sock puppet symbolized the disastrous collision of two vanities: the marketers', for believing that all they had to do was build the product and people would come after simply being made aware of it, and their ad agency's, for believing that the only responsibility of advertising is to be noticed and talked about. But awareness isn't a business result. People pointing and laughing aren't the same thing as people buying. The ING Direct team, uncontaminated by this mainstream thinking, knew at a gut level that advertising, in its broadest sense, had a serious job to do, a job as big and important as any in their enterprise.

Part of that job, of course, was obviously to stimulate business. Yes, advertising had to create awareness. But awareness is easy. You can buy it. ING Direct's advertising couldn't stop there (nor, I'd suggest, should anybody's). Advertising also had to make people willing to figure out a completely new way of interacting with a bank, and to reconsider the savings account, a product they thought they'd left behind along with their paper routes. It had to create desire out of thin air and, in the beginning, before ING Direct had perfected its Web and direct marketing channels, push that desire all the way to action. For ING Direct to stay alive, people had to pick up their phones and, in a gargantuan leap of faith, give personal banking information to complete strangers working on behalf of a brand they'd never heard of before it interrupted them in the middle of *60 Minutes,* seven months after that pitch.

But for a new brand with an essentially invisible business, in 1997 at least, that's only the beginning of advertising's job. Ads have to fill the cultural space that would normally be occupied by a brand's history, its physical presence in communities, and the observable, sharable experience of being a customer. Advertising *is* the brand, in the beginning. And because ads so often come first with a start-up, advertising ends up guiding the brand experience as it evolves, both for the customers who are having it and the employees who are creating it. When employees or customers are trying to figure out what a new brand stands for, ads might be the only evidence they're going to have to work with. The very last thing advertising can afford to be for a new economy brand is an amusing frippery. Brands like this can't afford to let a puppet speak for them. You can't send a puppet to preach revolution.

So, yeah, trust was going to be an issue here, because these guys weren't just selecting another vendor. They were drawing a line in the sand with their corporate sponsors. They were creating a mold for the organization they would build and a cause for it to live up to. And they were making damn sure that their "ad agency" was in just as deep and for the same reasons they were.

AK: Advertising may be the oldest business in the world after prostitution. As a business, we need to sell our products and services. We need to get the message out. The challenge is, how best do we do this when consumers are all different and the methods of communication are so many and varied? We have lots of information at our fingertips, and the task finds itself burdened with too little time and too many options for sending or receiving information in the public arena. Meanwhile, life is ever changing, dynamic, and charged with the pressure of everyday living. That any business would think it lives in a steady, static world seems far-fetched. A market is a moving target. The task of selling stuff quickly becomes daunting!

If we break down the tasks of marketing and then selling products and services, we'll find an order that looks, at least on paper, logical. The trouble is, it's all created by and for people, and it's judged and criticized by people. Should the measurable results rule the day, or is there more that maybe can't be measured objectively? To me, a good starting point would be to keep it simple. Describe the product. Good. Clear and to the point. Next: How does it work? Good. Clear and to the point. What are the benefits? What is the value? Good. Clear and to the point. Next, set up a budget and make it attractive. Last but not least, go and get it done!

To do this well, a lot of research and analysis goes into answering these questions. You have to understand the customer and how he or she thinks and behaves, but, just as important, how he or she dreams. It seems extreme to say "dreams," but I am convinced that good advertising engages consumers in a manner that helps them in more ways than meet the eye. Yes, what gets bought and sold is straightforward, but the opinions and ideas that surround that process find themselves wrapped up in our stories about who we are and who we wish to be. The things we have and the things we do become a part of us and define us.

Does this sound a bit academic? Well, if a product or service has this kind of impact on consumers, then it must also have an impact on the company providing it. So the image of the company and the staff delivering on it are part and parcel of the same story. The brand is the label for this, but more than anything it is the flag for a reputation and what a company and its products stand for. We humans love to organize ourselves and the world around us in very clear, personal terms. Generally with most things, the more directly we are involved, the more specific we like to be. As the saying goes, you are what you eat, but you are also what you buy and what you otherwise consume. In this regard, your actions and your buying decisions tell more about you than all the words you might use.

ING Direct had a mountain to climb, and there were two ways to do it: one, be like everyone else with probably average results in all aspects or, two, attack the mountain and gamble with the money, resources, and opportunity. Seldom do managers confront it in these terms, but there is always that second, unspoken option. Whether you have an existing company or you're starting a new one, the risk and the challenge are the same. It is my belief that how you see the challenge and describe it is key to your success and, most important, to making a difference. If you wish to make money and change the world, you need a bold idea and you need a plan to get to the top of the mountain. The leadership's role is then to remove uncertainty, show conviction, and thereby marshal the resources. All business does imitate life, and we are wise to see it up close and personal.

BP: ING Direct's advertising debut did more than imitate life. It dove right into the thick of it, having been filmed on the street in the financial district of the country's largest city in the middle of a business day. There were no extras milling around in the background, just ordinary working people on their way from somewhere to somewhere, and one very serious-looking man in a suit stabbing his finger in the direction of a movie camera as he spoke. The actor's name was Frederik de Groot, and he was anything but a conventional choice for an ING Direct spokesperson. For one thing, he was Dutch. Being a Shakespearian actor, his English was superb, but his accent was unmistakably European. For another, he was out in the street among the people, and not in a Hollywood bank branch set or strolling past happy customers reclining by their swimming pools living their bank-enabled dreams. He was not (and is still not, as he continues to be the brand's spokesperson in Canada at this writing, surely setting some kind of record for the longevity of a bank advertising campaign) a typical squared-jawed, carefully coiffed, central casting spokesperson. He wasn't the kind that consumers in focus groups had told us they thought would work best. His television persona was stern and austere; his look was tidy, conservative, and professorial; and his delivery was a mix of contained fury at the injustice of the status quo, chiding of those who accepted it, and the agrarian common sense typical of Netherlanders.

And he did something that banks generally avoid in advertising: He looked viewers in the eye and spoke directly to them. Frederik was no puppet, and there was nothing remotely entertaining about what he had to say: "Your bank is not treating your savings with respect. You accept this because you never had a choice before. But now you do. At ING Direct, those savings will earn high interest and not be eroded by fees and service charges."

The simple logic of this pitch was a gauntlet thrown at the feet of the consumer, and the boldness of it lay, paradoxically, in its complete *lack* of showmanship. It was the opposite of advertising as it was practiced at the time, and its plain language became a basis for the way ING Direct would speak to its customers in North America from that day to this. And, as if to underscore the brand's blunt, unsentimental advocacy for consumers, every commercial message delivered by ING Direct ended with three words that amounted to nothing less than a dare: "Save your money."

AK: Save your money! A battle cry to the market. A need that is both personal and collective for society. Who doesn't need to save? Who doesn't need to consume a little less or make better use of the financial resources he or she has? Money is the oil in the economic machine, humble but essential, and it works according to a set of laws most consumers often don't seem to understand very well. It gets mixed up with all sorts of psychological issues, issues that blind people to the fact that spending more than you earn, or buying things you can't yet afford, will enslave you in chains forged out of compound interest.

Money is sexy when you spend it, but boring and emotionally unfulfilling when you save it. Trying, then, to build a brand around the cold and boring idea of saving would be a challenge worthy of the best. Trying to make money for the enterprise as part of the adventure would be even harder, and making it sustainable would be the biggest mountain. Sure, our proposition was based on values and goodness that were solid and unassailable by critics. And, sure, the payoff was guaranteed. But that didn't mean people would listen. We had to make it cool, even hip to be a saver. We had to give it social currency. We could see that if this ever became part of the mainstream conversations and debates among consumers and ripple to all corners of society, then our mountain could be climbed and won.

The way ahead was a revolution, and advertising would have to fire the first shot. When do you have a revolution? When you sound like one, act like one, and everyone you speak to, unprompted, calls it one. If it walks, talks, and looks like a duck, it's a duck. Of course, revolutions are relative and in today's marketplace they are going on all the time in one way or another. What made this different was that it was about something very fundamental to people's lives: money and banking. Savings were regarded as a dead issue and consumers wanted to hear about buying things. Banks responded by promoting products and services to help them spend. We would have to really stand out to get noticed in an environment like that. Then, we would have to be very different from the rest and very consistent in our story. Simply put, we'd have to provoke a revolution and get consumers to join it. ING Direct started to climb that mountain back in 1997, but none of us really knew how big a mountain it would be or how the goal and the story would sweep us all away.

Starting with the idea that you need to set up the operation differently, staff it differently, and have an advertising plan that clearly stood out helped to set things on the right track. ING Direct was going to get built by us and by the consumer. It was clear then as now that you can shape it and nudge it but you cannot completely control it, so building the brand into the core of the advertising was like pouring concrete: It would harden into a foundation. If the consumers knew what we were trying to accomplish, they would help us; if there was any uncertainty in their minds, nothing would change. We were lucky, but we were also right in our conviction that it had to be big and creative.

The brand pieces on the table in the fall of 1996 were unique and easily understood. They are still there today, and they are the key to the revolution

BP: If you sense a blurring of the line between ING Direct's advertising message and the rhetoric of its real-life leader, you're not imagining things. When ING Direct has been at its best as a marketer, it's because it has been at its most authentic in its advertising. Every time it has resorted to, as ad legend David Ogilvy called it, "the disease called entertainment," there has been a kind of deflation of the ING Direct brand's energy, inside and out. It has had the same sort of unsettling effect as your dentist wearing a red Styrofoam clown nose while he's admonishing you to floss regularly: It's briefly amusing, but you soon start to wonder how seriously he takes his work, and therefore how seriously you should take his advice.

But every time ING Direct has spoken its own truth in its own voice, it has walked a little taller and resonated much more with the people whose money it was asking to be put in its care. And this, I think, is what was really behind the tough and personal process of choosing the brand's first advertising agency, and behind the sometimes painful iterative path we took to that seminal campaign and those that followed. It was about trust between the consumer and the brand, and between the marketer and its agency. If the latter isn't there, then the former will eventually suffer. Somehow, these guys knew that for them at least, advertising could not be a golden wall built to separate the consumers from the company they were going to do business with. It had to be, instead, a window into its soul.

Advertising and the Rebel Brand: Three Things Leaders Need to Know

BP: Here are three pieces of advice we think any leader can use to make sure their brand says what it is, and is what it says.

Think of Advertising as the Boss Talking

Today's consumers—and today's employees—want, above all, to know that what they're buying into is authentic. This is even more acute when you're asking them to take a chance by trying something new and unproven. Whether a company intends it or not, advertising in all its forms is that company's most public expression of what it thinks is important, and how seriously it takes its customers and employees. Ignore this, and the most you can hope for is an amusing advertising experience that might make people briefly remember you, if only for that. But be authentic in your commercial messages, and people will do better than remember. They'll believe, and belief is the root of loyalty. A good rule of thumb: Don't ask your ads to say anything your CEO couldn't say with a straight face.

Keep Your Friends Close, and Your Agency Closer

Maybe some of the outside services a company contracts can operate almost without supervision. Maybe some need supervision, but not from enterprise leaders. But, today, the reputation of a company and its brand is too valuable and too fragile to trust to suppliers who are disengaged or have their own agendas, and too important to trust solely to middle managers. Whether it's a mass media ad agency, a public relations firm, a corporate design company, or a direct marketing or Internet agency, if a supplier is being given work that the public can observe and interpret, then that supplier should feel accountable to the very top, and maybe even fear it, just a little. A brand is a leadership responsibility, not a management one—a central theme of this story and this book—and that makes the choice of a strategic communications partner no less important than, say, the choice of an auditor or corporate law firm. And the consequences of getting it wrong are infinitely more public.

It Doesn't Matter That People Are Going to Judge Your Advertising; What Matters Is How They're Going to Judge You for Doing It

In the age of YouTube, everybody's a critic. But you can't afford to care about what people think of your advertising in a creative sense, short of it being offensive or damaging to your credibility. You should care only about what your advertising makes them think of your company for doing it and, ultimately, whether it makes them *want* to want what you've got to sell. Popularity isn't a business result. Neither is awareness. All that matters is whether your messages brought consumers any closer to becoming your customers. That path starts with curiosity, which becomes desire, which then seeks trust, and finally becomes action. Everything else is just vanity.

Chapter 5

You Say You Want a Revolution?

The Opposite of a Bank

Managers look at marketplaces as zero-sum exercises: To grow, you have to take share away from someone else. But the ones that are most successful create new territory, a new market, new shelf space. The minute you say, "How can we create?" you break the cycle of zero-sum thinking.

—AK, CEO Message # 73

BP: You just can't make this stuff up.

A couple of years before starting GWP, my partners and I had worked closely with one of North America's largest banks to help it rehabilitate its image. It was a long process, fraught with debate and, frankly, lacking a certain urgency. One particular day, we were ensconced in their posh 68th floor boardroom preparing to give yet another presentation to the chairman and vice chairman of this institution, when the two men strolled in a few minutes early. As we busied ourselves plugging things in and sorting out Foamcore presentation cards, they stood together by the window looking at the bustling city below. The vice chairman, an earnest, practical man, addressed his colleague and said, "You see all those people down there?" The chairman nodded theatrically, and the vice chairman pressed on with his awkward joke. "Those are customers." The chairman, with perfect comic timing, squinted imperially for a moment at the throng below, and then replied:

"But they're so small!"

Working with ING Direct, I find myself recalling that moment often. It's such a perfect encapsulation of what's wrong with banking today, in the age of empowered consumerism. There, in that mahogany-lined, hermetically sealed box hundreds of feet above the street, it was—and apparently still is—possible to believe that nothing has changed for the past century or two. It's possible to believe that banks are an oligarchy by divine right, a royal court from which favor and excommunication are dispensed to consumers who are supposed to consider themselves lucky to be allowed to bank at all. Banks are not evil, for the most part. But their institutional self-interest combines with their legacy systems and habits of thought to produce an arrogant anticonsumer dynamic. It's a dynamic that, every day, leaves customers with the uneasy feeling that they need their bank more than their bank needs them.

This is both unhealthy and plain wrong. Too often, in all kinds of industries, the enterprises that grow the largest somehow end up looking down at consumers from ivory towers and seeing their customers as nothing more than the tail end of the value chain. Though banks may often be among the worst offenders, they are far from alone. And if you doubt that's a problem, ask any retailer: No matter where you are in the world of commerce, the customer is anything but small. No matter where you are in the world of commerce, the customer is, in fact, huge.

ING Direct got a lot of things right: its mission, its leadership, its brand, its culture and team, and so on. But underneath all of this, there really had to be a different way of doing what a bank has to do so that success would never lead to arrogance. For us all to believe, for the consumer to believe, that things would be different at ING Direct and, more important, to prevent the organization from devolving into the very dragon it was created to slay, ING Direct's banking business model had to be drawn on a clean sheet of paper. And the objective would have to be quite simple: Align ING Direct's operational imperatives with what's good for the customer. Invent a financial services business model in which, when the customer wins, we win. And vice versa.

Create, in other words, the opposite of a bank.

AK: If you could start a bank with a clean sheet of paper, why would you not go about it differently? If you want to achieve a better result, be more successful, and stand out, how would you redefine your business? What conventional business thinking would you have to tackle head-on? How? By not compromising your principles unless it really hurts, sure. But, banking is a regulated business, so there are limitations that are tied to the handling of money that you have to accept, too. How do you overcome these challenges?

As I pondered these thoughts, I was sitting in my car at the airport, waiting to pick up John Bone. John and I go back a long way, having spent time in corporate deals, traveling the world and crossing paths in the mining and gold business. John looks like a statesman. He is blond with a friendly smile, and you just sense he has a heart of gold, too. John generally made money for others, but what was most distinctive about him was that he had clear ideas of his own about business issues and people. I had not seen John for a while, but I always felt connected with him. He was like a brother I never had, but as close to the real thing as I can imagine. John, sharp and wise, has a sense of humor and a way to disarm you that lets most problems just fall into their proper perspective.

I was onto this new project for ING. The first four months of stirring all the questions that eventually fall into a business plan. What was the name we were going to use? Where would the offices be? Who would we hire? What skills should they have? These were the normal business questions you have when you get the go-ahead and the capital and it's suddenly real. The project was gaining momentum, and I knew that the early decisions would have lasting impact. I was sure that confused thinking such as "Let's just get going and we can change or fix any mistakes later" was a real death trap. I had to do better than that. Moments like waiting for an airplane lifted some of the fog.

The arrival doors opened and shut. The buzz around me was like a cloud over the crowd. Everybody was looking for eye contact. Gotcha. There he is, smiling and walking with that diplomatic gait, none other than John.

"Well, how are you, brother?" I greeted him.

"What have you been up to?" he asked.

"Onto a new venture with ING."

"Really? What are you going to do?"

"Well, we're going to build a new type of bank, of course."

"I see. But . . . why?"

That "why?" stopped me in my tracks.

It was not the predictable "why me?" or "how much?" or "when?" but simply "why?" We walked into the parking garage to look for my car. John was visiting at just the right moment. It would be a long evening of sharing ideas over a pot of hot tea.

John always believed that I was a corporate guy. He saw corporations ebbing and flowing as a natural order. So building, breaking up, or burying firms was part of John's thinking and business life. You just move on. In truth, however, this did not sit well with me. I imagined myself to be beholden to no man or company. I believed in a lot more permanence than John did. John is not much of a romantic. His view was that you needed to be able to function in a corporate environment, but not get lost in it. He was, of course, right.

This gap, so to speak, was my drive for change. It was clear that the reasons for building a new business included a personal agenda. I wanted a crack at the financial industry. I believed it could and should change, faster and for the better. Technology was moving fast with cell phones and computers and the Internet. Marketing was going electronic. More in-the-street and live experiences were happening everywhere, from sports to entertainment. Different types of retail businesses were sprouting up, too. Big box stores, factory outlets, mail order businesses, and Internet businesses were on the rise. Why not a different type of bank, too? Why couldn't it be time for a revolution in retail banking?

After I conveyed these ideas to John, he offered equally clear advice: "Be creative; have fun. Give it a crack at bat and see where it goes. And sell the story. The money guys love a story. Storytelling is what makes people believe." But then, he saved the best for last. It was 11 PM, time to hit the hay. John smiled and put his hand on my shoulder before he headed upstairs. "Don't worry so much about the project," he said. "What else do you have to do with your time?"

With that, my old friend was off for a night's rest. But all I could think about was that "why?" question.

BP: Looking at it, you'd think that banking is the last place that any real innovation is possible—certainly not innovation that would benefit a customer, anyway. The category is, not surprisingly, very inhospitable to risk taking. It's also tightly regulated. And everybody who competes in it has to do so on a compatible operational platform. In other words, in certain basic technical ways, your brand-new little start-up bank has to work just like the enemy's big, old institutional one. The more Arkadi thought about the problem of why banks don't work for consumers, the less likely it seemed that anybody could actually fix it. At least, that's how it might have looked at first.

Years ago, in another life, I worked in the marketing department of a very large Japanese consumer products company. As you'd imagine, it was a great learning experience to be immersed in a different way of looking at business, and often at life. A great example of this was a durable piece of wisdom a colleague was fond of reciting to me on the subject of problem solving. Though I suspect it owes a debt to W. Edwards Deming, it had the ring of a proverb, and it poetically describes the approach the ING Direct team took to the challenge of reinventing banking: "To learn the truth, ask why seven times." When you ask yourself why things happen the way they do, the first answers are almost always misleading. They reveal only the logic of each isolated decision that created the situation you're looking at. They don't reveal the interconnectedness of all those problems, or the root cause in the system that created them. Ask why seven times about the problems of banking, and the answer doesn't turn out to be that banks are evil or stupid. The answer turns out to be about the way that banks have to make money, compounded by decades of accumulated adaptive behaviors.

Thus, asking "why?" was the first key to ING Direct's banking model revolution.

AK: The answer to John Bone's pointed "why?" was, more than anything else, that the time had simply come. It's not that I was waiting for a chance like this; it's that it came at a profound moment. There was a sense of destiny to it. Things were changing and converging—in my career, in technology, in banking, and even in society. It was a crossroads.

My view is that values and how they are continually born and reinterpreted are a necessary social evolution, and values—yours and your customers'—are a necessary consideration when you're thinking about a business model. Today, we consumers are voting as much with our e-mails and dollars as we are with the political ballot box. The democratization of money is on the rise! The more things appear transient due to change and the more things are commercialized in everyday life, the more we as consumers yearn for meaning in what we do with our time and our money. We yearn for values that reflect who we are and what we stand for. Money becomes an important way of expressing this. Save your money. Be self-reliant. To me, these are watchwords for a stable foundation on which anybody can manage each day's ups and downs.

But where is this going? I believed then, as I do now, that business is essentially spiritual. A spiritual approach to business gives it a sense of purpose and stability that cannot be created in any other way. Business is not a religion, of course, but it has to do good and really serve somebody. To do good, you have to think of customers and their lives. It is in the eye of the beholder. A company with a cause that evolves into an authentic brand has an emotional dimension that appeals to the everyman. You can feel it, it but you are always one step away from touching it or putting it into words. It's spiritual. That's the best way I can describe it.

Now that the emotional direction was set, we also needed to look at the operation, the enterprise model of the business, so to speak, in a new way. Our simple, disruptive idea was to look at retail banking from a truly pure retail perspective. Instead of thinking of our business as moving money around, what if we thought of it as selling something? What could be learned and done better if we copied successful principles from another industry, one that thought more about customers? If consumers were to think differently about money and how they dealt with it, then our enterprise model would have to look and work differently as well. It quickly became obvious that to make it work we needed to be a rebel. It was a way to succeed that had not been tried before. We needed to be contrarian.

When we talked to consumers and asked them to share their thoughts about money, savings, credit cards, and the like, a few concepts kept surfacing in the dialogue. People did not like the activity of banking. They did not like the whole service approach they experienced in a branch or bank office. They also saw little value for bank fees and service charges and considered transaction work a chore. Consumers of all walks of life thought that banking processes were organized to suit the bank and not them. Last, the trust and likability factor was low. If consumers thought that paying $6.50 for popcorn at a movie was okay but paying a $1.25 service charge for a bank statement was an outrage, then who was going to argue with the customer? It seemed like it was time to adjust the concept of service and the pricing to what the market thought had value.

But how?

Most banks try to have good customer service. They mean to be good corporate citizens. They are, however, driven by supply-side thinking that starts with getting a return on capital, then organizing the bank, determining the cost structure, and leaving until last the setting of prices that the customers must pay to support all of this. Banks have traditionally always chased financial assets, meaning loans and mortgages to customers. Bankers make loans first. Then, those banks fund them as cheaply as possible with deposits from customers or some other source of debt. The rates they charge for the interest on these loans and deposits determine the margin or the net interest income that a bank earns. That's the revenue for the bank, the money that pays all the costs and that returns the required profit. The profit a traditional bank makes is the master key to its return on capital, and to the health of its license to carry on business.

Why is this so important? A bank maintains only 8 cents of capital for every 100 cents in deposits. If a bank loses too much money, then the risk is that the bank will lose deposits, be unable to make loans, or, worse yet, lose the market's confidence in its ability to operate. Cash flow is king for a bank. The ability to raise deposits wholesale or retail is a matter of life or death. Confidence! This is why most banks want to look and sound solid. The trouble is, they are all backstopped by a federal regulator and the federal government. In the broader sense, no one can or wants to argue with the system.

Therefore, our challenge in developing a new bank was rooted in the idea that banking, even though it must be safe and secure, does not have to be so onerous or complicated for customers. Customers don't need to be tied up in this bureaucratic complexity any more than they need or want to understand how a car factory works. In all businesses that protect some kind of safety or security for consumers, companies try to make the burden for the customer interface as easy as possible. In banking, this thinking has never really trickled down to the product or service level. Could we rethink the way things have always worked and make banking better? How can we build a bank that is an advocate for the average person, and is still a strong, stable institution?

BP: Rethink, not fix. This was the second key to revolutionizing the model.

Starting over is a theme that turns up often in the ING Direct story. "What if we started over?" is a brave little question that unlocks the door to real innovation, and a hypothetical premise that challenged ING Direct to imagine what it would do if there simply were no banks at all. Though hypothetical, it's a powerfully clarifying way of thinking, because it forces you to identify what really matters. If you were marooned on a desert island, would erecting traffic lights and parking meters be the first things you would turn your attention to in the cause of survival? Of course not. And if you were starting a new bank, would you think first about structuring your service charges or what color of velvet rope you should use to manage the lineups in your branches? No. As Arkadi put it at the time, the first order of business should be: "What does the customer really want to pay for?" And hard on the heels of that, of course, is: "What do we absolutely need in order to profitably deliver it to them?"

Instead of trying to create customer value by trying to overcome the basic nature of an institution, Arkadi and his team focused ING Direct on the point where the bank and the customer meet, and built its solution outward from that moment of truth. For ING Direct, that felt an awful lot like something much more familiar and comfortable to the average American: a retailer. And not just any kind of retailer, either. ING Direct was going to be about saving and would exist for savers. They were to be its cause. So, the kind of retailer it needed to be was the kind that delivered amazing value. The way forward for this clean-sheet-of-paper bank was to do more of less: reduce services and its product range from what was normal for the category, and then maximize its potential for economies of scale.

At launch, it described its operational mission this way: "Redefine financial services through relentless simplification." Arkadi looked around and saw successful companies doing this with fashion, with furniture, with hamburgers, and with airlines. And those companies seemed to be able to do it without turning themselves into dreary, Soviet-esque factory outlets. On the contrary, a lot of these brands seemed to enjoy great customer loyalty and affection, and even a certain cool factor. But could you do it with a bank? Nearly seven million customers and counting ended up proving that the answer was yes, but that didn't mean it would be easy.

Arkadi was working a shift in the bank's call center, as he regularly did and does, helping existing customers with routine transactions, helping new ones get signed up, and listening to the voices of real people. A woman from Florida with a substantial balance in her account was on the line, demanding that a printed statement of her account be mailed to her. Being so affluent and presumably valuable to the bank, she figured she was entitled. Arkadi politely explained that ING Direct did not offer this service, one of the ways it keeps costs down. The woman pressed her case, getting crankier by the minute. A printed statement, she said, was the law. Arkadi, beginning to lose his patience, corrected her. "The law says you have the right own a gun," he retorted. "It does not say you have the right to a printed bank statement every month."

By this time, the customer was in high dudgeon. "Has nobody taught you that the customer is always right?"

The unfortunate customer could not, of course, have known she was dealing with the company's founding CEO, or how deeply committed he was to his business model. So we can only guess at the look on her face at the other end of the phone in sunny Florida when Arkadi had finally had enough.

"That's it. You're not ready for this way of banking," he snapped. And closed her account.

You could call it "The Hamburger Doctrine," because that's the parallel Arkadi has often used since to explain why, while ING Direct *is* for everybody, not everybody is for ING Direct. You wouldn't pull up to a fast-food drive-through and demand a filet mignon medium rare, and the restaurant would be crazy to give it to you. The secret to making money selling cheap-but-good hamburgers is to sell a lot of them quickly, meaning no variety in the menu, no personalization in the delivery, and no special treatment even for people who eat a lot of them. That's the only way to preserve the value proposition.

The firing of customers is something that has come up often when the press writes about ING Direct, and if you aren't listening carefully you might assume that it's all about fairness. That would certainly be in character. ING Direct's brand has a broad streak of egalitarianism in it. "We will be for everyone," says the Orange Code. Yet, in a 2007 *Time* magazine piece, a similar episode is recounted, this time not with a wealthy, spoiled brat but with an older woman who is discouraged from opening an account because she was uncomfortable with branchless banking. The café manager who let her walk away told the *Time* reporter, "Customers who don't fit our business model don't fit our business model, and that's totally okay. The bank just wasn't for her." Not that anyone at ING Direct would put it as harshly as this, but if you're a threat to the efficiency that produces all this customer value for everybody else, you're not welcome here. Not even if you're rich. Not even if you're somebody's grandmother.

This stance is tough, but it's necessary to preserving both the business model and the soul of the enterprise. There is an ugly little paradox in conventional business thinking, though most leaders would never think of it this way: Companies work very hard to create the impression that they're giving their customers what they want at the price they want to pay, while behind the curtain the organization perpetually scrambles to figure out how much less than what's being promised they can get away with actually providing. The difference between what the consumer hopes for and the truth is called profit. It might be a cynical way to describe how a lot of business gets done, but it's not an inaccurate one. And it creates tensions that distract an organization from that fundamental job of creating value. The root of those tensions? Companies assume that every unmet customer need is a problem, and a business opportunity for the taking. That single-minded focus makes marketers do crazy things, things that increase production costs, add complexity to product lines, and drive up the expense of having relationships with their customers. And these things, in turn, cascade into more expensive marketing, all eventually resulting in compromised product quality or lousy margins, or both.

Companies that can't say no eventually end up liars or broke.

ING Direct had a better idea: Instead of letting the customer tell them how to run the bank, they made the customer a partner in it.

AK: ING Direct's proposition was straightforward and in-your-face: Doing business with us is as easy as buying a cup of coffee. Commodity products are easy to understand. You get what you see; there are no surprises. Everyone is treated the same way: fair, polite, and fast. If we could actually do what we would promise in our marketing and sales messages, then this different business model would have a chance. But the customers would need to see ING Direct differently. Their expectations would need to change, and we'd have to convince them that the value they would get would be worth the standardized way of delivering it.

- How do we make money? No branches.
- How do I do it with you? Direct call or on the Internet.
- Where do I find you? At these locations and, yes, at these cafés. Here are the addresses. Hang out with us.
- Is this all you offer? Yes.
- Everyday great rates and good service? Yes.
- Will you do introductory rates and bait-and-switch tactics? No.
- Can I get monthly paper statements? No.
- By law I am entitled to an annual statement and a tax receipt. Okay, you can get what the law demands, but no more.
- Will you stay in business? Yes. We have a huge corporate backer, and our deposits are federally insured.
- And there's only one way to do this? Yes.
- Will a live person answer the telephone? Yes.
- Will I be bounced around or left hanging? No.
- Will I be talking to someone in another country? No.
- Will you sell my mortgage to a servicer or a bondholder on Wall Street? No.

You can see we weren't just trying to please the customer. We were making a deal with them.

The overall customer response turned out to be fantastic. It sounded almost too good to be true for many visitors to our web site or to our call center. "You sure are not traditional!" they'd tell us. "You sure are rebels!" That's right, but we are real—real people who are committed to serving you well, in a very specific way. That was the corporate challenge for us. As with any good revolution, it had to be easy to understand who or what the enemy is. Spiritually, the enemy was banks; Operationally, the enemy was complexity. We had to execute a retail strategy in an unambiguous, unapologetic way so that customers would recognize it for what it is, and adjust their expectations accordingly. That was essential to revolutionizing our business model.

Taking this revolution to Main Street was going to be fun. Most banks don't have fun. Sure, money and banking are serious. A bank needs to be dependable and inspire confidence. But can't there be more? When traditional banks try to please everyone with everything they do, it can't be a lot of fun. A good retailer, however, knows that satisfying everyone all the time is a bridge too far. Only accepting customers who like your products and how you sell to them—this is a different way to do business for a bank. Fire customers? That might be harsh. Say no politely to the customers whose behavior does not fit the business model, and you are halfway there? Yes, and watch customer satisfaction go way up as a result. Do it consistently, and you begin to see the other side of retail success. Most of all, stick to what you know. It makes you better and better, and word of mouth really drives business when customers can get something done in a way that's easy and fast and makes them feel good.

We zig when everyone else zags. Other banks and financial companies have copied our marketing, used our words, and even used our corporate colors. They copy our rates and our slogans. They even tell customers outright they are like us. In the real world, however, not everyone can sing the same song the same way. A lot of our competitors stop at logic and rational thinking. They miss the brand principle that being different to stand out, and then staying that way consistently to make it stick, has to be in your DNA. They're only trying to look the part, but it's almost never who they really are. Besides, in the end, you still have to make a profit, and you have to bet on your business. A business needs to be a cause that everyone can believe in if it wants to be powerful in the marketplace. Most can never stay the course, because they simply do not believe their own rhetoric.

A revolution? Yes. Customers like to be on a winning side. They want to do good. They like a challenge, especially when they can benefit from it. And the best thing about this revolution is that we can stand with our customers on Main Street, and the only thing we have to worry about is getting trampled as more and more of them come to love what ING Direct stands for and, more important, want to be a part of it.

How to Revolutionize a Business Model in Three Easy Steps

BP: For a company with a cause, change is not a defensive tactic; it's the way forward. Here are three ways to start your own revolution.

Ask Why Until You Can Hardly Stand to Hear the Word

Three-year-olds are onto something. It's a big job, figuring out how everything in the world works. And how do little kids do it? A bit like management consultants, as a matter of fact: by asking why, relentlessly, until they have the answer to the answer to the answer to the answer. If a child asks you why the sky is blue, you can be sure that it's only the beginning of the interrogation. It seems obvious, but it's amazing how often people stop short of understanding the root causes of a broken business model, and the true nature of the opportunity in it. It's amazing how often people accept the corporate version of "because I said so."

In the years following the launch of ING Direct, many other financial institutions tried to do what they believed we had done. Many failed, some ending up bought or merged and some disappearing completely. Some of these efforts came even from large, established banks. One memorable example was a so-called direct bank created, ironically, by the selfsame major institution that was the subject of the anecdote that opened this chapter. To thwart ING Direct's launch in Canada, it created a new brand and built a comprehensive remote-access infrastructure. It was launched some six months ahead of ING Direct, in what I'm sure the parent bank thought was a brilliant preemptive move. The marketing for this launch reportedly ended up costing about 10 times what ING Direct spent when it finally arrived. Between this investment and the sterling reputation of the parent brand, you'd have expected this to be a slam dunk. Yet it wasn't. In a matter of a year or two, this flashy new direct bank was quietly folded back into the parent institution, having failed to attract new customers, and its brand was eventually retired altogether.

Why? Why did an institution with nearly two centuries of experience fail at this seemingly simple enterprise—a new business that didn't even require a single brick to be laid, but was merely a digital storefront for what the parent already had? Or why did so many other virtual banks disappear soon after their launches, or so many of those that remain continue to spend so much more to acquire customers than ING Direct does? One reason is simply that they didn't ask that "why?" question enough times. They tried to build a new, technology-enabled proxy of the old thing. In understanding how that old thing needed to be fixed, they didn't spend enough time figuring out why it was broken in the first place.

Start Over

Arkadi and his team understood why banking was broken, from a consumer point of view. Like a good journalist does, they followed the money.

And it led to what might seem like an unsurprising conclusion: Banks make it by lending. Everything a bank is has its roots in that basic truth. They are, as the CEO of one American bank put it, "in the moving business, not the storage business." Their core business is to provide a service that consumers are grateful to receive, and not all that loyal or brand sensitive about. People will put up with a lot when you're handing them money. It's no surprise, then, that the banking machinery evolved in such a way as to all but forget that it even had customers. And it wouldn't be a surprise, either, that it would be about as easy to fix this as to turn the proverbial supertanker on a dime. Any effort to revolutionize a traditional bank would quickly find itself drowning in "yeah, but's."

Starting from a clean sheet of paper is easier for a new enterprise, there's no doubt. But the exercise of pretending that you have a clean sheet of paper is powerful for anybody trying to make change in a business. How many of us at a certain stage of life have silently wondered, "If I'd only known then what I know now"? Leading an established business is like that, too. But, as with people, a business doesn't need to be a prisoner of its past. Even if true invention isn't practical, disruption often is. It can wake organizations up. It can make them realize that they don't necessarily have to live with the layers of past management thinking that build up like paint on the walls of an old apartment. It can make them realize they really can get out of their own way.

The simple question "What if we started over?" in a real sense built ING Direct, but anyone can ask it. And it's hard to believe there's a business that couldn't benefit from pretending, just for a day, that it's looking at a clean sheet of paper.

Make the Customer a Partner

Defending a business model from being subverted by outside forces is not a new idea. Companies do this all the time. But the battles are more often fought with shareholders, or with legislators or in the courts, constituencies that have the power to force unwanted change on the way a company operates. ING Direct, with its dependency on low operating cost and high volume, saw a threat where you wouldn't normally look: the customer. If the company was built to serve the customer but not to also serve itself, it would sink in no time, becoming an unviable version of the kind of organization it was trying to reinvent. They couldn't just create a new, lean, and efficient banking model. They also had to create an equally new and efficient kind of customer.

To make this work required some guts, because ING Direct would have to do two potentially unpopular things. The first was to build a service structure that rewarded the right kinds of customers, but was an obstacle to the wrong kind. They also followed this through in their communications, relentlessly and candidly driving prospects and customers to the least expensive channel they would tolerate. The second was to be willing to lose business to defend the model. ING Direct did this many times and continues to do so, parting ways with customers and prospects who want the bank to change for them. But they've done this with an interesting and potent twist: They don't have these conversations quietly, like a maître d' telling a restaurant patron that ties are required. ING Direct has been more like a diner where the first thing you see when you walk through the door is a sign saying, "No shirt, no shoes, no service." Their demand that the customer play ball in order to preserve the value proposition has become part of the brand lore. And it has had the effect of making those who save their money here feel somehow even more empowered.

In a world where CEOs have to think from quarter to quarter, it's easy to forget that long-term sustainability is just as important a leadership responsibility. The threats to profitability quarter to quarter are pretty easy to recognize and, for a while at least, relatively simple to manage. The threats to sustainability can come from more surprising places, including a potential customer with money in his hand. As Abraham Lincoln said about fooling people, so it is with pleasing customers: You can only do it for all of the people some of the time, or some of the people all of the time. Nobody can do it for everybody, every day—or not, at least, for very long.

Chapter 6

Saving the Savers

Walking the Talk

*It's your constitutional right to own a gun in the United
States, but having a bank account is a privilege.*

—AK, Innovation & Design Conference,
Phoenix 2007

AK: Once people call us, write us, or look for ING Direct on the Web, they start the conversation about saving. It's a very personal subject, and everyone has their own ways of talking about and relating to saving and what it means to their lives. Sure, saving is not as exciting as buying things like new cars and the latest computers, but it's still true that most people do not budget their money. Too many live from paycheck to paycheck, rich and poor alike. The bigger issue, though, is that few really understand the concept of compound interest, the idea that your savings can actually work for you. Interest is rent on money. You are either paying it or earning it. The cost, or how much the rent is, depends on the interest rate. That rate of interest combined with how much you borrow or save determines the size of the savings mountain you build, or the depth of the debt hole you dig. You have money control with a mountain of savings, but you're wearing a ball and chain in the money hole you create when you borrow.

BP: I'm not sure if this grease stain on the carpet is going to come out, but there's no time to worry about it now. They'll be here to pick up these bicycles any minute, the spunky kids in the orange windbreakers. The machine I'm tinkering with, sitting cross-legged on the floor of our brand-new office, still isn't shifting gears properly, and we've yet to load up the saddlebags with Tic Tacs.

It's still bootstrap time, for ING Direct and for GWP. It's 1998, and both of us are still short of our second birthdays. The kids in the orange windbreakers are the ING Direct Bike Patrol, a street team of politely enthusiastic proselytizers who will today pedal down to Toronto's waterfront to ambush people disembarking from streetcars on their way to the Canadian National Exhibition (CNE). Despite its grand name, the CNE is no more than an oversized example of an annual tradition that's affectionately observed in towns across rural North America: the fall fair. The people getting off those streetcars are hardworking, regular folks, about to show their families a cotton-candy-munching, Ferris-wheel-riding good time and, in the process, lighten their wallets not inconsiderably. Our militantly cheerful Bike Patrollers are going to intercept them for a moment, offer them a tidy little postcard that explains how they can make their savings work harder, and, as a gesture of respect and gratitude for their attention, a little box of orange Tic Tacs.

And I, president of the company proclaiming its intention to reinvent branding for the twenty-first century, am in charge of keeping the bikes' tires pumped, chains lubed, and shifters shifting. Jim Kelly had grudgingly agreed to the two-wheelers, but drew the line at having them professionally maintained. "We're trying to acquire customers for $70 per account," he reminded me. "Unless your bike mechanic is going to open one every time he oils a chain . . ." So here I am.

Those Bike Patrols remain a very fond memory for us, and a symbolically important one for ING Direct. It's not just nostalgia, either, nor is it because they were the inspiration for an ongoing series of similar (and sometimes legendary) guerrilla actions that ING Direct would undertake in the streets and transit systems of New York, Boston, Atlanta, Los Angeles, San Francisco, Miami, and other American cities in provocative, headline-grabbing acts of savings subversion. These Bike Patrols made a clear statement about who ING Direct serves: "We will be for everyone," the Orange Code says, and the Bike Patrols proved we meant it. There was no target group, no segmentation, no proto-consumer—just people getting off a streetcar; regular folks. Anyone old enough to open a bank account, and with a dollar and a hunger for independence, was welcome to join us, and we weren't above taking it to the street to tell them so.

It's hard to overstate how important it has been to ING Direct's success that there was no formally defined target group for what it had to offer. ING Direct was created for someone called the saver, a creature that, when the bank launched, seemed Sasquatch-like in its rarity and reclusiveness, if it existed at all. In a very real sense, ING Direct invented its customer, a consumer defined by attitudes and values rather than by its demographic characteristics. You'd think with something as tangible and measurable as liquid cash, it would be both tempting and easy to fish where the fish are, marketing-wise, to serve the people who could objectively benefit the most, right now, from a high-yield savings account: people with money. And yet, pore over the pages and pages of press coverage ING Direct has received, the hours of television time and the countless selling messages it has broadcast, and you will find not one mention or hint of the age, gender, education level, or net worth of the person who should own the ears and eyes that received those messages. Other than in the technical documents used by people who plan and buy commercial media for ING Direct, you rarely even hear anyone there even use the word *target*.

Why has this been so important? Well, one obvious reason is that there was no market for a high-yield savings account when ING Direct came to town. We *had* to invent one. Another is that ING Direct's business model depends on scale and on low cost of service, but isn't particularly sensitive to how much money its customers have. ING Direct really could welcome anyone, as long as they would play by its rules. Who wouldn't want a pool of prospective customers numbering in the hundreds of millions? Marketing doesn't get much more efficient than that. But the most important reason, the one with the most enduring consequences, has been that it has helped drive the organization to purpose itself for advocacy. With a traditional defined and measurable target market, a company inevitably ends up guided by what those customers think they need, and obsessed with whoever is competing with them to meet that need. A defined target tempts a company to pander to it. The customer, in essence, ends up running the business. But when a company is trying to save everybody, whether they realize they need to be saved or not, the question that drives its behavior is a much simpler and more focused "how?"

AK: In the beginning, there was excitement, and it was infectious. But there was also a certain amount of chaos. Those early days at the conference table were a confusion of agendas and personal desires. Some people wanted to be with a winner. Some wanted to prove something to themselves or someone else who mattered to them. Some wanted to be part of a good story. And some just wanted to make money and move along. In many ways, this is not unusual when you're building a team. In any new start-up or big push forward in business, many personal agendas need to be reconciled and accommodated along the way. As with any army marching off to battle, it gets organized by having a shared, larger objective in mind. It marches on its stomach, the saying goes, but it fights for a cause. In the end, the result is glory, and the human spirit triumphs by having done something good and just for man and country. If people's personal goals got met in the process, that's fine, too. It just can't be the focus.

It did not take long in those conversations and planning debates before that larger objective took center stage, so to speak. I knew our goal was to save the saver, but how? We sought clarity by getting above the tactical confusion. Why are we here? What are we going to do? How are we going to do it? When and where just completes the menu. Should we make new savers? Help old ones save more? Save all savers or just a few? How about young ones versus old ones? Well, it really doesn't matter. Saving the saver was good, worthy, and to the point. The obvious was staring us in the face; we'd had the answer all along: The saver is everybody.

We weren't the only or first group of people to worry about this, of course. Teachers and parents and organizations from state to church have taken an interest in and have made their own efforts on this topic. Despite it all, though, it looks as if, individually and collectively, we are all sliding backwards. The statistics just don't lie. Everyone spends too much and lives for today. The belief that tomorrow will take care of itself is rooted in a need to be happy today and enjoy the here and now. We are confident that we can handle tomorrow when it comes or, at worst, that we can make it up in the bottom of the ninth inning, just like in the movies. Our parents and grandparents were good with money and knew what a dollar was worth, but look what it got them, we seem to be saying to ourselves. Meanwhile, the headlines focus on the score in all aspects of life, and why not? Money has unfortunately also become a sport, a game. We either dream or live that hope.

But I didn't see hope in this at all when we started ING Direct. Our society was turning into a huge casino where people were gambling with their finances, hoping to score. A few were winning, but many lost. From my perspective, the pendulum had swung too far. We needed a return to basics, a way of thinking that would give everyone the chance to benefit and improve their standard of living.

"Save your money": a call to action and a plan, simple, yet breathtaking, because nobody was talking like this. It goes against the grain, and that would work only if it could stand up to the test of truth and relevance for us as a people. Now, saying "Save your money" and asking consumers to do that is tricky business. You can't preach. You can't be boring. You can't be yesterday's nostalgic story. You can't just make a moral case that saving is right. We had to make saving cool. We had to make it a smart thing to do, give it bragging rights. More important, we had to do it in a way that actually works as a business. Financially, the results had to be measurable and real, for the customer and for us. If you're going to build a savings bank, well, then a balance sheet and income statement are how you're going to keep score. Building ING Direct, the cause was always clear and all the other executional challenges of building the bank and running it as a business just got sorted out (well, mostly anyway). But even with the clarity that "saving the saver" brought to the task, there would be hundreds of conversations and interpretations of "Save your money" in the months and years to come.

BP: For Arkadi and the leadership team at ING Direct, purposing the organization to "save the saver" kept another threat at bay, too: the threat of becoming the enemy. As a business, ING Direct was still a bank, at least in the technical sense. And ING, the organization that was capitalizing this venture, was a financial institution, too—a huge, prosperous one with a lot of history and culture of its own and, as an insurance company, a natural and necessary conservative streak. The very people who were signing the checks could, with all the best intentions in the world, drag the new enterprise back toward what was familiar and safe for them. By continuously referring to the customer, especially in such dramatically human terms, Arkadi could keep the conversation focused on innovation.

AK: Now, getting bankers, corporate executives, journalists, and analysts to understand this was another thing altogether. I must admit it surprised me and generally frustrated me to no end. In meeting after meeting, I would sit and listen to the typical corporate business discussions: financial ratios, managing for value, six sigma, and risk models. Governance of the bank and compliance with regulations would grind on and on. Banking is a regulated business; that is clear and necessary. Holding deposits is a responsibility that goes beyond capital and good intentions. My responsibility is to the customers whose deposits we are supposed to manage well. *Safety* and *soundness* are the operative words, of course. For me, it was not that these aspects of the bank were unimportant. It's just that they were table stakes. They were, in my mind, not the point of what we were trying to accomplish.

Emotionally, this is why I felt the most at home with customers and, next to them, the associates who made it really happen every day and truly built our brand into a living idea. They bleed 'Save your money,' and we called them Orange with pride. The further up the legal structure of the bank you went, the more confused and disconnected things seemed to get from the true power of the idea. My own role as leader was to reconcile this divergence as much as possible and make it work by relentlessly championing the vision and our mission. I used the platform my title gave me and my own powers of persuasion to force this connection at every opportunity. It is a strange feeling knowing that I was getting paid for reasons that you'd think had nothing to do with what I wanted to accomplish or the cause that I secretly believed in so passionately. It was a double life, in a way. Well, if you can get $6 billion in capital, I guess it comes with strings. Making sure that one does not get hanged with those strings was a tough and highly disciplined act to perform.

I have no regrets about having to walk this tightrope, but my views can easily be summarized with this recap of a meeting in a boardroom in Amsterdam.

Debate raged about whether the ING Direct concept was viable as a business. It was one thing to sell a high-interest deposit product, but to build a business and a brand franchise around it? "When did anyone ever believe the idea that paying high rates of interest on savings could build a profitable bank?" said the practical corporate guys. "The financials are the real scorecard of things that get done in this world. The only franchise that is worth anything is the value of the customers who are willing to do business with us and continue to do so. They are not going to do business with us because we tell them we care about them or that we have great buildings or that they see our name on the back of a runner's T-shirt or on the side of a car! It's the offer that matters, not the brand," they argued.

Paying great and better rates is meant to do two things, I would fire back: One, yes, to prove that there was a good deal here: value for customers. But, two, it's also symbolic proof that we can do money with them in a way that is better than the other banks out there. The high interest rate was only the start! It was the equivalent of planting a seed. You need water and a lot of gardening before it turns into a sustainable crop. Yes, things get done because someone wants to get them done! So, the right thing to do is invest in innovation, automation, and the best possible people. Paying high rates was just the beginning, but not the whole concept. Driving and leading this bank with top-down thinking would be a bit like planting seeds in the ground and then looking for the vegetables in your refrigerator.

I generally at this point had to hold my breath.

When it came to marketing specifically, it was often just as difficult. There was always a lot of debate about why consumers, visitors to ING Direct, and those who finish the journey and become customers, will do it and why they will stay. Cynical betting goes on in banking circles, with regulators, and among analysts about what it will take for our customers to leave. The more we have tried to explain our cause and how people voted with their money for the brand and what it stood for, the more those professional eyes glazed over. Best of all were the data modelers, who insisted that consumer behavior could be predicted and manipulated, and that all any brand amounted to was a fancy, expensive label. How wrong they were.

Along the way we have always had lots of critics. No phones will ring, they've said. Deposits won't come in. Deposits won't stay. Not enough customers will sign up. Deposit accounts will be too small. Interest rate is all that is important to consumers, who, the doubters have insisted, are just greedy. Over time, we slowly proved them wrong with results and facts. The criticism continues, of course, because we are still in a very different mode than the rest of the industry. A turning point in this debate came when we had to allow the Orange Savings Account interest rate to fall behind its major rate competitors. The resulting rate differential got as high as 1 percentage point, as competitors tried to buy market share with unsustainable pricing. But our customers stayed and new customers kept coming. It really ticked the critics off because they couldn't explain it. We held this differential for over a year. True, lots of folks do not track rates or even generally know what they are getting, but there are rate watchers and rate followers, and they are vocal. And even they stayed. Some left and then came back when they found out that the service or the customer experience was not great across the street. From a retailer's perspective, this is fundamental. If you sell a product but deliver a poor experience afterward, then customers will not come back and they will not support your brand in any way, no matter how great the price was. They'll become negative promoters having learned a bad lesson about value. In banking, few understand this concept. For us, though, staying close to who we are for has been good business.

BP: It's pretty easy to talk about saving the saver, or about advocating for any kind of consumer. But this is still a business. If this rescue mission was allowed to become nothing more than the rhetorical theme of speeches and public relations and regulatory charm offensives, then the experience real customers had would still end up being created by professional managers with bonus targets and short-term profit motives. The organization would turn inward and become operationally focused. Good people need a purpose. For ING Direct, that meant finding ways to weave the habit of empathizing with the consumer into every aspect of the way it went to market. It didn't mean denying that a business needs to make money; it meant that doing so in the service of people, in some real way, was a condition attached to that profit. When you think of the customers you want as targets, it's easy to begin to see them as a statistical variable in a business model and, in a sense, lose sight of them altogether. When the customer you want is everyone, anyone, all Americans "yearning to breathe free," as it says on the Statue of Liberty, then, suddenly, you can't take your eyes off them.

Looking back on ING Direct's march to success, these are the ways that they've most consistently, most effectively, walked that talk.

Reaching Out

BP: It's a pretty universal human truth that first impressions define you and are hard to overcome. It's true with the people we meet and the communities we join, and it's true of new brands. A mentor of mine years ago was fond of saying about the art of launching a new enterprise, "Begin as you mean to proceed."

Imagine, then, that you are a commuter in one of America's bustling cities. You're crawling along in traffic or you're lined up on a train platform, and there appears before you like a mirage a cheerful person dressed in orange, offering to pay your train fare or fill your gas tank for free. And, while you're waiting, they also offer you an energetic reminder of the benefits of saving money (the free ride is meant to help you get started), along with a small incentive to open an Orange Savings Account so you, too, can enjoy those benefits.

To maximize the efficiency of its media spending, ING Direct opened for business in North America one city at a time, rather than the more typical all-at-once national launch. It was slower this way, and it took some courage to leave rich markets untouched so that marketing costs could be carried by the business as it grew. But it had some benefits, too, and one of the biggest was the chance to meet consumers on the street, face-to-face. And so, if you live in one of these cities, the chances are very good that you didn't hear about ING Direct first from an ad or a direct mail package. The chances are very good you heard about it while you were stopping for gas or waiting for a train. You met ING Direct in the faces of friendly, happy-looking young people in orange who approached you with a gift and a message, or you met it in the faces of commuters whose days just got better, as they smiled into television cameras. In a wonderful twist, this so-called virtual bank almost always introduced itself in a most human way. You couldn't help but feel that this business was about people and that it was here to help—that it was, more fundamentally, here.

AK: People really notice this about us. It has an emotional impact. Here's an example of the kind of moment that happens many times a day for us: Our new Chicago café is humming. It's midmorning, and I find myself sitting anonymously among students with laptops and people milling around drinking coffee and pulling chairs from one table to another. Seeing the café associate I'm sitting with, a couple comes to my table, and says without prompting, "We're visiting here in Chicago, and we just want to tell you that we love your café. You guys are so friendly and the atmosphere is so positive that we just have to congratulate you." Shaun Rowley, the café manager there, is grinning from ear to ear, knowing that I have just witnessed a "here" moment.

I understand the science of marketing pretty well, but I trust this kind of human experience more. No ad can make a first impression like this, or leave people feeling as good about you.

BP: In new economy circles, the ideal virtual business is often cynically described as "a server in the corner printing money." That's not how it's been at ING Direct, not by a long shot, and this policy of outreach didn't stop at launch events. Its cafés have become rather famous as iconoclastic gestures to the traditional bank branch. "Memo to banking's old guard:" said *Fast Company* magazine, writing about the Philadelphia location in 2003. "Meet the new guard—and have a chai latte." The ING Direct cafés make a genuine effort to join the communities in which they reside, to make its brand somehow part of the street life there. They also function as physical points of contact, where you can sign up to be a customer and do business. But the most interesting function they perform is as a kind of living, vibrant (and even self-funding) temple for ING Direct's cause. "The design of the cafés tells people," Arkadi has often said, "that we're going to be simple and easy and human." And that opening a savings account is as easy as buying a cup of coffee.

The idea of outreach even influences the more traditional and basic aspects of how ING Direct goes to market. From the earliest days, billboards and other street-level advertising media have been a core element of ING Direct's paid media strategy, despite persistent challenges in trying to quantify its effectiveness. Whether it's a conventional billboard exhorting consumers on I-95 or taking over every available piece of advertising real estate at New York's Grand Central Station, even our most commercial messages say, "We're here. We aren't granite bank branches with velvet ropes and prim tellers hiding behind mahogany wickets, but we're here."

Simplifying

AK: It's 2:15 PM, and I'm taking one of 25,000 calls we'll receive today, each one of them a moment of truth. Each will be a moment that builds or hurts our reputation and shapes the way customers feel and think about the ING Direct brand. But this next call starts off on a very bad footing.

"You guys sound good, but it won't last, right?"

Wrong!

"I mean this is an introductory offer, right?"

Wrong!

"You know, the old bait and switch. Little tricks in the fine print, right?"

Wrong!

"Are you for real?"

"We are for real," I assure him. A pause.

"Okay, I'll open an account. But I can close it with no cost, right?"

"Right. So, now that we've got you started, why did you call?"

"I need to save, but I want to feel confident about where my money is."

"Sounds like you have been thinking about this for a while."

"Yeah, and I am totally turned off by my bank now."

"Where did you hear about us?"

"I saw your commercial on TV, and it sounded straightforward and easy. I wanted to see if you guys really answer the phone with a real person who lives in this country."

"Looks like we do," I said.

We finished the call with a joke about who we are. He thought ING Direct sounded like an Indonesian courier company and not a bank. I told him we left out the word *bank* so that customers would think differently about us. That would focus us on the retailer's challenge of just selling a simple product. "Why?" he asked. I said it means we have less to screw up. He laughed and replied, "You guys are too much." He was a convert. I knew he would mention us to his friends.

BP: If you make things hard for people, nobody is going to believe for a second that you're here to save them. Words, if they're long enough and you use enough of them, make walls. Complicated processes and clever catches and conditions are like gates and moats. Eventually, people get the message they aren't welcome.

Simplification, as obvious as it might seem in hindsight, has been one of ING Direct's most fundamental ways of saving the saver. The products themselves must be simple. The process of signing up for one must be simple. The experience of using it must be simple. And this drive is not motivated by the belief that people aren't smart enough to handle complexity. It's motivated by the understanding that simple means honest. Simple means nothing to hide. Simplicity is an invitation to customers not only to act—because doing so won't ask too much of them—but to act with trust. And it's a challenge to the people who develop ING Direct's products, its customer communications, and its marketing: If it's any good, it can be simple. And if it can't be simple, maybe you've still got some work to do. Selling an idea at ING Direct—and believe me, I know—is like selling a script in Hollywood: If you can't explain it before the elevator doors open, don't bother trying.

Having Conversations

AK: "I don't have any money to save!" It's the most common response I hear when people are challenged to save their money. "I should pay off my debt first, right?" Not necessarily. You will never get there if you don't get into the habit of saving first. It has to be part of your everyday thinking about money, a reflex. Let me give you an example: You need a break at work. It's time to have a cup of coffee. Do you really need to pay $3.25? Why not go somewhere cheaper than your usual café or order something simpler, spend $1.75, and save that $1.50 for yourself? It's not about suffering; it's just about choices.

It's 10:15 AM and I am on the telephone talking to a single mom in Chicago. She has received an ING Direct mail piece that offers her $25 if she opens an account. She has a young daughter in school and wants to save for college tuition. She is interested and really wants to save, but she's not sure how to make it work. As it is for many people, saving is a game of Snakes and Ladders for her. Up one year down the next, she never feels like she's getting anywhere. I listen for a while, and then I ask her what she and her daughter do for fun. "Movies on Saturday are our big mother-daughter outings," she tells me.

"Movies are pretty expensive," I sympathize.

"Yes, but it's our treat," she explains. I decide we're going to figure this out together.

"So you pay $18 for two tickets," I say. "Do you buy popcorn?"

"Yes, and a drink," she replies, sounding nervous.

"How much would that be?"

"Another $16. Oh yes, and parking for $8."

I offer her a suggestion: "Save the popcorn and soda drinks. The movie and parking are important, but you can skip the popcorn."

"Really?"

"Yes, and the result is $800 a year in savings."

"You're kidding!"

"No. It's easy to do this if you really want to. You'll have pretty nice savings in the bank at the end of a year, for not really giving up much. And for a movie snack, you can just bring something small from home. The movie is probably good value. The popcorn, well, it's popcorn."

These very human conversations with people about their money happen every day, and not just on the phone.

I'm at my workstation and reading an e-mail from a customer who wants to talk about fees. "Your savings accounts don't have fees," he points out. "You advertise no fees. Yet you charge a fee to provide a mortgage."

I can tell by his tone that he's afraid we aren't what we say we are. In the beginning, we would get this all the time: ING Direct is too good to be true. Still today, the chances to break faith or disappoint are enormous. The e-mails are usually kisses or kicks. And some need reassurance of one kind or another. Most customers just want to know that what they are doing is the right thing. They wouldn't bother writing if they weren't engaged. I draft a reply.

"Thanks for writing," I tell this gentleman. "I don't think fees are any good unless you receive clear value in exchange. Mortgages are expensive for any bank to write. For our mortgages, we recover just $800 of $2,300 in fees it costs to put a mortgage on the bank's books, and we're up-front about it. Fees are like sand in your bathing suit," I tell him. "We don't like them any more than you do. Have a great day."

Short and direct was the reply, and frank. There is no sense in wasting his time with condescending education or big explanations or dodging the question altogether. Save me money or save me time. Every customer forms an opinion and then looks to reinforce it. That alone is a big reason why all the associates who work at ING Direct need to be savers and good with money themselves. You need to talk, think, and believe in the principle and the mission if you want to convince and support folks from Main Street that what they are doing with their money is right.

BP: Reading Arkadi's accounts of working the phones in ING Direct's call center, you might be impressed by the fact that he does it at all. It's admirable, there's no doubt. The benefits of having the CEO hear the voice of the customer firsthand are obvious and powerful. But look again at his stories, and you'll see something more surprising: There is no script for dealing with customers. And it's not just Arkadi who works without one. Every associate talking to customers on the phone is at liberty, and encouraged, to listen to what it is that individual wants or wonders or is worried about, and then, within reason and the practical limits of what the bank can do, to help them get it. Because they're so clear and certain about what they are there to do (that would be save the saver), associates can be trusted to not need a script for everything. These people can engage customers and prospects as fellow humans and really talk to them. One call center team leader puts it this way: "There are three things we can do on a call. We can build the brand, we can be neutral to the brand, or we can destroy the brand. The key is empathy."

Being a company that talks with people rather than at them is something ING Direct grapples with constantly. In a call center environment, time is money. Associates need to be able to speak in the voice of the brand and as advocates, yes, but a single phone contact with a customer can also cost the company more than five dollars. Still, in the age of the Internet-empowered consumer, the impact of a brand experience gets amplified quickly. On the day this was written, there were 37 active ING Direct groups on the social networking site Facebook alone. It would be somewhere between ludicrously expensive and impossible to reverse the kind of damage a bad experience can do out there. It's far more efficient to just make sure the voices of customers who had a great conversation with their rebel bank are the loudest and most consistent ones. So, the keys for ING Direct have been accessibility and responsiveness. Write,

e-mail, or call ING Direct with a point of view, and you may be assured
it will land on all the right desks very, very quickly. Write the CEO himself, and you may be assured that he will read it, and that if it's a criticism
it will cause some heartburn, for him or for whoever is responsible.

And if you call to close your account, you'd better be sure that's what
you want to do, because you never know who'll be on the other end of
the phone urging you not to give up.

Holding Hands

AK: As with any company that has a high profile, ING Direct has always
attracted the attention of countless charities looking for support from us.
They've all been worthy, too, which has made it all the more difficult to
say no. But we have said no, often. There are three things that drive our
approach to charitable activity: We want to make a real difference, we
want to be hands-on and engage everyone at ING Direct in what we are
doing, and we want to focus our giving on causes that reflect our own
values as a company and, yes, as a brand.

BP: That more or less explains the brightly painted dinosaur that adorned
the lobby of ING Direct's *Orangerie* building on Wilmington's riverfront
for months.

It had to do with a charity auction in which citizens and corporations in Wilmington, Delaware, would buy dinosaur sculptures, with the
funds going to a children's literacy group operating in the city. The sculptures were meant to be decorated individually, after which the donors
could do with them as they wished. ING Direct bought one, had a noted
artist paint it beautifully, and donated it to the city's Cops 'n Kids Reading Room; Arkadi also bought one, painted it himself, and displayed it in
the lobby to promote the cause of children's literacy and, not incidentally,
set an example for community involvement among the Orange faithful.

Corporations across North America do good in countless ways, and
make their communities beneficiaries of untold millions of charitable
dollars. On this score, ING Direct is neither unique nor a pioneer. The
way it goes about citizenship, though, is very much its own. And it does
more than simply give back, as the familiar platitude goes. It completely
erases the line between ING Direct the enterprise and ING Direct the

corporate citizen. After all, if this rebel bank really has a cause, how could there be any difference between the two? From this, two themes emerge that, in my experience, make ING Direct's brand of corporate citizenship a bit special.

The first theme has its own soundtrack.

If you were in San Francisco on a Saturday morning in July of 2004, you might have noticed the 723 Harley-Davidson motorcycles rumbling across the Golden Gate Bridge, which had been closed for the occasion. It was the start of a tradition called the ING Direct Independence Ride and, though you'd have to look closely to recognize him behind the goggles, that was CEO Arkadi Kuhlmann leading the pack, raising money for the ING Direct Kids Foundation to support the community's Honoring Emancipated Youth initiative. It's only the most dramatic—and loudest—example of an important distinction that characterizes the best and most enduring acts of ING Direct's communitarianism, the distinction between charity and activism. Arkadi didn't just sign a check. He was out there. So are the associates who build homes for Habitat for Humanity, or who stuff backpacks with school supplies for underprivileged children, or who ride bicycles—dressed, of course, in bright orange—in community fund-raising events. In 2007, in fact, ING Direct invested 15,000 person days of its associates' time in community service across the United States, incredible for a company of about 2,000 people.

Communitarianism even finds its way into the bank's operations. The team of executives in charge of building ING Direct's headquarters in Wilmington, Delaware, were activists, too. Instead of renting space in a sleek, anonymous office tower, they decided to rejuvenate the Christina Riverfront in Wilmington with beautifully renovated heritage buildings, park space, and covered parking, making a forgotten neighborhood into a lively and welcoming community center. From the Golden Gate Bridge to the Cops 'n Kids Reading Room, the people of ING Direct get personally involved. And in doing this, ongoing, they make their corporate family so intimately a part of their communities—local and national—that it's not only impossible to separate public relations from genuine communitarianism, it's actually unnecessary.

The second theme has to do with the source of all of ING Direct's power, and much of America's: optimism. At the very core of the belief system behind this organization, its culture, and its brand is the certain knowledge that confidence in the future is the real dividend of saving money. People who save have more of this confidence than people who don't, and the capacity for self-empowerment is what it takes to be a saver in the first place. Money in the bank exchanges fear for courage. Without faith in the idea that tomorrow can be better than today and that we each have the ability to make it so, there is no ING Direct. And the broader social impact of such a poverty of optimism is too terrible to contemplate.

Consider this, and you begin to see a strategic pattern in the kinds of causes ING Direct works for in its communities:

- Children, who *are* the future: Primarily through the ING Direct Kids Foundation, children are given the chance and the means to learn, which, in turn, empowers them to believe in themselves.
- Financial literacy: There is more to self-determination than saving, and yet even this simple habit is one that too few people learn early enough, too often condemning them to life on the treadmill of debt.
- Housing for those who can't make that all-important start on their own: For Americans, there is no more fundamental symbol of security than a home, no more powerful step in the journey to independence; and, for those who might not otherwise have been able to take that step, no more persuasive proof that the future might just be theirs to write after all.

The nature of ING Direct's community involvement is in some ways about economic sustainability: This bank can't expect to profit from leading Americans back to saving if it's not willing to do all it can to include everyone, generation after generation.

And this, in essence, is the key to ING Direct's way of holding hands with the communities in which it does business. ING Direct offers its cause as a contribution to the common good and a reason to belong. It chose a founding purpose for itself that would benefit society as much as it would benefit its own business. That has made choosing charitable causes to support a simpler matter, and it has meant that ING Direct has never had to quiet its voice of advocacy, even when it is just trying to help.

Defending

BP: Reading the headlines as this book is being written, with the damage of the subprime mortgage crisis swirling through the media and the world's economies, the irony is bitter: "Who Will Save the Savers?" The sober black-and-gray newspaper ad ran in March of 2005 in the *Washington Post* and the *Wall Street Journal,* a plea to legislators to think again before signing into law a new bankruptcy reform bill. The bill, the ad said, would be punitive to consumers and overprotective of financial institutions, particularly those whose predatory lending practices might play a role in causing consumer bankruptcies in the first place. It isn't only irresponsible people who go bankrupt, it argued. It's people who have been lent too much money by banks that should know better, people who have been blindsided by medical disasters, and people who have been victims of identity theft. Banks own some of these problems, the ad said, even though it was a bank logo that appeared at the bottom. "We can't let this happen. America needs to save its savers." The ad was aimed at the nation's elites, decision makers and opinion leaders, and it was the first time ING Direct had ever spent a penny talking to Wall Street rather than Main Street. But desperate times had called for desperate measures.

With the Bankruptcy Reform Act of 2005 looking increasingly likely to pass and the clock running out, Arkadi dropped everything and went to Washington, D.C., to lend his support to Senators Russ Feingold, Charles Schumer, and Edward Kennedy, stumping against the pending bill, which he had publicly decried for more than a year, in the press and against the American Bankers Association (who were supporting the bill as written). In the end, that battle was lost, but the fight wasn't over. As *American Banker* dryly reported, "Mr. Kuhlmann said . . . he would continue taking controversial public-policy stands if he believed legislation or regulations were hurting consumers."

And so he has, and so ING Direct has, more than once, not always in the public eye, and seemingly oblivious to the risk of making enemies among regulators and powerful competitors. ING Direct, usually in the form of Arkadi riding into town like a vigilante, has advocated passionately for laws and rules that favor the people over the institutions that depend on them. In that same year, there was a call for reform of the Real Estate Settlement Procedures Act, and for more protection of consumers' private information when it is entrusted to banks and credit card companies. And it continues today, with a quiet initiative to have government reconsider the wisdom of blanket mortgage interest deductibility— because it encourages people to borrow too much money—and semiserious exhortations on national television that credit cards should have warning labels on them like cigarette packages do.

In the final analysis, standing up for savers is like standing up for anything that really matters: Sometimes, you're going to have to take risks, do unpopular things, be a burr under the saddles of powerful people, or expend effort that might never earn you any public recognition, credit, or profits. But being willing to do that is how you remind yourself that your cause is for real. That's how you keep the fire lit, how you can look customers in the eye when you're asking for their business and have them know you mean what you say. That's walking the talk.

AK: What people do with their money is often a reflection of their values. The way they spend says something about who they are. I think the same is true of corporations. ING Direct doesn't just contribute to charities to ease our consciences or look good. We do it to prove what we believe in. It authenticates our values, and it makes "saving the saver" something we're all here to do, not just an empty marketing promise.

The most important thing we have to remember about saving the saver is that it's a cause that has no end. It's so fundamental that any progress the brand makes will be for the better. ING Direct also proves that building a bank on more than capital can work and is worthy. Nobody knows how long we can keep the cause alive, but we know that it has already made a difference and will continue to have a lasting impact in the lives of many people. Believe it or not, I even think it's good sign that many other banks are now offering higher rates to compete with us. That will force them to become more efficient. They are redesigning their branches and online offerings. There is a pressure mounting on how credit cards and mortgages are sold. These are all strong signs that ING Direct has helped put pressure on public opinion by publicly defending its cause: by saving the saver.

For us, living and working with our brand, there is no better or softer pillow than a clear conscience.

Chapter 7

It Takes a Village

Building the Orange Brand Nation

> *With the right culture, the problems of commitment,*
> *alignment, and motivation go away and hierarchy becomes*
> *irrelevant. . . . [Managers] tend to set strategy and plans*
> *first and then try to put the right people in place. Great*
> *companies do it the other way around.*
>
> —AK, CEO Message # 47

BP: "We're probably going to get a bonus."

The speaker deadpanning these words is Arkadi himself. He's talking to a video camera and sitting at a makeshift table in ING Direct's Wilmington café, with desultory Thanksgiving week traffic gliding past on Delaware Avenue in the window behind him. He has just rhymed off business results for the previous month—226,000 new accounts; $1.2 billion in new mortgages (for "nice people," he reassures the unseen viewer in a reference to the gathering storm at other institutions in the mortgage industry, a subject he'll return to in a few minutes); $657 million in deposits; $160 million in profits so far this year—and wraps up by saying that the corporate goals for the period had been met and exceeded. ING Direct was on track to have a very good year. Applause erupts from somewhere behind the camera, sounding for all the world like a studio audience.

He continues, mischievous, animated, off-the-cuff. News is next: A new television commercial is in production. The St. Cloud office has won an award for civic volunteerism. Electric Orange has been named by *Kiplinger's* as the year's "Best Checking Account" (the team working on it is congratulated by their names). The New York café has been wrapped to look like a stack of enormous dollar bills. A scoop: ING Direct is opening a café in Hawaii (this one will serve beer). Then a guest, Bob George, Customer Maximization Leader, is there to talk about the customer experience for mortgage buyers. From here, Arkadi springboards to the ridiculous fees mortgage customers have to pay at other institutions (except in Indiana, where there are laws against some of them. "Go Indiana," he intones), and then wraps up with a quote from *American Banker* about the growing subprime mortgage crisis. "Make no mistake about it," he reads from the publication. "This crisis was caused by the financial service industry's grossly lax underwriting standards and deceptive marketing." Then, looking up at the camera, he says earnestly, "Those of us that are doing solid, great work for affordability and suitability, for financial products that actually make sense for savers and borrowers . . . we're on the right track." He concludes with a humorous list of "Top Five Reasons Not to Pay Bank Fees," and then the screen fades to black.

Officially, this was to be called "Good Morning Associates!" in homage to the movie in which Robin Williams famously played a maverick Armed Forces Radio DJ. But the marketing team that was frantically trying to backstop Arkadi's latest idea for engaging ING Direct's staff had already given it a more informal handle: AKTV. It was going to be a weekly television show, conceived, produced, written, and hosted by ING Direct's CEO. And it had an audience of just 2,000 people (if everyone was at their desks, that is), because every pair of eyeballs would belong to an employee of ING Direct, who would have it broadcast to their computer workstations. Nobody was ever going to see AKTV who wasn't already drawing a paycheck from ING Direct and "bleeding Orange." Arkadi Kuhlmann was preaching to the choir.

Does any leader always enjoy the task of motivating a team, or find it easy, or even always productive or worth the cost? Sure, it has its moments.

Lots of us affectionately recall this or that successful sales meeting, or the popularity of a branded polo shirt or tote bag that was handed out a Christmas or two ago, or the time the CFO sang "Oops! . . . I Did It Again" on the karaoke machine at the summer picnic. But that's just the point. We can remember the highs, and all too often those highs are extrinsic to the real job everyone is there to do. The task of motivating a workforce has a Sisyphean quality about it. We roll the boulder of employee motivation up the hill, and then wait for it to roll back down so we can start again. Students of organizational theory might be reminded of the infamous Hawthorne Effect, named for a series of worker productivity experiments at a telephone factory in the 1920s in which everything worked, but only briefly.

Little wonder, then, that so many businesses built on low-operating-cost models run screaming in the opposite direction of engaging their workforces. Everybody from discount retailers to dot-com giants surrenders to the futility of trying to make frontline people into ambassadors for their brands. Instead, they choose to manage on the principle that any consumers who don't want to serve themselves should get the sullen, disassociated, low-wage, regularly recycled help they deserve.

It's a harsh generalization, but it's a necessary one if you want to really understand how utterly contrary ING Direct's approach to developing an internal culture has been. Good leaders try to motivate their employees. Great ones try to inspire them. But at ING Direct, they went further, declaring the people who work there to be the brand incarnate, and a full-fledged community, one with its own language and customs, its own obligations of citizenship, and its own gathering places. It's called being "Orange," and the experience of citizenship in this community begins the day they walk through the door: The first training material they receive is a booklet called "Your Official Orange Passport." "Get ready," says the subhead on the cover, "for the adventure of your life."

AK: I find myself sitting in the Wilmington ING Direct café, by the window with a mocha coffee in front of me. Cafés, coffee, friendly people—this is a social ritual as ancient as history. It still works. Everyone can relate to the stress-free moments that go with coffee and conversation.

It's Monday morning, a little after 8 AM. The sun is shining and it's early spring. Business always hums on Monday. There are big inflows and lots of calls from customers moving money and wanting to add to their accounts. The staff associates are busy, smiling and handing over cappuccinos and chai lattes, the caffeine for the energetic conversations to come today. It seems that the mood is positive and strong, with a few smiles and a bit of encouragement. It feels great just watching them talk and do their thing. Having just finished my morning workout in our Wellness Center, I'm thinking about the lineup of fellow associates ordering their morning cups of coffee, and glad to be one of them.

These cafés of ours are not very traditional—they have a clean, modern, yet relaxed feel to them—and they aren't all the same. It always surprises me that even when things like this are not identical, they can still give you an impression of being shaped by one underlying idea, and by what we as visitors wish to see. It's a bank? No, it's a café that has some banking talk around it. Okay, you'll think, maybe ING Direct is different. For a bank, a brand is a clear point of differentiation. Who would have thought? Don't get me wrong. The cafés are good in their own right. They're relaxed; they make you feel that doing business there is as easy as buying a cup of coffee. The quality of the coffee beans has to be good, and it is. The price has to be right, and it is. If the service is good, then, as a package, it's good value for the customer. But what else? How does it feel? The design and the colors say a lot. They communicate something about us, and so does the atmosphere. So does the lack of clutter, which seems to promise simplicity. They say that retail is detail, and in my experience it's true. As with any good play or performance, you have to hit every note right on. The thing is, you've got to prepare for it and understand it. What you don't plan for will, in the end, plan itself. Then, of course, you may or may not like the outcome. Experiences like our cafés are not accidental.

In walks Rick Perles, head of human resources (HR) for ING Direct. He's not on coffee but is sipping a juice drink. Rick walks a different path than most. He's dedicated, loyal, and very focused. He would have made a good Marine, come to think of it. Never at a loss for words, Rick, you just know, is turning the wheels in his mind.

"Hey, Rick, how are you?"

"I'm just won-der-ful! So, Boss, what can I do for you?"

The "Boss" thing is really not Orange, culturally speaking, but Rick feels proud that he can make his plays behind the scenes, including for me. I have had the privilege to serve with Rick for five years, and every meeting over that period of time has started with the same opening lines. I've come to think it's like a lucky charm for the two of us. Rick has managed to get our HR in line with the ING Direct brand and the culture throughout the organization. Rick does bleed Orange. The thing is, he is practical about it, not fanatical. He does not push our culture on people, but he defends it to the hilt. In a subtle way, his upstate Pennsylvania upbringing shines through. He is direct, honest, and holds strong fundamental values that sit well with ING Direct's brand.

BP: The word *values* comes up a lot in the ING Direct story. Values are the structural components of ING Direct's sense of purpose, its "pixie dust." This company's ability to inspire consumers and be nearly immune to being copied by competitors comes not from a proprietary business model, but from the cause the model serves. So it's natural that the team ING Direct builds has to be made up of recruits with an affinity for those values. And it's essential that the company appear to be guided by those values in the way it sells. But if ING Direct stopped there, its values could quickly become abstract and irrelevant to the way work gets done from day to day. They'd become an artifact of its culture, maybe, but not necessarily central to the way it operated. You'd hear them preached at pep rallies and holiday parties, but not in business plans and performance evaluations. And the only obvious way to prevent this would be to codify them into a book of rules and processes, creating the kind of organization that appears to be principled but is, in fact, just a corporate robot, automatically mouthing the right words but feeling nothing—and giving customers exactly the same warm feeling they get when the touch screen at an ATM flashes the words "Have a nice day."

For Arkadi and his team, that wasn't going to cut it. Such a lack of authenticity would be devastating to their credibility as a cause. And it would be terribly unsatisfying to the people who worked at ING Direct. This was supposed to be, after all, a revolution. You can't have people just "phoning it in," as they say in Hollywood. They have to have evangelical fire in their bellies, and a book of rules isn't going to put it there. The leadership of this new bank needed something more organic, a way to make the organization live these values almost without thinking. And it needed the people who work there to expect this from one another just as constantly as their leaders expect it from them.

The solution was to prove one of the defining decisions in ING Direct's success: They recruited the brand as the key instrument of leadership.

The word *brand,* for most people, instantly evokes marketing. They think of it as the name a company gives to its value proposition, making it recognizable to prospective customers. Most companies confine the subject of brands to their marketing departments just as they'd confine the subject of dental benefits to their HR departments. ING Direct made it mean much more. What it calls its brand is actually the moral standard to which everything the company does is held. It's what everybody and everything has to live up to. As Arkadi once put it, "Everybody thinks that the leadership of ING Direct shaped the brand. But it's not true. It's the brand that shaped the leadership." This turned the creation of ING Direct into something akin to nation building.

Turn a company into a "brand nation"? It might sound crazy, but consider this: Nations are built on common ideals and shared values, not on business models, and they have a habit of outlasting corporations by centuries. Long after everybody has forgotten the insurance-selling lizard or the hamburger-selling clown, they'll still revere the Magna Carta and be able to quote from the Declaration of Independence. If you want to integrate governance, culture, productivity, and customer experience in your organization in an almost infinitely scalable way, nation building isn't a bad model. Just start with a constitution. . . .

AK: There is nothing better than the truth. Once you trust the people you work with, you can't stop the process of bonding that eventually leads to love and respect. It has often been said that we accept those we care about with all their strengths and their faults. The Orange Code has this idea of oneness and mutual respect as its source of relevance and energy, and it includes all of us.

I'm sitting with Jim Kelly and Rudy Wolfs on a Friday afternoon in the ING Direct Pakhuis offices. The end of another week is upon us, a brief moment to reflect on the week that was and the battle to come next week. As it happens, we're in the very same corner of the same floor where the three of us had stood in the summer of 2000 when it all began for us in the United States, and in a quiet moment I was carried back to that day. We had been talking about the ongoing work agenda, and I had asked Jim, "What's really on your mind?" It took Jim a while to put his thoughts together, but then in pure, concise form he said, "I want to do good." Rudy, understanding exactly what Jim meant, nodded in agreement. Whatever came, we were going to be on the side of the angels, as I so often put it. Doing good has always been the soul of how I feel and what I care about in this business. I wonder how many times in a man's life he gets a chance to experience that true feeling of partnership. The memory of that conversation stayed with me all weekend. Anyone would follow Jim anywhere on the promise of doing good. The line might not have the punch of "Do no evil," but it reinforces the positive. It's active, not passive, and the commitment it makes is at the heart of what the people who come here yearn for and have in common.

We all need our work to be important, no matter where we are in the corporate hierarchy. I remember, for example, a conversation I had at Hans Verkoren's retirement party. The party took place on a floating barge with a room full of smiles and warmth, a typical corporate celebration of a great career. But when we finally had the chance to speak alone that evening, I told Hans that the real value of what he has accomplished is not to be found in the corporate suites. It's found in the appreciation of the millions of customers for whom we have created value in spite of all the challenges. Their thanks are returned in service, which those of us who live the Orange Code understand. So did Hans. Conversations like these show how important it has been for us to feel that we are in it together, and never above it.

When the work on this brand began, about three sentences after the idea of a new bank start-up, we asked ourselves this question: With a blank sheet of paper in front of us, what should the bank look like? It was both daunting and exciting. Imagine the opportunity! Not the commercial aspects; that would come later. The business plan would take care of those challenges. The staff, the customers—what would they look like and how would they behave differently? What would set them apart that can be easily understood and nurtured? How would we create value for customers and, in turn, the shareholder, through the strength of our people? Could that be our competitive edge? Could we disrupt the status quo in financial services? What would it really take?

We knew that we wanted to win and make it a success. We wanted to win big, but also to make a real difference. We wanted to be on the side of the angels when it comes to doing business. An unspoken view was in the room at all times: If we are to fail, then it must be on good grounds and dished out by the market. We must not fail because we tripped over ourselves in execution or management skills. At some level, I always believed that great things got done because someone wanted to get them done. I held the same classical view about failure. It was a thought that would surface continually at ING Direct. It should not be hard, therefore, to articulate the way forward. What would we write down on this blank sheet of paper?

Well, the Orange Code was eventually written, though it took some time to find the words that really resonated for us. Before the Code, there was something called DIRECT Values, which we expressed in an acronym: Direct, Integrity, Respect, Excellence, Customer-oriented, and Teamwork. It was a bit forced, having to dream up words to fit "DIRECT." Then there was GRASP. It stood for Great deals, Responsive, Accessible, Simple, and Passionate. These were a start in that it was important that we were talking about it. But neither of them felt "Orange" enough. They were about what we sell and how we do it, but not about who we are. Eventually, though, the discussions took shape and the Code pulled together. I say "pulled" because it reflected a lot of debate. The Orange Code is unique in that it declares a set of principles in the form of a challenge rather than just dictating lofty goals. It's a realistic approach, and it invites ongoing conversation about how the people at ING Direct can live those principles every day. (We'll talk about how we understand the Orange Code in detail later in the book).

The 12 statements in the Orange Code are not linked to a single theme, but are a collection of thoughts that express a philosophy. The Code states how things should work in our business by stating how we should be. We did not turn it into a rules-based formula. It's not a "Thou shalt . . ." kind of document. Like many testaments, this was based on the principles that first sparked our revolution and brought together like-minded people. It also sought to inspire employees with a set of values that everyone could use to connect with customers as well as each other. This isn't entirely new as a concept, but it's a large and blank canvas for a financial services business. It is true that the brand must be bigger than the business, and a challenge to conventional thinking. It must be inspirational. The Orange Code is those things.

As customers were asked to trust the brand and send their savings to ING Direct, they all demanded proof again and again. Are you federally insured? Where do you operate from? Who are you? Whose capital is behind it? For staff, it was just as challenging. Where is this company going? Are you in for the long haul? The cornerstone of the brand would from this point forward be shaped by the Orange Code. We'd be honest, say it like it is, tell the truth, be consistent, do and say the same thing every time for everyone, make no apologies, and, above all, choose only the right customers, the ones who get it. Yes, we'd choose customers based on their behavior and belief in our brand's values. The consumer was not always going to be right. If you fit, you were right. Trying to please everyone was not going to work. And an amazing thing happened. People wanted to talk about what fit and what didn't. They either reaffirmed their choice or told all their friends that this bank does not work the way they wanted. In either case, a lot of conversation and noise was made, and we needed it. A clearly defined brand has to differentiate, but a rebel brand has to polarize people. You like it or hate it, but you cannot ignore it.

BP: It started, like so many important things seemed to, with a Friday-afternoon phone call from Jim Kelly. He was about to be made "corporate culture champion" on the executive team. Arkadi was becoming restless and concerned that the bank's entrepreneurial rebel spirit might get suffocated by the growth and success that ING Direct was about to experience. Three years in, you could feel things starting to tip. Growth was accelerating, and with it there would be hundreds of new hires and, with them, enormous pressure on the culture of the company. From new people who didn't have the experience of ING Direct's start-up, and, more worrying, even from some current staff who might be tempted to get conservative or complacent. With the head count set to double in the next 12 months, Arkadi had challenged Jim to figure out how to get all of them to, in Arkadi's words, "organically act in a way that is consistent with what our brand stands for."

Jim Kelly is no fool, and there's nobody closer to ING Direct's spiritual flame than he is, short of Arkadi himself. He knew that the answer to the leader's challenge wasn't going to be a policies-and-procedures manual, nor would a beer-soaked, backslapping corporate bonding retreat do the job (though these aren't without their own charm, he would hasten to add). This was a cultural challenge. The job was not to invent something to solve the anticipated problem, but to make concrete something that was already in their hearts. "We already have corporate values," he said. "What we have to do is make them drive the way we operate."

"What," he challenged us, "is our *internal* brand?"

The white paper that followed from this conversation put some pretty fundamental stakes in the ground for institutionalizing this internal brand. First, we agreed that ING Direct already had one. "There's already a culture in here somewhere, and that culture is experienced as something functional and effective . . . something that has made money, careers, and shareholder value. . . . [This will be] a process of discovery and refinement, not invention," the document said. Second, even if we formalized what was already there, the existing core team would hardly stand for having it imposed on them by a so-called corporate culture champion in a tidy, prefabricated package. They'd been there all along. They'd been part of its creation, including both the triumphs and the messy bits. That opportunity, in fact, was a big reason they'd come in the first place. We had to have them "nod in recognition . . . [because] we need today's 800 to instruct tomorrow's 900." And, finally, the way forward could not be allowed to have an operational focus, however strong that urge might be. At moments like this, companies are always sorely tempted to prescribe their culture in terms of how people are expected to do their jobs. "As a company gets bigger and more successful, the organizational imperatives increasingly favor protecting its status quo—putting process ahead of mission, worrying more about protecting than growing . . . and this would be deadly for a brand founded on *challenging* the status quo."

The constitution itself was easy. It required almost no discussion. The Orange Code had its roots in the manifesto that was proposed in that dreary hotel conference room in Toronto back in 1996, before it was certain there would even be an ING Direct. These words had inspired and united the original group to wear the Dirty Dozen badge, and those who gathered most closely around them in the months that followed the launch. It was already in the genes. It just needed to be crafted so that it read like a fact rather than like a dream. The real puzzle was how to deliver it.

The Orange Code made its formal debut at a birthday party. ING Direct was five years old in the United States, and that called for a celebration. How? Well, most companies celebrate the way individuals do: with a party. In corporate life, such parties amount to rewards in the form of brief escapes from work. Nations, however, seize celebrations as opportunities for mythmaking, knowing that myth is the armor that cultures wear to protect themselves from boredom and cynicism. Rather than being an escape from the reality of nationhood, a celebration raises it to a more pure, intense level. They aren't escapes; they're reminders of why nobody would ever want to.

Arkadi and Jim treated the fifth anniversary as if it was the greatest and most improbable victory since Henry V's at Agincourt. And the centerpiece was a book, archly referred to as an annual report while it was in development, called *What If?* Part corporate milestone, part scripture, part testament, the book celebrated not just the monumental accomplishment of business success, but the countless small accomplishments that had led to it. It was a story of stories, with every other spread a pictorial time line that started with President Bill Clinton signing into law the act that would make banks like this possible, and marched heroically forward through dramas like Arkadi Kuhlmann's fight in Congress against the Bankruptcy Reform Act, touching scenes of ING Direct employees building affordable housing and packing knapsacks for kids who can't afford school supplies, proud commemorations of new products and technologies that ING Direct had pioneered along the way, and epic images of snarling packs of Harley-Davidson motorcycles symbolically assaulting the ramparts of the cruel banking status quo. And it was all arranged in one magnificent narrative arc. "You," this book seemed to say to employees and the bank's corporate sponsors alike, "are all heroes." And punctuating the time line were the company's principles, reconstituted as a testament to its accomplishments. What if everybody could win? read the first. What if we started over? What if we weren't alone? What if we were meant to be here? What if we shared the work? What if the idea had a name? What if we gave something back? What if we aren't finished? Under each of those headings there was a solemn and earnest explanation of the shared principles and values that had made this team great, and that had made them do these great things.

And the Orange Code was its first page. The key to defining ING Direct's culture, its internal brand, was the nation-building practice of mythologizing the past. Who would argue with being called a hero? Who would resist the brand's principles when they were proven valid by that selfsame heroism? And who could fail to fiercely internalize those principles when they are presented in the context of such an intensely emotional and happy moment? Not the first 800, that's for sure. Arkadi and Jim gave them ING Direct's success to own, and in exchange got hundreds of evangelists willing to sing from the same songbook, no matter how big and hairy this business got. It was a heckuva party.

This communitarian approach to the brand and its culture didn't end there, though. Day in and day out, it's at the core of what propels ING Direct forward.

AK: "Orange Days of Giving" sounds normal enough, but it has a touch of magic to it. Many companies have employee charity events. Giving back and helping children is not so unusual. All of our employees participate at a number of locations to do things like help rebuild a Girl Guide summer camp, build playgrounds, repaint a school, and build a baseball field. These events bring everyone together and let our purpose of doing good take tangible shape. For me, seeing their faces always brings joy that this makes our people feel good about themselves. It creates a collective meaning that belongs to us all. It's just us. The schools and people who receive these projects and efforts are always overjoyed. The best phrase I heard at one school event in St. Cloud was, "How could so many people all want to do this?" The answer is that we're a community.

The Orange Code, the Orange Journey, Docking, 2.0, town hall meetings, brown bag lunches, and corporate charity work provide the opportunities to discuss and debate how to bring the Orange Code to life. The process of joining the bank and working at ING Direct was called the Orange Journey. It was and is important to think of this business and its people in it as being on a journey. The journey is the point, while the destination is not. This was not about people covering themselves in orange and repeating slogans mindlessly. There is a certain arm's-length perspective people need to maintain, and we didn't want anyone to have an excuse to stop thinking. This will never be finished for the business or the people working in it. The ceremony for each new associate finishing his or her first 90 days is called Docking. It includes cake and skits, and it's fun, but also serious. Celebrating the joining and making it on the team is a milestone, and recognition is important on many levels. I often think that the act of bible study is even more effective than the book itself, so to speak, when it comes to building culture in a business. Town hall meetings and brown bag lunches with staff in an open format make possible a great exchange of information and ideas. Everyone wants to be heard, and part of the ING Direct brand is about letting people be heard. That is the point of advocacy: You have to be heard.

Leading by example is hard in this kind of culture. You are emotionally vulnerable, yet at the same time you are required to show conviction and confidence in your direction. You need empathy as much as you need authority. The two go together. Judgment about success or failure is always one step ahead of you.

I regularly exchange jobs with people throughout the company. This, too, is not easy and you come to understand very intimately how difficult a lot of jobs are here. But the experience of walking in someone else's shoes teaches me a lot about how things work, and the empathy I learn gives me some moral authority. And for our brand, we get a bit of pure folklore, too: "You mean he did . . . the garbage!? . . . And he . . . !?" The Orange Code is something nobody is above, not even the CEO or the board of directors. It's not about managing up or down. It's not just about listening and team building. It is viral, virtual, and networked. The village has a common identity, but it is an organism that envelopes and one that individuals can relate to intimately. The brand becomes a great leveler and connects the business to the customers. It's a modern form of a village.

Storytelling and myths that get created daily are important tools for getting the brand tone right, reminding us who we are and giving our village its own history. We could have had a prophet or a medicine man doing that job for us, I suppose, but our brand does it better. As a leader, I try to present myself as the messenger.

"Good Morning Associates," my live 15-minute morning show, Podcast to the whole bank, has also worked to personalize leadership. It lets everyone see who I am and that I, too, am inspired by our cause. In addition, my daily CEO messages are short, thought-provoking ideas for the whole bank to read and comment on, and they've worked to keep the dialogue going. The telling of stories and the reinforcing of our message are key and help create the energy and momentum to move the business forward. Most leaders underestimate the sheer volume of communication that is needed to move an enterprise like this forward. I don't mean just the ads and the newsletters and the web site. I mean the real, authentic conversations between leadership and staff, and between staff and customers. Conversation creates communities and makes ING Direct feel dynamic and alive. That seems to influence the way our customers, in turn, talk to the people in their communities, and in fact this has always propelled the brand at a great clip. The referrals, the confirmations, all added up to people wanting to join and belong and be supported in their choices. The Orange Code was created to make that happen. The ING Direct idea has always spread like a small-town rumor.

BP: Every day, ING Direct evangelizes to its community of employees. You can hardly walk down a hall or look at a piece of corporate literature without feeling like you're being sold on what this brand and this company stand for. Even before you sign on as an associate, ING Direct's recruitment ads sing from that Orange songbook, looking indistinguishable from consumer ads and featuring savings-y headlines like "High Growth Potential." Reading this, you might be tempted to dismiss it all as mere propaganda and corporate jingoism, and I think in a lot of companies that's just how it would feel. But not here, and for three very important reasons.

First, I believe that selling anything to anybody, if it's done with integrity, is an actually an act of respect. It acknowledges that the person you're trying to win over is freethinking and autonomous. But a lot of the things that corporations do to motivate their workers aren't predicated on this assumption. Rather, their leaders believe that the result they want can be achieved in a more Pavlovian way, one in which all that's required is to get an adequate reward linked to a desired action. But people aren't drooling dogs in a laboratory experiment. They are, indeed, freethinking. And they do have power—the power, at least, to not perform or not stay with the company. They also have hearts and souls, and it's an ancient human truth that you can get more from someone who is emotionally committed than from someone who is simply being adequately paid. ING Direct wants the first kind of person to be on its team—the kind of person who was converted rather than bribed.

Second, there is hardly anything more cancerous to an enterprise like this than cynicism. Can you imagine what it would feel like to work in a company like ING Direct, a company that has declared itself a challenger to the status quo and hurled heated antibank rhetoric around at every public opportunity, yet have your daily experience as an employee be routine, bloodless, and bureaucratic? And your leaders cool, professional, and disengaged? At best, you would be the same. At worst, you would feel licensed to talk out of both sides of your mouth, because that's what your employer does. Creating a kind of wink–wink, nudge-nudge culture around what a company claims to stand for versus its reality, it's not an exaggeration to say, is the slippery slope to serious corporate ethics problems. In contrast, an ongoing internal-branding effort authenticates the brand. The people who work there are constantly reminded of why they came. The seamlessness of the way the cause is promoted reassures them that it's genuine, and not just a ploy. And the wall that usually exists between a company's culture and the outside world is removed. Employees see the people they're trying to serve, and those people can observe these employees doing so, all in the context of a common understanding. Paying as much attention to how employees see the company as to how consumers see it proves it's for real.

And third, there is the rather important matter of what customers and prospects experience when they touch ING Direct. A brand is as a brand does. In the moments that you're talking to sales associates at ING Direct, those people *are* ING Direct, and not just in what they say and do for you. Whether consciously or not, you'll judge their enthusiasm; how much they seem to care; whether they like being there; whether their values seem compatible with yours, at least as far as taking care of your money is concerned; and whether you're both there for the same reasons. The result of a "yes" to all of those things is trust, and that's a pretty valuable thing to have when you're asking people to give you their savings. Employees who have joined a cause, who are reminded daily of what the cause is and why it matters, and who believe firmly that it's authentic will deliver that experience naturally, consistently, happily. Propaganda? I don't think so. Affirmation is more like it.

AK: The core competencies in the ING Direct business model are marketing and information technology (IT), but it was the HR drive and the focus on culture that would glue the business together. Staffing comprises 40 percent of our expenses. It's the most important resource and the one most critical to get right. You cannot have a good business without a good culture. Many say that people are important and customers are important. How do you make it really work? It's the belief that something successful, authentic, and good will get done. Determination will see it through. It was the virtual village that the brand was creating that kept the business nourished and sustained. The personal stories were heartwarming and true, but above all they made it all real. They allowed staff and customers alike to believe.

The people hired at ING Direct have always been an odd lot in some ways. The company is a business and, like any organization, has a structure and rules. The key has been to let the sheer volume of the business drive the organization by necessity, to sweep people along with the momentum. Leadership came by way of the vision and the mission, and they became the only constants the organization could rely on.

Margaret Rose, head of operations, is a no-nonsense executive who just gets things done. Her tough approach tends to hide her passion and commitment, but she has them in spades. The battle to fix processes and straighten out the volume of problems and situations a young company faces took a "get to it" approach. The willingness to take a problem or a challenge on and see it through was a characteristic that stood out among the staff members. When choices have arisen either to stay true to the brand and the mission or to compromise too much, most of the staffers have dug in their heels. There was to be no bait-and-switch funny business, either with customers or with one another. For Margaret, this is pure energy. She worked in Delaware and then in St. Cloud, Minnesota. She has moved her family and charged into the task at hand. She has earned the respect of the staff in the bank and among customers as well. With no differentiation between the back office and the front office, the Orange Code would enter into all discussions. Faced with one of these challenges, she would simply ask, "Is this how the brand would deal with this?"

I have often said that resurrection has happened only once in history. It can't happen with people like you and me. Building ING Direct as a challenger brand in the financial services industry cannot be done with people who have worked at traditional banks or who were hired directly from other banks. It's not that staffers recruited from other banks are poor employees or that they do not have enough skills or even enthusiasm. They can be good people. Unfortunately, though, we are all products of our environments, so working for a traditional bank inevitably makes you think like one. That's the point here. If we want to copy a retail business model, then we need to do this with the people we hire, as well. Walk like a retailer, talk like one, and act like one. Of course, it has to be a good retail example that we decide to follow and there can always be exceptions. But they must be exceptions. A willingness to change always runs into a clear conflict with the need to standardize and formalize business processes and how things get done. Finding a way to reconcile the discipline needed to handle large volumes of business with the need to be creative and open to new ways of doing things is the hardest management challenge. It's a bit like learning how to run and sit still at the same time. I am not sure if both can be done very well at the same time, but within a great brand that stands for a great business you have to make it look easy. New associates joining ING Direct always have that puzzled look on their faces that says, "So this is it? It's that straightforward?" Yes and no. It looks easy but it's very hard to do.

We run an orientation class for new associates every month. It's my opportunity to see new faces, tell stories, and set expectations. Once I get through the history and why we are here, we then talk about why *they* are here. Most new people talk about how they heard about ING Direct and why they like the Orange Savings Account. They all get connected by word of mouth. Of nearly seven million ING Direct customers in the United States, 40 percent found their way to opening an account by word of mouth, so it's not surprising that some want to come and work for the cause. What does surprise me is that few ask about the capital, the color, or the name behind it. Most want to talk about our brand, what it stands for, and why we should never change it. Still, a few in every class are surprised when they realize what we say is what we really do. They get visibly pale and wonder what it all means. Okay. . . . Eliminating titles and not having offices allows everyone to focus on something bigger. For the same reason, employees get no special treatment if they are also customers. They ask: We get the same rate as the customers for all products? Yes. No employee discount? No frequent-flier points? No. That is fundamentally different. Then, everyone listens in on real customer calls and eventually gets on the phone themselves. It's an eye-opening experience when you listen to what a customer has to say.

I usually end the orientation session with something that goes like this: I am thrilled that you are here. We need you. We need your energy and your ideas. You have already made the contract with us—your time for money. But what else? This could be a great chapter in your life's journey, maybe some of your best years. You can make a few good friends, develop your skills, learn to control a conversation, and above all find out what you want to do with your life. The only responsibility that we all ultimately have is to find our destiny. What are we meant to do? Your time here at ING Direct is a great open door to exploring and finding out about yourself. It matters less how long or short the time. It's the impact you can have and the difference you can make that counts.

The focus and dialogue then moves on to the Orange Code, and slowly the ideas begin to flow back and forth. These orientation sessions last three days, and the group is made up of people with all types of backgrounds, skills, ages, experience, and walks of life. To me they always look a lot like people on an airplane, waiting to go somewhere.

Yet they are picked because they want to prove something—maybe to a parent, to a loved one, or to themselves. You hear it in the stories they are living. There is a need to prove something. They are without doubt looking for something to connect with. All of us walk to a purpose. At this moment, here and now with the world turning, it is ING Direct and the brand it is building that offers purpose. It has been more than a decade and it still has momentum. Some do not make it through the first 90 days. Those who do always love the brand and what it stands for. They may not like everything, but they like what the brand means to them. They want to be on the side of the angels and do good. They want to help people, and, yes, they also want to beat the competition.

In the Los Angeles office of ING Direct there works a most unusual guy. His name is Bill Watt. Funny, I don't know much about Bill personally, but his value to the brand experience is without measure. A seasoned mortgage executive, Bill joined the start-up effort in LA to get ING Direct into that business. Bill got the Orange Code really fast. You can trust Bill. His word is good, so it rang true for him. He did it all: hire, work with premises, manage IT, set up the processes. Bill made it work with everyone, anywhere in the business, and never gave up. He is pure inspiration. He just believes that you have to do everything well, one day at a time. The thing is, we have some older team members and some very young ones. Some, like Bill, came from big industry players, and some only knew that bank was a four-letter word starting with *b*. Finding the right combination and trusting how the team works depends on understanding the personal agendas. Bill was one who took the brand mission and the

Orange Code at face value and ran with it. It was just in his nature. It's not surprising that LA is working so well. If St. Cloud has been the heart of ING Direct, then LA is its shoulders. Give them a challenge and they carry it off well. The Orange Code was written for people like Bill.

It takes a village. It is, by design, a bit disorganized and unusual. Most companies try to dampen all talk of people and their lives. But a brand needs human energy to survive. Having more time and conversations about our lives and why we are on this journey is the most important factor in creating this energy. To my way of thinking, the more clearly the brand is understood, the more unruly the human platform that creates it must be. It's somehow logical that these opposites attract.

BP: It's a few weeks after the inaugural episode of AKTV. We're hard at work with the mortgage group at ING Direct, led by Scott Lugar, trying to figure out how to position the bank for the tough new realities of the mortgage business in the United States today. Publicly, ING Direct has taken a strong position against the irresponsible practices of mortgage lenders, but mortgages can be easy money for a bank. Would we walk the talk? Without a doubt. ING Direct won't lend indiscriminately, and it will refuse the games other banks play to make money at it, games like selling mortgages to Wall Street or surprising people with fees when they can least afford to walk away. For ING Direct, advocating for borrowers doesn't mean just trumpeting a seemingly hot interest rate. It means doing the harder work of being honest, respectful, and transparent with customers, and sometimes saying no. It might mean selling fewer mortgages, but Lugar knows that will be the lesser sin compared to becoming the enemy. He doesn't have to ask. And he also knows that the organization will be proud—needs to be proud—of doing the right thing. Bracing for the potential cost of standing on principle, the mortgage team doesn't punt the responsibility elsewhere, and it isn't apologetic about where they stand. In an e-mail endorsing the position they've decided to take, Lugar writes, "Let's [spread] this message internally as well—would love to put this in front of our sales associates—it would really give them confidence and another reason to brag about being on the side of the angels!"

That's what you get for preaching to the choir.

The Lesson: Don't Try This at Home

BP: The valuable experience we want to share in this chapter is pretty simple: ING Direct got phenomenal performance out of its organization by making its brand an instrument of leadership. As a consequence of that leadership decision, the traditional wall between marketing and operations was torn down. Each served the other, and both served the same greater purpose. The wall between the consumer and the organization got torn down, too. The people who touched the consumer in any way became the brand incarnate, creating a classic virtuous circle: The organization stands for something, hires and operates in that image, efficiently attracts customers who share those values, who then have their attraction to the brand authenticated by their experience with it. You can see the power of this virtuous circle in ING Direct's numbers, whether it's the high percentage of customers acquired through referral, the phenomenally low cost per acquisition, and behind this the phenomenally high conversion rate (often hovering in the 40 percent range), strong staff and customer retention, or exceptionally high satisfaction ratings. Nothing in the business model technically explains this holistic excellence. It takes a village to raise a brand. This all works because everybody is pulling together, and they're pulling together because more effort was put into culture than into process. Manage the culture, and the culture will manage the business. Manage the culture with an idea, and it will grow it.

So, can any company be a brand nation? Not any company, no. It's simple enough to decide to sell what you stand for to your own people as ardently as you do to your customers. It's simple enough to have your ad agency write recruitment ads and training materials so that the brand experience appears seamless, or to get your team together regularly to hear sermons about the values for which your brand claims to stand. But you shouldn't do it if you don't mean it. A group of people has, collectively, infallible instincts. If the people who work for you think they are really just being fed propaganda, you're setting yourself, them, and the enterprise up to fail. Cognitive dissonance, as psychologists call it, is just as toxic and soul-destroying to an organization as it is to an individual. The next best thing to an authentic brand nation isn't an inauthentic one. The next best thing is probably just to be a well-managed company.

Before a leader decides to try to substitute a moral purpose for a commercial one, he or she should try this simple gut check: What is the very last thing anyone in my company could get fired for? At ING Direct, I think it would be quite difficult to get fired for anything you did to help customers save their money, so long as it was legal. If the last thing you can get fired for sounds a lot like your company's declared mission, then hoist the flag. You are a brand nation.

And if it doesn't, then a beer-soaked, backslapping corporate bonding retreat might just be your best hope. Be sure to bring a karaoke machine, though. Some of those CFOs can really belt it out.

Chapter 8

The Money on the Table

Winning the Battle, Losing the War

No bank should ever sell a mortgage it wouldn't put on its own balance sheet.

—AK, Miami Savings Summit, 2006

BP: "This is BOOL-s—!"

Speaking is Sebastian "Bas" Lichter, a strapping, usually affable Dutch fellow who is on the ING Direct launch team, and about as pro-consumer as they come. He repeats the invective, pacing back and forth in the dark behind the one-way glass of the stuffy little observation room. We're there to watch a focus group in which concepts are being tested for ING Direct's very first lending product. The new bank is still in its infancy in Canada, and two years in the future for the United States, but with the savings account product off to a roaring start, there's a lot of pressure to solve this. A lending product is essential for the balance sheet, and customers are expecting one, anyway. After seeing what ING Direct could do with something as mundane as a savings account, they're busting to see what it would be like to borrow from these guys.

But ING Direct has a frustrating problem, and it's not one it has made for itself. It's a product of accounting rules and banking regulations: The better the interest rate is on a loan or a mortgage, the higher the borrower's credit rating has to be to manage the bank's risk in offering it. But that could make a lending product too exclusive, and this bank is supposed to be for everybody. However, if it offers to lend money to anyone who's reasonably able to borrow, the interest rate would have to be too high to compensate for the likelihood of more defaults. And this bank is supposed to be about value, about saving.

So far, tonight, it's not going well. Consumers are on their guard, and they aren't really understanding the newfangled product idea for a line of credit, which has been built to try to address the knotty problem of how to be at once fair, inclusive, and profitable. They've never really seen anything like it before, and that makes them nervous.

No matter which way it turns, getting into the lending business seems to face ING Direct with a moral dilemma. When it comes to lending money to consumers, especially with mortgages, ING Direct's cause and its business model are on a collision course. And the men behind the one-way glass don't like it one bit. The leader of the asset team is sitting Buddha-like, sipping Evian and taking it all in. Jim Kelly is histrionically looking skyward, presumably for inspiration or perhaps hoping to be struck by lightning. And Bas Lichter is in high dudgeon.

"*BOOL-s*—!"

That night in a Toronto focus group facility, all those years ago, was a watershed. From that day to this, nothing has brought ING Direct face-to-face with its own rhetoric, and tested its conviction, the way that offering mortgages and loans has done. No product in banking puts the needs of consumers and their banks in more direct conflict than these ones do, and yet none are more lucrative. Lending money, a simple process so central to banking, seems to taunt both ING Direct's business model and its cause: It can lend like the rest of the industry does, make a liar of itself, and make more profits. Or it can stick to its ideological guns and leave that money on the table, risking its potential for growth.

It's an ugly dilemma.

AK: The word *risk* has many meanings in banking, but one of them is familiar to rebels in any business: the risk of change. All business models that are disruptive to the status quo are complex in their makeup. The strategy and the principles involved look easy from the outside, but in reality are far from it. This is, however, the case with many things in life and business. Changing the way things get bought and used by consumers means uncertainty and risk for both the buyer and the seller. Those of us who see value in changing the world know that there are corporate and personal risks that must be taken. The changes may be small or large, but they all come with these risks to some degree. It's part of the game.

So is the tightrope walk of innovation. Many ventures start out slowly, get traction, and then gain momentum, while some others just storm into the market. ING Direct was a slow idea that just kept on growing. For us, the business ideas came in small packages over time, countless little innovations either building on our basic concept or solving the challenges we met along the way. No branches? Well, then let's just use telephones only, or let's do better and more direct marketing, for example. Let's use more automation in processing applications for new accounts so consumers handle more of the process themselves, almost like ATMs. We all know that money is information, and information is what computers do best, after all. But for a very long time nothing really changed in a big way for retail financial products. Then, slowly, plastic cards became more commonly used. ATMs expanded their presence, then to be followed by direct debits, all taking out much of the paper that clogged up retail banking processes. These general trends continue today, and, by and large, consumers have ended up pulling each change along faster than banks were willing to push them.

And then there is the people challenge. Debate is in the nature of the kind of people who work in start-ups and who have an entrepreneurial interest. They all have strong, very different personalities. They are curious and full of energy and motivation to make something happen. I always believed that something gets done only because someone wants to do it. So, organizing a team of managers and getting them to work together is, as I've said often in this story, a never-ending struggle. Discipline is defined differently. Goals are argued over, and corporate agendas are often confused with personal ambitions. By nature, the teams in start-ups often don't last very long. Success breeds complacency, which bores the best start-up people, while the rest are constantly pulled toward the center. Building a business that challenges the market and wants to grow and prove that it can make lasting change is a tough order. Staying focused on the vision while dealing with the complexities of working together and keeping things moving is difficult, and usually underestimated. Why? The glamour is addictive and the emotional investment everyone has in it is enormous. And the more intangible or philosophical the corporate vision is—leading Americans back to saving, for example—the more of a contradiction this whole piece becomes. People who want to be part of a start-up aren't typically followers, yet ING Direct had set out to be a cause.

When it came to mortgages, this was a perfect storm for us: the risks in disruption, the uncertainty of whether consumers would embrace something new, and the personal ambitions of the people on the team.

It was a hot Wednesday afternoon in Wilmington in June 2003, and we were in our fifth straight month of discussing the challenge of selling mortgages on a direct basis. This seemed like an opportunity to do something positive, as we had done for savings, because the market as it existed seemed anything but consumer friendly. The mortgage business was deeply reliant on brokers who were selling very profitable 30-year amortization-type mortgages. These mortgages were then originated by lending institutions, which then turned around and sold them to Wall Street as securities. Even hairdressers were signing up overnight to become mortgage brokers. The word was that making money in mortgages was easy. And it sure looked like it in those years. That was interesting to us for a few reasons: One is that any bank needs assets, of course, and for a bank that's what a mortgage is. Another was simply that this was a booming product category in financial services, and it could start to seem strange for an up-and-coming rebel bank like ours not to be competing in it. But most important was that here, again, was a product being sold by our competitors for their own benefit, while putting consumers at risk. Somehow, we needed to be there.

BP: There's a good reason why greed made the list of seven deadly sins: It does the most damage. This is no less true in corporate life, in leadership, and in marketing than it is anywhere else. And although the popular belief is that the worst, most socially damaging greed is the corporate kind, the truth is that we all—consumers and corporations alike—are motivated by the primitive urge to get whatever we can.

More times than I can count, I've seen companies destroy value and lose their way in the marketplace simply because they were trying to satisfy the urge to get as much as they can, as fast as they can. Typically, the story starts with a great product at a fair price, met by an eager marketplace. Companies, seeing the potential, market aggressively to preempt competition, saturating the market. Consumers, sensing competition, expect better and better pricing. Companies, not wanting to disappoint the always-right customer or lose market share, comply, and then resort to taking value out of the product to get their lost margins back. For a manufacturer, this might mean lowering quality standards; for a bank, it means sneaky fees and service charges. In any case, it doesn't end well, and everybody goes home disappointed. While it's not always inevitable, and though the details differ from case to case, the essential story is all too common. If you're, say, in the entertainment business (or, perish the thought, an author), the cycle of value destruction can be cruelly over in just weeks. In the fashion business or the stock market, it can take only months. If you're in the car business or in packaged goods, years or decades. The value in a brand franchise can disintegrate before your eyes, or dissipate slowly to nothing before you even notice the decline. However it ends, though, the common denominators are the same every time: Consumers who want too much, and businesses who use that desire as an alibi for taking every last cent off the table.

What separates these sorry tales from the enterprise success stories we all admire? In a way, it comes down to this thing we've been calling a brand. For many of the companies that are on this value-destruction treadmill, a brand is a marketing tool they reach for when it's useful, and otherwise let languish. For the ones that resist it and become icons and unstoppable value-creation machines, a brand is the conscience of leadership.

Conscience matters because money on the table is a test—not just of an organization as a whole, but of the conviction of every member of its team. So imagine, now, that you're leading a young ING Direct in 2004. You know nothing will validate this concept in the eyes of its shareholders and the business press like a healthy bottom line. Vindication would be sweet. Meanwhile, American consumers are madly borrowing every dollar any bank will lend them, especially in the form of mortgages. And many of them are completely unconcerned with the real cost of these loans. They just want a monthly payment they can handle, an interest rate they can brag about, and the house of their dreams. Mortgage customers are roaming the land in vast herds like the Plains buffalo, and there's a trainload of bankers with breach-loading carbines leaving the station any minute.

Rarely had the opportunity to give consumers what they think they want—and make a fortune doing it—ever been so ripe. But it was a temptation Arkadi Kuhlmann could easily resist. His idealism had gotten him and ING Direct this far, and he certainly wasn't about to turn into a cynical banker now. There was a right way to do this, but only if everyone had the same strength of their convictions.

AK: Our challenge was to design a standard mortgage product that could be self-serviced on the Internet, with a good rate of interest and an interest rate term that was five years long and not 30. (Thirty-year mortgages give consumers a feeling of stability, but they are horrendously expensive. If people added up what they paid in interest over the whole life of such a mortgage, they'd faint from shock.) We wanted and needed to sell large volumes—that's key to our business model—and keep them on our balance sheet. Our mortgage customers would stay ING Direct customers, and their mortgages would be serviced by us. This was essentially the total opposite to the way mortgages were now being done in the rest of the marketplace. But how to pull it off was a contentious subject, and the internal debate forced people to show their true colors.

The argument in the conference room on this day deteriorated very quickly. Nobody was shy about their views and expressing them. The sales team wanted something that consumers could recognize—in other words, something like our competition was offering. Consumers were not ready yet for trusting a very different product or way of buying it, they argued. The technology team worried about the lack of systems that could do a different job with mortgages. This would be pioneering stuff, which presented risks for us. The finance team could not seem to make the economics work. The legal team worried about complying with regulations. There were 25 of us in the room, and 25 sets of concerns. After charging into the savings account business so fearlessly and successfully meeting these same kinds of challenges, I was stunned. I jumped in and argued the case for charging ahead. That was not very well received. Half the room started to tune out and hoped that I would just wind down eventually, while the rest tried to get on board and figure it out. Two, however, took my pushback very personally and were truly upset. Their way of dealing with this issue was to question my leadership. The objectives of making money and remaining true to our vision were so at odds that this had become a crisis of confidence.

This cause of ours, was it for real? Should it not sometimes demand risk and sacrifice? They feared that I was taking them into too much risk and maybe onto a hopeless path. This had become much more than a product problem, and it would take some serious work to set things right. We could not fall apart now. Leading up to today, I had spent more and more time selling the mission one-on-one to key team members, and stayed away from group meetings on this topic. It was like lobbying, and it cost us momentum in mortgages that year. I continued to emphasize the good things that were happening to keep the faith in our vision strong, but realized that this elephant in the room was just not going to go away. We broke up the meeting at 4:15 that afternoon, and one of the objectors, a member of my executive team, walked me out to try a little lobbying of his own. He lit a cigarette and said in a quiet way, "Maybe the best thing to do is buy a mortgage broker or a mortgage bank. That would leave all the brand questions off the table, and the mortgages can be done just like everyone else does them without harming the brand." The logic might have seemed tempting, but the name on the door said "Direct." I wasn't sold, but I wasn't a fool. Not wanting an out-and-out mutiny, I responded, "Well, maybe that's what we have to do, so see what's out there." I wanted to see where his commitment was and how far he would go. Pretty far, as it turned out. Three months later we had our first potential acquisition deal on the table. And three months after that we had a different executive with a different personal agenda in that role. But the hard feelings in the rest of the team would simmer for 12 more months before we finally got beyond it. Not every test comes from the marketplace.

It was time to put a stake in the ground. We needed to be in the mortgage business, so we cobbled together a compromise. The resulting mortgage had some innovative features in it, but it still ended up being a product that was already available in the market and one that consumers already knew. We would sell it a bit differently, mind you. We'd offer lower fees to get it set up. We'd have standard pricing, so people wouldn't have to negotiate or play competitive shopping games. But still, for me, this was not yet a product that created a wow or a differentiated experience that customers would rave about. All the same, some still did. Volumes did pick up, and people loved the simplicity and directness of borrowing from us, but it did not shake the world. And there was still the tough job of getting here with our own team. It was not until we battled over our payment account years later that this kind of process got a bit better, but it still was not great. A number of members of the team who worked on that original mortgage imitative would ultimately leave the bank, but not before undertaking a quiet program of sabotage. It was very destructive. They couldn't stand the idea of leaving money on the table for the sake of principle. I knew about the dissent, of course, but in the real world of management it's not so simple or quick to eliminate malcontents. Finding out who and how many of your staff are truly committed to a vision and a mission is never easy. It was certainly not easy for ING Direct.

BP: Money on the table, like any temptation, can take many forms.

The mortgage business posed a special challenge for ING Direct, because developing a mortgage that truly served its mission resulted in a product that the marketplace didn't think it wanted. It was a good product, as much in the best interests of savers as it was possible for a mortgage to be. It was just hard to sell. Still, even after the wrenching philosophical test the mortgage debate put Arkadi's team through, the challenge eventually became more comfortingly familiar: Integrate it into ING Direct's low-cost service model, and then market our hearts out. This we knew how to do. This, in the final analysis, was still advocacy. Coming from us, consumers would listen to that.

Opportunism, on the other hand, is a more difficult kind of greed to fight. It is difficult because it seems harmless. It sometimes comes disguised in marketing euphemisms like "cross-selling" or "leveraging," and the logic that, as long as the customers are in the store, why don't we see what else we can toss in their shopping baskets before they get to the cash register? A global chain of cafés decides to sell breakfast sandwiches. A hamburger giant decides to sell pizza. An athletic apparel brand adds street fashion. A grocery store makes space for prescription drugs, houseplants, and lawn furniture (while the drugstore in the same strip mall makes space for milk, eggs, bread, and snack foods). A conservative luxury car brand decides to make a sports car, and then a truck. In each case, the marketers are motivated by the fact that they've got the consumers by their wallets for a moment, and in this moment hope to sell them nearly everything else they might have on their shopping lists. Thus, the marketers reason, they can spare those consumers the effort of shopping elsewhere, and deepen the supposed relationship they have with them.

Sometimes, it works and you know it. Cross-selling can offer real value to consumers and earn marketers legitimate profit, while building their franchise and broadening the definition of their business. Everybody's happy. And sometimes, it *doesn't* work and you know it. You end up with a product nobody wants, or you accidentally start a competitive war you can't afford. You cut your losses and move on, and consumers generously forget the whole thing. But sometimes, insidiously, it only *seems* to work. The product begins to sell. It starts to smell like a winner, and attract corporate attention and resources. The trappings of corporate activity spring up around it, adding structure, processes, and costs. New power bases get built and they compete for marketing resources, which then get divided and reallocated in the name of investment. The brand's meaning in the marketplace begins to become uncertain, hazy. Dry rot sets in, and the real damage to the momentum of the business and its brand doesn't become apparent until long after the whiz-kid chief marketing officer (CMO) who sanctioned this so-called brand extension has sailed off into the sunset.

AK: Losing one's way in a brand-driven business is as easy as losing the beat of a song. It's strange, but the most dangerous challenges to our brand always came in the disguise of new products. Well-meaning staffers will say to me, "Customers love us and they really want a mutual fund product. Can't we sell them one? They are just asking and asking! It won't cost us anything to add this product!" Well, maybe not right away. For one thing, cost creep happens incrementally in the same way that one's house gets dusty: one day at a time. For another, the customer is not always right. They expect that if you sell them the next product, it will be as cool, easy, and low-priced as the last, whereas the bank often has not figured out how to do exactly that. It's just opportunism. The erosion of the brand then starts, and it continues like rust on steel. It doesn't seem bad at first, but it just keeps on eating away at it, quarter after quarter, year after year. Bankers fall for the volume numbers and the increase in cross-selling opportunities and think that if customers have more products they will stay longer and become more profitable. That's good in theory, but not in practice. For years, the industry has been promoting these share-of-wallet arguments and "deep experiences" with customers, not respecting that what a customer thinks and says is critically important to the energy and resilience of the brand. You have to earn it every day with each and every product and transaction, and nothing stands still. The great players are successful over time and can reinvent the energy and the ideas that are relevant with customers. But they don't do it by piling up compromises one after another.

No, not every test comes from the marketplace, and being a rebel can come at a price when there's money on the table.

Back the spring of 1998 we'd had a very successful cover story that showcased our vision and mission in *Canadian Business* magazine. It stated on the cover that the competition should be afraid. Well, okay, that kind of thing does make you smile. David-and-Goliath comparisons often come to mind, and they always evoke a little grin around ING Direct. Anyway, we were pleased with the coverage, especially at such an early stage. Then, a couple of years later, in the fall of 2000, the author of that story wanted to do a follow-up piece to see how the ING Direct team was doing in the main arena, the big American marketplace. Do we have legs? How are we going to do it?

The story did not go well from ING's point of view. It was truthful, but it reported the inside debate that I was having with my colleagues in Amsterdam over our mortgage strategy. The story told of my frustration with trying to get permission to launch mortgages in 2001. In contrast to the opportunism of some on my team back in Wilmington, ING held the opposite view. The thinking there was to stay out of originating retail mortgages altogether for now. We can do that later, if we have to, they said. The story was a real slipup. I had let my guard down and opened the kimono too far. With my resignation in hand I flew to Amsterdam and did my rounds of explanations and apologies. The rank and file wanted blood. Among my executive colleagues, reactions ranged from concerned but supportive to being outright worried that this was part of a chain of events that would ultimately harm the business. The outcome would boil down to Michel Tilmant, and he wanted to get the U.S. project launched. He was not concerned with the press or stories in the United States. My resignation was not accepted and I survived once again. And I was, of course, more motivated than ever to make a successful launch.

Now, flip the calendar forward from that uncomfortable moment to the announcement of our 2007 financial results. Michel put forth a confident showing and exhibited a steady hand on the wheel. In addressing the issue of retail mortgages on the ING Direct USA balance sheet, he explained, "If we could grow our own originated mortgages fast enough, we would not buy any in the market. We have confidence in our own credit assessments." In other words, we had done the right thing. We hadn't put the business at risk with irresponsible marketing, but we hadn't turned our back on the chance to improve our balance sheet. Our cause had guided us to a solution that made business sense. Those of us who remember the *Canadian Business* story found a simple vindication. The wheel had come full circle.

There are many examples of strategic compromise and of what a successful business can absorb and still work versus what will cause it to fail. The challenge of finding the balance lies in understanding the business fundamental (a bank has a balance sheet with two sides) and the brand fundamental (ING Direct's cause is to lead Americans back to saving), and the fact that it can never come down to a choice between the two.

Our parent company, ING, has mutual funds that it distributes through all types of intermediaries such as brokers and banks. It was only a matter of time before the corporate push would come to sell them through ING Direct, too. The funds themselves were not exceptional on performance and the fees were pretty average. The record keeping and customer interfaces, as with most providers, were old-fashioned and cumbersome. "So let's give them to the ING Direct customers and make some money" seemed to be the logic. Customers liked what they saw and they were tempted, but they were tempted because they assumed that the deal would be good. They trusted ING Direct to do right by them. In the end, though, the experience for the customers was just average. This did not help our reputation. There was no harm done in the end, though, right? Wrong. Customers are always watching and they never forget. They came to the conclusion that ING Direct had a good start-up idea with savings but could not deliver on mutual funds. The money spent in promoting a damaging mutual fund offering was not financially or brand accretive. The product managers and marketing staff who worked on mutual funds had mutual fund experience from more traditional companies, and they believed that the answer was to attain scale. It is still surprising to see how many managers think that scale alone is the answer to everything. You can't make a flawed product better by selling more of them. The simple truth is that the product, the experience, and the final value to the customer have to be better than the competition's. Scale benefits will then take care of themselves. Productivity, specifically the lack of it, is always masked behind scale arguments and their promised results.

In some international markets, the ING mutual funds worked better. If a market's prices on fees were high, the program worked better because the value proposition was better. In countries like Canada and the United States, where fees are already low and the competition in mutual funds is already intense, the value proposition was not great and the results were predictably poor. Most difficult was the reasoning from the traditional bankers in the organization: "Well, we just never invested enough money to market the funds." Or maybe we didn't listen to the market. As ING Direct grew larger, we were finding it hard to avoid hiring more staff with banking experience, and sometimes this eroded progress in a hurry. Transfer pricing, managing for value, customer profitability, customer relationship management (CRM), six sigma, and the like all steered us to an ever-greater financial perspective. It could get hard to think sometimes with all this analyzing going on.

BP: While Arkadi fought the battle to stay focused in Wilmington, the proof that he was right was quietly unfolding an hour's flying time to the north, in Toronto. It was April 2004, and a bunch of slightly freaked-out-looking ING Direct Canada executives were assembled in GWP's boardroom. The very first ING Direct in the world—the business where Arkadi and his team had honed this concept before taking it to the United States, and a crown jewel in the growing ING Direct global network—had a problem.

A new management team had just taken the helm of the Canadian unit, the second since Arkadi's posse had headed south to take on America. The previous few years had been difficult but prosperous for ING Direct there. A stock market crash and economic uncertainty in the wake of 9/11 had created a favorable environment for ING Direct's savings product; Canadians typically liked to put a little money aside for a rainy day, and there had been plenty of those. But this positive momentum had been despite the fact that some influential executives on the departing team had never exactly been evangelists for the brand. Rather, they had been what one might generously call professional managers: pragmatic, unemotional, detached, process- and numbers-oriented. They had been handed the baton of a successful and fast-growing start-up some four years earlier and, seemingly, had kept the machine oiled and running well.

But the deposit business had inexplicably started getting soft. Yes, the stock markets were recovering and some cash was flowing out of the bank and back into equities. But that didn't explain all of it. And some important leading indicators were suggesting that things might be about to get worse. Key image scores in ING Direct's quarterly brand-tracking study had flattened out, or even tipped downward. And one all-important measure had declined significantly, a measure called "unaided awareness." It didn't make sense to the ING Direct executives. They had certainly been spending money on marketing. They hadn't changed their core marketing campaign, they believed. There was no rational reason why consumers should suddenly be losing interest in ING Direct, and it was making people very nervous.

It was this "unaided awareness" number that was worrying us all the most, and the reason was pretty simple. "Unaided awareness" is a market research measure, often collected in one of those telephone surveys we all love so much. It quantifies the number of consumers who are so familiar with your brand that they can spontaneously recall it in association with the business you're in, without any assistance from the pollster at the other end of the phone. For us, it was the percentage of consumers who, when asked if they can name an institution that offers savings accounts, would answer "ING Direct," unprompted. This group of people was where the next wave of potential ING Direct customers would come from. The job of advertising is to create that pool of aware consumers, people interested enough in you to mentally file your name away for future reference. And since it's pretty hard for a virtual business to sell anything to someone who isn't first interested enough to do that filing—and since this was still a young business—the size and rate of growth of this aware population was of paramount importance. And, in the spring of 2004, it was in decline. The new ING Direct leadership team was in our boardroom to find out why.

The answer had seemed pretty obvious to me just from looking at media plans, but one of ING Direct's marketing people and I had spent a couple of weeks analyzing the data to confirm it: The issue was the money on the table, or, more specifically, the departing management's inability to resist leaving it there. Over the past several quarters, marketing money had been diverted from our strategy of building the ING Direct brand through the universally appealing and distinctive savings product, and redirected toward television advertising for mutual funds and mortgage products. Worse yet, the money had been divided yet again by using two separate advertising campaigns, each with a different look and a different spokesperson, supposedly optimized to each product's selling characteristics. It was all very logical, and all very wrong. To the professional manager looking at a media plan in the comfort of a boardroom, it seemed as if the brand's voice would be as loud as ever, but would sell more products. To the consumer, though, it was as if the advertising budget had been halved and halved again. For one thing, while everyone can relate to our savings message, only investors pay any attention to mutual fund ads. And only potential home buyers and people whose mortgages are about to be renewed pay any attention to mortgage ads. Consumers are deaf to messages that don't matter to them, so the diversion of marketing resources ended up hurting, not helping, advertising efficiency. That's a trade-off a well-established company, or one that was in investment mode, might plausibly choose to make. But for a company whose business model depends on a simple product suite, efficient marketing, and an orderly, profitable building of scale, it was like driving straight into a snowdrift. Their strategy had not failed ING Direct's cause in any obvious sense, but it had betrayed the business model that served that cause. People were losing interest because they weren't hearing our voice anymore. We had more stuff in the store, but fewer people coming through the door.

AK: It was Bert Derksen, a great marketing man who worked with Hans Verkoren at Postbank in Amsterdam before joining ING Direct, who said, "Don't hire product managers." His reasoning was that if you create product manager positions and fill them with good people, they will work hard to create more products. They'll come up with plenty of ideas to create revenue with new product features and for how they might be sold. But in a direct, high-volume business struggling to be a pure commodity play, this would add the wrong type of pressure on the business. No product manager ever sat down at a year-end performance review and said, "Please give me a bonus because I did not create any new products last year." Bert had a good point.

After the battles over how to introduce mortgages and mutual funds, our next battle centered on checking accounts. It was hard to face the truth that not enough emphasis had been placed on innovation and investing in product design and process reengineering, when that was the key to future growth and profitability. Being in a defensive mode so much had discouraged it. Besides, the success of the day and the bank as a whole seemed to be rolling along, and we remained emotionally and financially dependent on our savings account product. As long as the interest rate market was favorable and the slope of the yield curve was positive, we could afford to be that way, even with the challenges of other products. We did need an asset product like a mortgage. We did need mutual funds to diversify the revenues and earn—in a fair and honest way—fees. The key problem was that success was being measured the wrong way, and expectations were clearly not in the place they should be. Customers were looking for new things and ideas from us. They wanted our products to demonstrate that there were real alternatives across the board. ING Direct couldn't be one great product and 10 ordinary ones.

Checking accounts are the major link between people and their banks. Depositing income and making payments is the most basic of financial activities. Our vision was to find a way to do this without paper, and change the way consumers thought of their checking accounts. The way consumers use checking accounts is well established and deeply ingrained. Changing those habits looked like an uphill battle, but that's the kind we like.

We started to list the gripes consumers had and design ways to take them away. Account fees and service charges were a big irritant. Earning no interest on balances came next. This is, in fact, why consumers kept moving money around: to earn interest. And it meant lots of work and attention for consumers, more than most were able to commit to the task. Getting the account balances right and not being charged for overdrafts was another issue, and a tricky one. Next came the need to be able to get cash and not be charged a big fee. Consumers were not happy, and the seeds of how to make it work better did not seem all that difficult to find.

So, we designed something called Electric Orange. It works like a checking account. But it pays interest. It doesn't charge fees. Access to a network of ATMs for cash is free. And it has no paper. To get customers to switch from standard checking accounts that use paper checks, we decided to have customers fill out online checks, and ING Direct would then print them and mail them for the customers free of charge. The idea was to get customers to see the benefit of doing everything with one account and have one simple, complete record of all their transactions rather than trying to manage two or more separate accounts.

I really pushed for this idea. The differentiation was big, and the impact could be very big, if we could handle the financial and operational sides of the product. Well, that internal battle took 12 months, with poor projections both for finance and for operations. The arguments were old and expected. Most people won't switch. It's too expensive. It's too generous a deal for customers who, in the end, will not appreciate it. But it was the most Orange product initiative we had undertaken in a long time. And the best was that most customers would see Electric Orange as a savings account with transactional capabilities. We would add an overdraft line on which we'd have to charge interest, but there would be no fees if someone went negative on the account by mistake. That might just work.

To combat rising interest rates in 2007, we got the product launched but soon found out that we could not explain it clearly enough to consumers. It was, ironically, unfamiliar to them—that old innovation risk. Still, the number of accounts grew steadily. And the balances grew, too. We added a 1 percent cash-back incentive for customers who used the credit/debit card, and this customers understood. They liked to see a deposit to their account from their bank, and that seemed to help them understand what Electric Orange is. But the struggle to educate and to explain the different features and their benefits was still a tall order. Central to our strategy for this was the idea that we would emphasize one feature after another as customers got to try the account and become familiar with it, rather than trying to educate them on everything all at once. The whole experience taxed our marketing, sales, and IT teams, but nobody said advocacy should be easy. The truth is that Electric Orange saved the day for us, and became the first wow for ING Direct in five years.

BP: At this writing, Electric Orange is still a new product, but it is already clear it's going to work. And the reason is not that it's a simple product (it isn't), or even that it's giving the consumers something they'd been asking for (they weren't). What's making Electric Orange go is the fact that everyone at ING Direct was motivated by a common sense of purpose when they created it. The scrapping over how and what it should be was no less heated than it had ever been for the Orange Mortgage, but this time everyone around the table wanted the same thing: to lead Americans back to saving. With that unity, people spent less energy resisting the challenges and more trying to surmount them. The marketing team focused on how to make people see the value in the product rather than questioning it. In the call center, associates pitched it sincerely and explained it patiently. And, soon enough, consumers felt that conviction. There were glowing reviews in the press, industry awards, bouquets from consumers in the blogosphere and in e-mails. The goodwill in the ING Direct brand made people want to listen, and the good intentions in the product made them want to buy.

The story in Canada eventually had a happy ending, too: ING Direct's then-new management team had the guts to return their messaging strategy back to savings. We would stop trying to hard-sell and start trying to help again. As we had done in the beginning, we would talk to the marketplace about the empowering joy of saving money, the obstacles traditional banks put in the way, and how we're there for them. By the fall of 2004, critical tracking measures had turned sharply upward again, in the case of unaided awareness posting a gain of more than 50 percent over the spring number, and business health followed.

Looking at the data, I could see we weren't the only ones relieved by this, either. Through the reams of statistics, you could almost hear the consumers saying, "Man, we're glad you're back. You had us worried for a minute there."

Three Good Reasons to Leave Money on the Table

BP: Offering more products and services is obviously not a bad idea. It can be quite a good one, in fact, especially if it's a leader's job to build shareholder value. But it can also be messy and unproductive, and it usually goes wrong in one of two ways: Companies either make the move into a new category too soon, before they have enough credibility and resources to support it, or they move into a category that's just too different, in the *consumer's* mind, from the one that earned their trust in the first place. This was what put Arkadi at odds with some of his original mortgage team. To them, a mortgage was another financial service, something a bank just does. But to the customer, Arkadi knew, the wrong mortgage was an invitation to spend too much money, coming from a brand that stood for saving it. It would be dissonant, and dissonance like that destroys trust.

No, it's not that going after the money on the table is a bad idea. It's just that trying won't be easy or free. There are some costs that no financial model can measure, but that a leader should consider carefully before making the leap.

It Can Change You

Bert Derksen's advice to Arkadi was profoundly wise, especially for a company that has made itself a cause. Adding products and services pushes an organization away from advocacy, and toward bureaucracy. Power bases get built. The organization Balkanizes around product categories. These little empires can start defining themselves by how they're distinct within the organization rather than how they serve its overall mission. New employees arrive, and their new jobs seem created more for what they'll sell than to further the cause of the company. And, for long-serving staff, the culture is disrupted by the question of what this company is really here to do. Meanwhile, where the cause-driven organization once had a single, clear enemy—the status quo—it now has a list of competitors for everything it sells. Slowly but surely, informal power in the company shifts from those with the vision to those with the information. And information without vision is just a commodity.

The keys to avoiding all this? First, use your brand as a compass. Does the new product do more of what your brand promised your company was here to do, or is it just trying to borrow against the consumer's trust? Second, don't delegate new business. The temptation to use new business lines as a way to groom tomorrow's leaders is noble but perilous. In the beginning, it should be the leadership's job to open up new frontiers. They have the best sense of context, of what's at stake. They have the authority to trade off the money on the table for the greater good. And they have to look at themselves in the mirror every morning and reaffirm their moral leadership in a cause-driven enterprise.

It Can Weaken You

The case of declining awareness in Canada shows what can happen when marketing resources get overmanaged. It was a classic case of blinkered boardroom logic: Somebody thought that as long as ING Direct was trumpeting its name out there, advertising was doing its job and, therefore, so was marketing. But it wasn't true. Consumers opened a different mental file folder when they saw mutual fund advertising, a folder that contained its own biases, desires, fears, comparative brands, and barriers to action. In effect, the only aspect of the brand this marketing carried with it was some implied endorsement, and a few familiar creative elements consumers might recall from savings ads. The result was, for a while, three weak marketing efforts instead of one strong one.

This risk of dividing resources is, of course, much broader than just to marketing. Leadership bandwidth gets divided, too. So do press and shareholder attention. So does the infrastructure of the organization—things like finance and HR—and it all has the same effect: It pulls the organization apart, bit by bit, creating a collection of pieces that are considerably weaker than the former whole was.

And to avoid this? Remember there's a difference between marketing and selling. In contrast to the difficult experiments ING Direct has endured trying to mass market lending and investment products the same way it did savings products, it has done quite well by quietly selling these things to existing customers in the comfort and safety of their saving experience. Talking to customers as savers and doing it in more intimate media like personalized direct mail, the ING Direct web site, and ING Direct's SmartSell (which targets selling messages in the Web environment on the basis of individual customer relevance) has been very effective. It has allowed customers to consider the merits of a new product while they're in a positive, engaged, Orange frame of mind, and has done it in a way that seems personal and momentary, so it feels less like a public declaration that the brand's meaning is changing.

Think of it like this: We happily buy the chewing gum and magazines displayed at our supermarket checkout while we're waiting to pay for our groceries. But the gum and magazines aren't why we came, and mass marketing them would only make us wonder how serious the grocery store was about the food we put on our tables.

It Can Make You Look Bad

For all of the marketing consequences of being greedy, there is a more basic danger, one that is especially scary if your business has publicly described itself as a cause: You can look as if you didn't mean it. Do consumers really want their favorite brands to sell a wider variety of products? Probably not. Consumers, in fact, would probably prefer that their favorite companies just stick to their knitting. They don't want their lives complicated. Brand extension is a selfish act and, like most of life's selfish acts, is best undertaken with care and humility. If you do it in a way that betrays your stated values, your customers might think that your advocacy for them, the thing that attached them to you, was just manipulation. At the very least, that makes a cynical consumer, someone it's going to be hard to sell to. At the worst, it takes the emotional content out of the relationship so completely that all that is left for them to judge you on is your price. Then, they start looking for the money *they've* been leaving on the table, too.

Here again, let your brand's code be your compass. In the entire bumpy history of ING Direct's effort to market a mortgage that was both good for people and profitable, there was one moment of true clarity when consumers paused, turned to us, and genuinely wanted to know more. It was a single line of copy, born first in a concept for consumer research, and reborn later in the script for a television commercial: "What if a mortgage could make you richer?" Its effect on the marketing team was galvanizing, and the consumers' response was much the same. Why? Because this *was* something we were licensed by our brand to talk about. This *was* a logical expression of ING Direct's mission to lead people back to saving. Jim Kelly had once rhetorically asked, "Why don't people realize that a mortgage is a savings account?" His point was that the better a mortgage is, the faster a homeowner will build equity in a house, and equity is savings. Looked at in this way, mortgages are naturally urgent business for ING Direct, the very opposite of chewing gum and magazines. If people just come to you for your products, you're starting over every time you try to sell them a new one. If people come to you for your point of view, they'll always be eager to know what else they can buy from you.

The moral high ground can be pretty expensive real estate. But, for ING Direct, it has usually turned out to be a pretty good investment, and worth hanging on to. And that's no "*bool.*"

Chapter 9

Steering by the Stars

Beyond Managing

A good manager should not be afraid of chaos. He or she should not try to control it but rather welcome its dynamic aspects. Through them, we can shape our desires and needs. Chaos is the place where a company's vision is created.

—AK, CEO Message # 65

BP: I don't usually include this piece of information on my resume, but I once took second place at a science fair.

It was in grade seven. I'd spent the previous winter watching my father curse a blue streak and endure smashed thumbs and vicious slivers as he built a wooden sailboat in our garage. I wasn't helpful, but I learned a lot from observing and listening to the colorful commentary as the vessel took shape. I acquired a spectacular vocabulary of invective, for example, which has been richly useful to me down through the years. And, more to the point, I learned how a sailboat works. So, as my homage to the project, I prepared an elaborate demonstration for the school science fair, involving a little wooden boat, a table fan, and a pink plastic washtub full of water, to share my revelation with everyone at Parkview Public School.

The revelation was this: A sailboat is not propelled by the wind alone. Unlike a motorboat, which obliviously churns itself from A to B by brute mechanical force, sailing is a more negotiated process. Yes, the wind puts pressure on the sail, but that alone doesn't move the boat where the skipper wants it to go. In fact, given the choice, the wind would just as soon blow the boat over to get it out of the way. No, what moves a sailboat is the way it fights the force of the wind with its keel. It's called a "parallelogram of forces." The tendency of the boat to be blown over by the wind is countered by the pressure of the water against the keel, and the boat squirts forward the way a watermelon seed pinched between your thumb and forefinger does.

In other words, a sailboat gets where it's going by finding some wind, and then leaning against it. It participates in its environment and makes use of it, rather than mechanically overcoming it or pretending it isn't there.

Though it might seem a little corny, this tidy analogy is hard to resist when I recall meeting with Arkadi in the summer of 2007 to talk about whether there could be a book in the ING Direct story. It was a warm, humid August afternoon, and we had sought relief from the heat on his sailboat, where we could talk without interruption about whether sharing our experience could possibly have any value for anyone else. Though he believed firmly there was something of value in the story and wanted to tell it, he didn't yet see this as a book about leadership or the ING Direct brand, and he didn't think the world needed another marketing book. Was it the right time to tell the story? Was it too soon? Was this business grown-up enough to be reflective? But having had a ringside seat since the story began, I thought he was selling ING Direct and himself a little bit short. The real power in telling it, I argued, lay not in the business case study, but in its proof that a company can do well by doing good. That principled leadership can accomplish more than a mechanical business model can. That's a message people need to hear right now, I prattled on, looking back toward the helm to drive home the point.

But I don't think he was listening right at that moment. We had almost stopped moving, becalmed in the still August air. We weren't making enough progress, and Arkadi was squinting into the middle distance, looking for some wind.

AK: We are awash in information, and in the many forms in which it seeps into our daily lives. We are bombarded with paper, data, and sound, from voice mail to e-mail to junk mail. Let's not even think about advertising flyers and the bumper stickers! Our urban world is looking more like New York's Times Square every day. For better or worse, information is like the waves in the ocean: endless and deceptive in their size and power. So, too, is the nature of information and the consequences it brings to business. The weather constantly changes, and we can't always see the horizon. Is that just a piece of real data or is it a reflection of something else? We have all lived through those moments. We often find that the course we took was wrong or not what we intended, but that's the nature of all journeys. In business, the challenge of navigation is the heart of all leadership and corporate quests.

You may be thinking now, easier said than done. Aside from the finite things in the world, the information about it is endless. We create more chaos every day. Today, the watchwords have become "perception is reality." Most leaders blend fact with belief to form perception, and then try to force a new reality. All humans who lead organizations have done and continue to do this, from ancient campfires to modern boardrooms. Leaders may no longer be snake charmers or witch doctors, but it's pretty close, sometimes, when you think about it. Selling themselves and the rest of us on the way forward, as a ritual, has not changed much, and it has never been just about information. People say knowledge is power, but I'm not sure I agree. I think awareness is power.

As with most things in my life, it just appears at the most unusual places and times, like driftwood in the ocean.

BP: A funny thing happens when an organization is completely sure of what it stands for. It suddenly finds itself more nimble. Instead of a massive strategic playbook-in-the-sky that anticipates every challenge to its goals and prescribes a process for getting from A to B, it simply has a center of gravity and a sense of direction, a certainty about its purpose that is so solid that it isn't afraid that circumstances might intrude and contaminate its plan. Instead, it's open and tuned in to its environment. Without the pressure of executing the prescribed process, it can be fully watchful for the next source of momentum. The clearer your purpose, the less fixed your plan seems to need to be. Or, at least, a plan serves the organization's purpose rather than the other way around. Chaos becomes a resource, resistance a source of power and direction, serendipity a gift.

A clear sense of purpose is strategically liberating.

The thing that Arkadi often calls serendipity has always been a theme in ING Direct's success. But serendipity has never meant mere luck or opportunism; the company has always known who and what it needed, and where it was ultimately going. Rather, in a direct reflection of its leader's own life philosophy, ING Direct has rarely passed up the truly relevant opportunities that fate has put in its path. Almost always, those opportunities have come in human form, as fellow travelers, and the enterprise has even been willing to change its course now and then to include them. It's the dividend of having a purpose instead of just a plan, and a recognition that the energy that comes from being among your own kind is, in the long run, a more powerful and reliable impetus than any map.

AK: I'm walking in the door one evening and Synthia, my wife, asks the predictable home-bound question. "How was your day?" "Fine," I say wearily. "We're still trying to find a back office system for the bank." A few minutes later, after the mail gets looked at, she says, stirring the spaghetti sauce for dinner, "HP [Hewlett-Packard, with whom she'd worked some years earlier] had talked to a company that has a good banking system. They have installed it in a few other banks, or maybe it was credit unions. Mnh! Remember their name? Yes, it's Samson . . . no, it's Sanchez." You never know what you'll come across in the ocean. One minute it's dark, and the next there's a lighthouse right in front of you.

Two phone calls later and I'm talking with Mike Sanchez from Sanchez Computers, located in Malvern, Pennsylvania. He sounds very interested and positive. I liked that they were entrepreneurial and had that go-get-it attitude. His focus was on helping us. His references from HP were good and we agreed to meet and get a proposal together. Now, the start-up work on systems for ING Direct was a challenge. There were no systems easily available that would fit our model, no off-the-rack solutions. It was going to take this kind of entrepreneurial creativity, and a certain amount of serendipity.

At the operational core of the bank, we needed an engine that would be low-cost and would run well. Being online and available was critical if we were to be direct and virtual for the world. The only system we had been looking at before then was one called Olympic. It was a European private banking system that would have been like a boot for snow, when we needed a sandal for the beach. Now, Mike and his brother Frank came to the rescue. They needed a sale, and best of all they were committed to making a partnership happen. And it was nice to deal with the owners and decision makers. Personable and determined, they really worked hard on the deal with us. Mike and Frank Sanchez always told the truth. Their word was good, and they were committed to winning. Here again, at critical junctures of a project like this, it was the individuals we found who really helped us build a successful start-up—individuals like we found at GWP Brand Engineering, Sanchez Computers, and later at Peet's Coffee. The big names can't help attack an industry establishment that pays 90 percent of their everyday bills. They aren't hungry, and they are committed to incremental innovation. It's risky to go with smaller players, but the internal friction is a whole lot less. The ability to see the personal strengths and values of these individual operators was like seeing the stars very clearly.

BP: My partners and I, of course, had been on the other end of just such a serendipitous process. Like Sanchez and Peet's, GWP Brand Engineering had been discovered by Arkadi and his team and, like them, we had been attractive to ING Direct because we had nothing invested in the status quo and something personal to prove. That meant our agendas were aligned. But we would learn very early in our relationship that alignment was only half the story. Like the steel rails of a train track, it wasn't enough just to be parallel and tied together. That track's real purpose is to go somewhere.

This came home for me when we were at the point of inking our first formal contract with this new client of our new firm. We could hardly believe our good fortune: We had won the ING Direct account in not one but two competitive pitches against formidable enemies. Meanwhile, these guys, Arkadi and Jim, had plainly spent a significant amount of political capital to get their colleagues in Amsterdam to support the risky choice of a small, one-office independent agency partner like GWP Brand Engineering. They believed in us. They also seemed to have the guts to buy whatever ideas we could throw at them, and were more than willing to let GWP make itself famous in the process if it so chose. And they'd accepted our fee proposal without blinking and without the usual ceremonial arm wrestling that usually follows an opening bid. There was even a performance incentive in it for us. Going through the contract document with Jim Kelly on the phone, in fact, I could find only one catch. But it was a whopper: If either of my two partners or I were to leave the company or even stop working personally on the ING Direct assignment, ING Direct could fire GWP without notice. And almost certainly would, added Jim.

"We bought you guys," he said simply.

Suddenly, this engagement wasn't just another new business win for us, however thrilling. It was a decision to alter the course of GWP's life as a company. And to some degree the same was even true for ING Direct. They were saying, to us and to themselves, and at this tender moment in their own growth, that branding and marketing this new venture wasn't going to be an easy, mechanical job that any reasonably qualified person could do. It wasn't a technical matter. It was something more human than that, and it mattered more than that. They knew they couldn't succeed if they poured their hearts into this thing only to have it brought to market by someone with nothing personal invested in it. And without a doubt, we knew that our own radical founding philosophy wasn't going to amount to a hill of beans if we couldn't find a client willing to bet some money on it. They needed us almost as much as we needed them, and we were both willing to change course rather than miss the opportunity.

Sometimes, the people you find are the stars you steer by.

AK: Good people are hard to find. But once they're found, you can do great things. It's ironic that all large companies spend time and energy on building leaders, but then do everything they can to kill leadership in the pursuit of being a team. You need to have good judgment about people and their leadership potential. My experience with the Orange Code was always to remind me that if there is doubt about an individual, there is no doubt. Seldom have my initial judgments been wrong. It's the lights of a passing ship that should not be mistaken for stars when it comes to the people you're working with. We have made mistakes and we have been fooled and, most depressing, we have sometimes been late to admit a failure, to make the hard call. The truth is, even in those moments, we always knew the right thing to do. It's just puzzling to understand why sometimes we hesitate and try to rationalize our way into a decision that for some unknown reason did not seem right in the first place! All leaders sometimes fall into the trap of thinking too much and not trusting their instincts when they make a decision about people, and then hanging on to their mistakes too long.

Now, not everyone is on board to steer by the stars in a business venture. Everyone has an agenda and few people really want to change the world or strive for perfection. I have known this a long time and realize that there is a price to pay for following the stars when all around are content to follow other agendas or goals. It can be lonely. For sure, when I see the stars alongside kindred spirits who see them in the same way, the joy is much brighter. Never underestimate the treasure of finding great people who get it. It restores your faith in what you're trying to do, which a leader desperately needs to have. The best celebration for any traveler would be a final "night of all nights" in the company of the star walkers: pure admiration and love to mark the real reason we existed on this planet.

Now, I have thought, of course, how this would sound to you reading this? Maybe a bit too sentimental or philosophical? There were on this particular journey with our Orange Code plenty of dangers and plenty of opportunities to fail. Success has many parents, while failure is an orphan, so the saying goes. For me and my team, though, the journey itself has had to be the reward. History is littered with claims of success and the labeling of failures, but you don't think of it like that when you're in the thick of it. That horizon is always moving. When success is working, however, there are clear signs, and the commitment to stay on course with the stars is core to understanding its mysteries.

The stars are always the clearest when the sky is darkest. In this sense, conflict has been very important to the human aspect of the ING Direct story, because the darkest moments have revealed who we are in ways that an easy passage never would. We had plenty of battles at ING Direct. On reflection, I now believe that the most underestimated struggles were the internal ones. The outside struggles with suppliers, customers, and competitors are critical and ultimately determine commercial success, of course. Yet to increase your chances of success you have to face and solve the internal battles, too, well and in a timely way—and not with truces, but with a true sorting out of agendas and ambitions. A leader has to read the situation clearly and anticipate how everyone will act and what they want and are willing to do. Taking everything at face value feels good, but it doesn't work for long. There is no forgiveness in the end. Remember, a business venture is like life: It's a blackboard you can't erase.

BP: They say the road to hell is paved with good intentions.

In the world of advertising, that road often seems like a superhighway. More fatal mistakes are made by brands trying to improve their ad campaigns than in any other aspect of marketing. But the lessons of those mistakes are universally applicable for leaders in just about any situation and, in what is really the point of this chapter, they have a lot to do with being true to yourself. In the abstract comfort of a boardroom, it's easy to get tired of an idea long before the consumer does, or to believe that all that matters is your product's functional benefit, or, conversely and just as commonly, to believe that a consumer who is entertained is a consumer who is ready to buy. It happens all the time—the evidence is everywhere from YouTube to the Superbowl—that brands lose themselves in the quest to make people giggle and like them, even if it means not selling them anything. Companies forget that consumers are no more looking for an ad to amuse them than they're looking for a plumber who tap-dances. Sure, it's a nice bonus if either of these things shows up at your door, but it's no substitute for relevance and trust.

ING Direct hasn't been completely immune to this urge. Every once in a while, there erupts an impulse to change things up, to make ads that people talk about and laugh at, to make consumers enjoy a brand as much as the people who work with it do, or to outdo some competitor's latest bit of commercial derring-do. It happens with ad campaigns all the time, but just as often with every aspect of marketing. Distracted by our own reflection, we lose sight of where we're going and, with pure hearts and total conviction, steer the brand into the worst kind of shallow water.

So it was that in the early spring of 2008, I was crowded into a small meeting space at ING Direct's Wilmington riverfront offices with several members of the bank's marketing team, a tray of sandwiches and sodas, and three earnest souls from a prominent advertising research company. We were a year into trying to perfect a television campaign for the Orange Savings Account that would somehow do it all: be relevant, selling advertising, and be entertaining, memorable, and likable in its own right, too. So far, it had gone pretty well, but we'd been careful and tentative about it and the results had, maybe not surprisingly, been inconclusive. That wasn't going to do it for us. We were trying to see how far we could go, and the researchers were there to tell us what this latest effort had wrought.

The formula for this campaign was pretty simple: On the rational selling side of the equation, we'd created a spokesperson for ING Direct, an affable evangelist for saving who wandered the land in a cool orange 1962 Chevy Impala, preaching the benefits of the Orange Savings Account to anyone who seemed to need to hear them. On the funny and memorable side of the equation, we created entertainment value by having our guy intercept people on the verge of making silly financial decisions anyone could relate to. He'd pounce on them, about to spend thousands on a purse or eight bucks on a cup of coffee, and merriment would ensue. Funny stuff, we hoped, and it led directly and naturally to a sales pitch. And it was working, sort of. I watched slide after dreary slide projected on the wall of the meeting room, as the research people used phrases like "quite good" and "at or above norm" to describe the results of our latest effort.

But I was grumpy, and a bit mystified. This campaign made sense, and it was fun—the best of both worlds. But if it wasn't hitting the ball out of the park in terms of entertainment value, what was the point of the compromise? We weren't looking for polite applause from the audience, here. We wanted them to roll in the aisles, and then go online and open an account.

Finally, the research people arrived at one of the more interesting moments in these creative research presentations, something called the interest trace. Basically, when an ad is tested with this particular methodology, the consumers watching are given an opportunity to register their level of sheer interest in what they're seeing, in real time, using a handheld device like a computer mouse. If they're interested, they move it one way, and if they're not, they move it the other way. The results are presented to us by superimposing a line representing the average level of consumer interest over the commercial as it plays on the screen in front of us. We can see, second by second as the line moves up and down, how engaged people were as they watched. I've watched more of these things than I care to remember, and the pattern is usually the same: Interest goes up when the consumer is being entertained, and it goes down when they're being sold something. That's the pattern we were trying to beat.

And we were beating it. But not the way we'd intended. I watched in amazement as the commercial played and the little interest line crawled across the screen. During the funny part of the story, people were, at best, amused. The line meandered into positive territory, but not with any real energy. Yet when our spokesman took charge of the story's situation and made his pitch for the Orange Savings Account, the line didn't sink into negative territory the way these things usually do. It shot up like the price of an initial public offering (IPO) on its first trading day. And it stayed up right to the end, even through the obligatory logo superimposition, until the screen went black. The ads hadn't failed; if they had, the consumer would surely have punished us by losing interest entirely when our brand spokeman made his pitch. Instead, I believed, people were simply telling us not to try so hard. They didn't want to be bribed with entertainment, not when the subject was as important as their money. They just wanted us to tell them what we could do for them, in our own voice.

Sometimes, customers are the stars you steer by.

AK: Consistency in advertising messages and other communication to the marketplace is the most misunderstood aspect of brand building. Even within our parent company ING, as in any large company, there is ongoing pressure to improve, manage change, and get better performance. When it comes to the brand, every year, it seems, they have new taglines, new advertising campaigns, and new graphics and, of course, a new vision and mission. Refining what your company wants to strive for in the name of continuous improvement seems hard to criticize. But the truth is that companies cannot and do not change that fast, and neither does the consumer's mind. Marketing is a process of battling in a competitive environment, yes, but its main function is to project a commercially useful image that will stick and be remembered. Any call to action for consumers stands on the shoulders of that image.

Even with employees and other stakeholders, the tendency in corporate life is to gain confidence by taking action and making changes.

Winners don't sit still. Growth, earnings, and market share are always viewed as the drivers in business. Yet the line going up is never straight for any company no matter how much we want to will it to be. You can't control everything, so you need constants that you and your customer alike can navigate by. The clarity of the mission, the clarity of the offering, and the clarity of the competitive advantage must shine through. They are your image in its purest form. How easily and well understood are they by everyone is this company? The ones that stand out are the ones that have those attributes and are confident enough in them that they never change. Look at the American flag or the Red Cross/Crescent symbol. They each simply say a thousand words because they have history. Think of any great brand in this way and you will recognize that distinctive quality. American Express is still that green card after years of willing it to be something else. Southwest Airlines is still the upstart discount airline no matter how much it tries to be a player and add things like business class service, of all things. For marketers, the message is clear: Stick to a logo, a tagline, a color, a message, and a campaign theme that does not change year to year. For how long? For as long as you can keep creating positive energy and ideas on the same fundamental brand values.

There can be other reasons that branding and messaging need to change. ING Group continues to go through marketing iterations in its many diverse businesses and with customers in different marketplaces. Trying to tie them all together is surely not easy. The motivation to manage the brand's image and messaging is as much internal as external, maybe more so. To get all the employees in ING's world on the same page is easier said than done. The need to leverage the whole organization's resources is a tall task in its own right. But the question is, do the customers care? The need for them to recognize and trust who the company is and what it stands for is critical. The rest is of less value. Shell and its logo and colors are recognized. The GE, FedEx, and Apple logos are also recognized and understood, and those companies don't tinker with them. Why, then, overmanage the rest of the brand formula? Branding decisions should not be made with corporate agendas, but by seeing things from the consumer's point of view. If a company does this, it will quickly realize that constant change to its image is just confusing and ultimately does no real good. A brand is not what you say but what you do.

I first saw the Peet's Coffee logo in Palo Alto. Peet's colors are brown and beige. The coffee was good and the whole thing felt solid and earthy.

Brand-wise, it was also complementary. When Synthia and I visited the Peet's home office and plant in Berkeley, California, it was like walking into a start-up. An industrial and nondescript building yielded a commitment to good coffee, expert roasting, and above all same-day fast delivery for freshness. Best was when I asked the Peet's marketing team to describe their brand. I was met with "It's all about the bean!" Unlike its big competitor that prided itself on the "coffee experience," this company looked for excellence in the product and saw its reputation as being built cup by cup. There was no fast-growth or drive-the-share-price mentality. If ING Direct as a financial brand wanted to use coffee to reach and interact with customers, then Peet's was uniquely suited to the job. They were very protective of their brand and how the coffee would be sold or used in our locations. They were also low-key, even modest. They wanted to make it work in a focused way and not compromise what they stand for in the process. I just knew we were not going to see Peet's ice cream in a supermarket store. I also liked that they split with the original Seattle team that later became Starbucks. The old "growth versus staying true to the brand" battle felt good and familiar to us at ING Direct: no flash, earn it every step of the way, just like we wanted to do. Doing a coffee tasting in their plant felt very down-to-earth and pure. I bet they wanted to steer by their own star.

BP: The governance of ING Direct has always been an invisible process to all but a few people involved in the day-to-day operation of the business. It hasn't been hard to guess why. For one thing, this is an operating unit of a very large, distinctly more conservative corporate entity. The cultural effect of being reminded of this every day could be very hard to manage when you consider how much ING Direct's entrepreneurial energy comes from seeing itself as the pirates and not as the navy. For another, although ING Direct emphatically positions itself as an alternative to traditional banks and is sometimes a harsh critic of them, it is nonetheless a regulated financial institution with all the financial stability and structural compliance that implies. Think about this too much, and you start to feel uncomfortably like the enemy. Still, I always wondered how Arkadi and his executive team managed it. Was it a constant struggle? Did Arkadi have to check ING Direct's cause at the door and transform himself into another Wall Street suit when it was time to face his own masters?

As it turns out, sometimes your own words, echoed back to you by those you've passionately persuaded, can be the stars you steer by.

AK: An almost-invisible part of our serendipity story was the group of directors who decided to join this start-up rebel bank. In Canada, the mix of backgrounds was not unusual for a bank board of directors: banking, academics, accounting, and government. In the United States, the mix was similar: regulatory, accounting, investment, and academic people. All the directors, when first approached, had doubts and reservations. Who could guess how this would play out? Individual director reputations after long, successful careers are much more important than most people realize. Who wants to take on the responsibility of being a director in a regulated business for a retainer if the marketplace is volatile and the business plan looks very unconventional? Yet eight of the 10 original directors in Canada and all of the U.S. board are still with us, having served 12 years and eight years respectively. It would take another book to tell the stories of each of these directors, but to a person they have played a large part in steering ING Direct's success. And not just because they attended every meeting, either. It's not just that they fulfilled their director's duty, but rather it was their clear understanding of what our mission was. Once they understood it and saw it as a strategy, they embraced it and held firm. They became part of our conscience, so much so that when I pitched other commercial initiatives, the board would play the "what mission are you on?" tape back to me. How much better could it get?

I'm at a board meeting in Fort Orange, one of the specially named meeting rooms in the ING Direct main office in Wilmington, Delaware. It's day two, and we're near the end of the predictable board strategy session. I'm coming to my concluding remarks, and I ask the board what they think about the choices before the company and the merits of each of the three directions I've proposed for ING Direct to grow into over the next five years. I'm saying all the right things for a CEO charged with growing shareholder value: We need to look at all the options. Need to think of all the stakeholders. We need to seize the market opportunities. There are trade-offs, but size is driving us to do and tackle things that maybe we would not have considered a few years back. I need to show

them I can be pragmatic, because, after all, a board doesn't want to think
its enterprise is being run by a zealot. But my body language is in total
contrast to my words. My words are saying go ahead, but my body is saying no, what a disappointment it is to be considering options we have
no real heart for. Finally, director Shannon Fairbanks holds her pen like
a wand and says something like this: "It seems to me that you have to
look at the options in a way that fits with your customers and what those
customers would expect of you. I know these other ideas are interesting
[from a shareholder point of view], but you have to do what makes sense
for ING Direct." Wow. No push on numbers or returns; let's get the basic
mission right. How much better can it get for the team when the board
challenges you to stay with the mission because they believe that it's a
winning strategy that is worth fighting for!

BP: Arkadi's relentless advocacy for ING Direct's cause, and its insepara-
bility from its business model, has been an internal quest as much as it
has been an external one, and it hasn't stopped on this side of the Atlan-
tic Ocean, nor with ING Direct's board. The ability to create converts
all the way to the top of the organization has been crucial in letting the
bank stay its own course when it counted most, against even the most
destructive hurricane.

AK: It's the summer of 2005 and I'm sitting in a conference room at ING
House in Amsterdam, a glass building shaped like a large ship stranded
on land. The architecture is symbolic in its transparency and the image of
venturing around the globe in search of new ideas, and profits to boot.
The ING Group mergers and acquisitions (M&A) team that looks for situations that might help ING develop its business mix was hosting a large
New York investment bank for a discussion of opportunities in the U.S.
marketplace. I'm there observing because it's always a good idea to listen
to fresh thinking and tie into ideas that might work for ING Direct. The
firm's London investment bank partner goes over a scratch list of ideas
with the group, and then, coming to his main point of the day, states
that the U.S. mortgage market is booming and that there are some solid
deals for us to do. The conversation went like this: "ING, you have done a
great job getting your banking business started in the United States, but
now is the time to step up and fix the asset side of the balance sheet. You
cannot just gather deposits. You need to let the real players on the field

and thank the boys for the good start." This subject is just never going to go away, I thought to myself. Everybody thinks they have the answer.

Neither the speaker nor the rest of his team had gotten a good introduction to who was who in the room, and did not know who I was or what I was doing there. Michel Tilmant, ING Group's CEO, looked at me and was wondering if I was going to speak or what I was going to say. Politely, I held my breath and thought how easily businesses get sold on this kind of hype and get caught up in the latest trends in the marketplace. Hey, everyone is doing it . . . don't be left behind! To Michel's credit, we carried on and promised to consider the options, which, in corporate-speak, means we'll keep looking until something makes it up the ladder. But all six of the mortgage deals we looked at in 2004 and 2005 have since disappeared in one way or another. We escaped the consequences. It is true that in large organizations it's very easy to say no and very hard to get anything approved, but there was more to this than corporate feet of clay. We were aligned on what ING Direct's business is about, right to the top. It took time, and it has paid off. Michel Tilmant's support from the first days of ING Direct in 1996 until today has been critical to our success. This helped us stay on course and steer by our own stars, rather than by the lights of a passing ship that might just be heading for the rocks.

BP: It would be untrue to say that steering by the stars is a simple, certain way to run a brand, an organization, a career, or a life. It's not. It comes with personal responsibility, since every decision you make is a product of observation and thought rather than a policy or a plan. It comes with uncertainty, since your choices always seem limitless, and success and failure are less than absolute concepts. It's lonely sometimes, since everything you do can be questioned and doubted in hindsight by anyone who wasn't in the boat with you. And like any form of unlimited thinking, it leaves you restless, since you never know for sure what else you could have done, where else you could have gone.

Yet, when your enterprise is a cause like ING Direct's, there really is no option. You can't be guided by science, because science is a leveler; there's no competitive advantage in it. You can't be guided by consensus, because you're trying to create something that doesn't exist yet. You can't be guided by market behavior, because you're trying to lead that market. You can't ask permission from consumers or anybody else, because you're trying to provoke and inspire them. To be free to innovate and to be able to keep your brand pure and authentic, you can't rely on the lights of passing ships. You've got to have your own horizon and simply accept, as the Orange Code puts it, that you "will never be finished."

AK: The Fort Orange boardroom just never worked right. It's hard to say if it's the light, the space, the shape of the room, or the sound, but it never felt right. It's been a constant irritant for me. We tried a number of times to fix it, but the result was always the same. Things could only be improved incrementally, but never really transformed. The constant tension between wanting to change everything that isn't right and settling down and accepting the imperfections in order to focus on getting things done is always with me, it seems.

The boardroom issue for me, symbolically, highlights the challenging tug-of-war between being creative and thinking out of the box, and just plain old moving on and executing. The truth is, that boardroom room cannot be fixed. We, of course, do not want to admit this, because it would mean a whole other set of questions. It's hard to be defeated by a physical space! We simply want to get some things done. Knowing what can work and what can't is never easy, and the answers come in all shapes and sizes. Thinking about the right outcome and being able to visualize it are something that seems to require training and experience. It also requires a clear understanding of risk. In management, there is too much "let's try this stuff" or "it's good to experiment and have an open mind" or "let's explore this!" Striking the balance among planning, executing, and controlling is a manager's most important tool in the toolbox, and it's impossible to do without really knowing who you are and being true to that. There are lots of situations where we did not get that balance right. This boardroom was one of them, and it stands as a constant reminder to me of how this work of ours is never finished.

As the work of building ING Direct is never finished, so is the work of developing the people who will carry it on when our turn at the helm is done. To develop leadership you have to let young leaders make mistakes and learn from them. You just cannot afford large mistakes that are life-threatening for a business. As a business gets large you can't control all that goes on or all of the decisions that get made on a daily basis. Managers learning the art of management look for inspiration in many places, but the crucial point remains that they need hands-on experience. In many meetings we have discussed an issue, hit a wall, and resolved things by asking, "What would Bruce say?" It's been another way of agreeing with all on the vision, the mission, and the code by which we operate—another star to steer by. You must set out the frame of the picture but let everyone else try their hand at the canvas. One does not work without the other. Steering by the stars is a singular experience. No two journeys are alike, even when you're in the same boat.

Why Celestial Navigation Beats Managing

BP: When a company is a cause, principles are more useful than strategies.

Okay, maybe that sounds naive. And we realize, of course, that in the cut and thrust of competition in any business, strategy is a critical skill, and strategies are useful things to have. Strategies are the bridges you build between your objectives and the operational solutions for achieving them. So you can turn the shredder off; even ING Direct believes in strategies. This book isn't about that. This isn't about goal setting, accountability, plans, and measurements, and it's not about a system. There are plenty of good books about those things. This is about strategic awareness.

Strategic awareness comes in two varieties: the kind that guides you, and the kind that keeps you vigilant.

For any business, but especially for a rebel innovator like ING Direct, the environment is never a static thing. It's in constant flux, and it's often you that's causing that flux. By definition, then, there is never any convention to fall back on—no well-worn path, no time-proven standard solutions, no industry norms, no defaults. So, when you set a new goal or face a new challenge in the marketplace, a playbook solution is always going to feel a little bit wrong, never going to fit quite right. For ING Direct, and it would seem for many disruptive innovators, the solution is to instead have the clearest, most deeply committed sense of who you are and what your mission is. The better people understand these things, the more naturally and organically they're able to improvise and innovate ad hoc, because they're not serving some kind of operational orthodoxy.

Imagine a manager, alone, hard at work in an evening or on a weekend, bumping into some kind of dilemma: Does she call her supervisor and ask what to do? Or does she just know what your way of solving this would be? Not the solution itself, but the principles by which the solution should be formulated and by which it will get the natural support of the organization on Monday morning? At ING Direct, that's what empowerment really means. It's not a matter of just granting autonomy to employees but of enabling it with a code that directs it. Think of this as the difference between having a conscript army and having a volunteer one: Soldiers in the latter always know, at least in the most general terms, what they have to do. The former will always wait to be told.

It's easy to imagine that there's an Apple way of doing things, or a Disney way, or a Virgin way; there is absolutely an ING Direct way, and steering by that star has made it a terrifically efficient and productive organization to helm.

The second kind of strategic awareness is a more literal one. When you're managing, you sometimes have your head down, so to speak, working the plan, focusing on the task at hand, like that motorboat churning its way from A to B. One of the points the stories in this chapter make is that having your head down can make you miss valuable things along the journey: golden market opportunities, amazing people, unexpected puffs of wind on the water ahead. By being sure and confident about your cause and your mission—what you're ultimately there to do, as opposed to only what you're obligated to do this quarter—you allow two great things to happen: You're more open and alert to whatever gifts the universe (or the marketplace, or a competitor, or an innovation from your own ranks, or an inspiration from your spouse) sends your way, and you have a natural ideological filter through which to evaluate them. It was this, and not a crystal ball, that kept ING Direct from getting into the riskier end of the mortgage business, for example. It was this, and not a crystal ball, that connected ING Direct with some of its best people, its most loyal vendor partners, and a thousand other seemingly random things that, if you stand back and look at the constellation they form, have created an authentic brand that people immediately understand, and that can sustain itself organically.

As way of leading, steering by the stars may not always be very scientific. But it will always get you where it's worth going.

Chapter 10

Herding Cats

How to Snatch Defeat from the Jaws of Victory

Silos get created by volume of work, specialization, and increased complexity. But the reality is . . . we can't work the way we bowl. There is only one lane to the customer.

—AK, CEO Message # 204

BP: All ideas are born drowning.

This cheery sentiment comes courtesy of a creative director I once worked with. I'm fairly sure he cribbed it from someone wiser and deeper than he, but he always delivered it with sage conviction and, after all, who would know better? The life of a creative director is an endless series of battles to have his work understood and respected by people who, though they may lack the talent to actually have an idea on their own, paid for the privilege of criticizing and participating in his. And if you're the kind of leader who is trying to build an enterprise on a singular vision and a sense of purpose, I don't think your lot is really much different. Arkadi's hasn't been. Mine hasn't been. If you have motivated your organization behind a cause and you have, as we proposed in the first chapter of this book, made it personal, then you are every bit as much a creative director as my colleague in the black turtleneck sweater. The only difference is that he fights a thousand little fights to protect a

185

thousand little ideas that, in the end, all have the shelf life of mayonnaise anyway. You, in contrast, are fighting just one fight, for one big, precious idea that's supposed to last forever, and that fight never ends.

The enemies of organizational integrity for an enterprise like this one come in two basic varieties: The first is more of a nuisance than a threat, though it can still be pretty destructive, and that's the disparate individual agendas of the people on the team. Arkadi has talked about this many times in these pages, and there's no doubt that it is particularly vexing for an enterprise like ING Direct. If a company is more managed than led, the fact that everyone has their own agenda is just part of the deal. Managing is, after all, essentially an ongoing process of negotiation. But in a company whose leadership is striving to unite it around some kind of mission, those moments during elevator rides when employees ask about why they can't decorate their cubicles or why they have no titles make the leader's job feel like herding cats. You sometimes wonder who is really working for whom, and how it came to be that a good day is just one where none of these cats pulled down the curtains or shredded the couch. Still, if you hire well and stick to your principles, this is a tolerable leadership challenge. Every good person, in the end, wants to play for a winner. They just can't all see as far, as clearly as the leader must, and why should they? That's what leaders get paid for.

The second kind of enemy is more worrisome, because they're here to help.

They're the professional managers, people with resumes studded with the names of corporate icons, and maybe even some management-consulting experience. Of course, not everyone who matches that description is a threat by definition, but the ones to watch aren't hard to identify. They talk exclusively about results. They talk about process and measurement and they toss data around like a circus knife-thrower. They think life is lived in fiscal quarters, and that every business plan is a chance to start over again. To them, an enterprise is a machine, not a community. Their horizons are always short-term, and their rhetorical style is characterized by rationality and coolly embroidered with numbers. They think that your brand's image, as they call it, is a luxury you can afford once those numbers are where you want them, as if it were that sports car you're going to buy when the kids are out of college. And they are irresistible because, for a while, anyway, they can fatten everybody's bonus checks—and because they seem so darned, well . . . so darned *reasonable*.

Still, two things remain certain: An enterprise must grow, and that means more and more people with no cultural memory of a company's founding cause. And as it grows, it needs professional managers, because the bigger and more successful you become, the fewer technical mistakes you can afford to make. The challenge for tomorrow's leadership is not to avoid growth, but to somehow keep the flame alive in the face of it. This chapter is for them. Think of it as a field guide to the cats ING Direct's future leaders will find themselves herding as a dividend of its success. Some of those cats are already here, tugging at the curtains. And a lot of them are by no means unique to this rebel bank.

Seven Deadly Temptations That Can Sink Our Business

AK: This book, *The Orange Code,* is not the usual sort of business story about ING Direct. It is about its brand, its marketing, and its advocacy. There are still, however, important business lessons linked to the Orange Code and how it gets interpreted and lived by everyone, lessons that have universal implications. Every day, a lot of time gets spent talking in the media and in coffee shops about successful businesses and why a business succeeds, about finding a formula that works well and provides an easy model for adoption. Copying and repetition as ways of managing risk in business, as in anything else, are as ingrained in us all as eating and sleeping! But there are also mistakes that inevitably get made, and we usually see them in evening news show postmortems and newspaper editions on Sunday morning with headlines like "What Went Wrong?"

The factors that lead to success and the ones that lead to failure are many, but most get headlined and labeled as strategy, execution, or leadership. Fair enough, but are these factors specific to a particular mission or are they universal in nature? Can they be predicted, or do they just appear without warning? Every business lists its financial opportunities and risks in annual reports. It's usually demanded by whoever provided the capital required. Once stated, the opportunities are pursued and the risks are worried about. But is there something more here?

Whatever the vision and the mission, however they are extolled by the leadership, written on the office wall, or explained in the company brochure, they still end up meaning different things to different people. We all interpret the world and how it works in our unique, personal way.

Now, most of the time this matters little and, generally, the canvas is large enough to accommodate all these different interpretations. The alignment of a corporate agenda and the personal agendas of all those agreeing to work together lies in shared values and principles. They are the heart, so to speak, of the commitment and energy being invested in the journey.

All business journeys are natural reflections of the world around us. It's as much biological as anything else humans do. There is a birth, a maturing, and eventually a demise and passing. This cycle is predictable, and it leads to rebirth and rejuvenation. There are cycles as short as catching your breath and as long as it takes to turn breath to ashes. Companies have short and long cycles as well, but eventually they all disappear and their ideas and knowledge get absorbed by society at large. We do evolve, kicking and screaming, and we want good things to last as long as we can make them last, but all we do is subject nevertheless to the cycle of life.

Understanding the nature of a business and how it works provides important lessons, but your personal involvement in it is a bit like choosing between watching movies and making a movie. It is a process that lays bare the real intentions and the basic motivations of all the participants. Why? Intentions matter. What's more, they are often concealed, hard to recognize, and difficult to understand. Some intentions are an innocent misreading of ideas and thoughts, while others are just not, and are premeditated, deeply seated, selfish needs that come into play.

Looking at the Orange Code itself, it's easy to see and understand the vision and the mission it speaks to. I have never had anyone disagree with any of the 12 principles. Its advocacy for consumer-empowering ideas is in some basic sense classical and universal. What could go wrong, then?

For one thing, it might all look and sound too good to be true. Good intentions can lead one to defeat as well as to victory. Here are seven temptations that, from my experience, could have exactly that result for ING Direct.

Thinking It's Just a Savings Account

Many pundits have looked at ING Direct and said it's all about the savings account. A revelation! Save your money! I get it. It's a business in itself! Just look at the customer growth, and at the deposit balances and their growth. It is a good and unique strategy to win customers and attract balances and thus funding for the bank. Unfortunately, it's only half the story. As a market entry strategy, it's original and great, but it's not the steady state or the end state for a bank to operate and survive upon. High interest paid on savings accounts is an expensive liability for a bank. You need to originate or buy assets, like mortgages, and they will yield interest income and, after costs, provide a net return. If you subtract the interest expense of the liabilities from the interest earned on the assets, you are left with a net margin. The margin must be big enough to pay the overhead and the risk costs. And there must be an adequate return on capital. Now, in a start-up, a lower return is rationalized as a justifiable initial investment in growing to scale. The trouble is, you still have to have the same amount of assets, which for ING Direct would be customer mortgages, to match the customer deposits—or liabilities—to make it work. If the proportion is out of balance, then you have to substitute other kinds of funding or financial assets for savings and mortgages. This imbalance can significantly affect the profit impact when the interest rate environment causes quick changes in the net margin that the bank lives by. Savings is not a business in itself. It's half the story.

Chasing Balances, Neglecting Balance

Next is the temptation to allow a mismatch of retail deposits with whole-sale assets. Traditional banks originate loans or mortgages and determine the yield from those assets, and then see how they can fund them as cheaply as possible. The cheaper the funding, the more margin you can make. Sometimes the funding is wholesale in the financial markets, and sometimes it comes more from retail customers' deposits. What is the most you have to pay for this funding? You see what the market offers and you make the best choice to earn the best margin, spread, and return. If you have relatively high-cost customer deposits and you have wholesale assets, the changes in value and availability in the financial markets can make your margin fluctuate sharply up or down. The key is to match retail assets to retail liabilities. Customer behavior in the savings and mortgage worlds is much more aligned than behavior of wholesale and retail financial markets. As with any business, you can't put all your eggs in one basket.

Sticking Your Hands in Their Pockets

And then there is the third temptation, the pitfall of fees and service charges. Since the early 1980s, banks have been moving away from exclusively earning margins as I described earlier, and collecting more and more fees. As distributors, they need less capital and do well on service charges and income. The trouble is, it's also the thing most customers hate and see little value in. If the industry was supply side driven, maybe you could get away with this. Where else would they go? Most customers would give up or put up with it. But if they are given a choice, they will move faster than you can say Orange Savings Account. If you, as a retail financial services player, want to stand out and be different and win over customers, you have to redefine what fees mean and how they are charged. You have to avoid them, and where they are necessary there has to be clear value for the customer in exchange. In any event, the amount that you can add to your revenue with fees is limited if you are a new-age direct bank like ours. With a commodity approach to products and service, you will not have the time or opportunity to provide added-value personal service, let alone advice. It will not fit a business model that delivers standardized commodity products like ours. If you get confused by this temptation, ING Direct will transform into an advice-giving business by default, and destroy its basic economics. The attitude of customers will change and your competitive distinctiveness will disappear. The urge to add fees and service charges is very seductive. It will be a nonstop temptation. It will always be a mistake.

Acquiring a Gambling Habit

The fourth temptation is to ignore the long-term and short-term time commitments attached to mortgages and savings. For ING Direct, savings accounts are on-demand. Certificates of deposit are on time schedules, but are mostly shorter than two years. Mortgages are amortized over 30 years, but interest commitments as to rate are for five years. In practice, savings stay longer in the bank than most savers originally intend. And mortgages are canceled or renewed more frequently than most customers expect. So, savings might stay on deposit an average of two years, while most mortgages might last three years. The capital behind the bank has to take the risk of this time difference into account. This is particularly important when you consider the fact that the bank is committed to that mortgage interest rate for a period of time, while deposit rates could change many times over the same period. It's obvious that when you change your interest rate, it's going to have an impact on margin.

Everyone understands that. But there is a less obvious, equally significant risk in doing it without considering the long-term impact, too: You might never get that margin back.

Most of the factors that influence the timing of major outflows from a savings account are natural facts of life: a job change, health issues, divorce, retirement, and so forth. A bank plans for this kind of variability. The big unknown, though, is the actions of customers who want to gamble using their savings and their homes as financial assets. Many people see a house as a financial asset that helps make money rather than just sheltering it. They gamble on the value of that house going up and the cost of financing the house remaining steady, hoping that their equity will come from that asset appreciating. The savers, meanwhile, are tempted to get into the stock market and score with their cash. The flow of greed and fear creates great swings in the volume of balances that a bank has to work with. More capital is needed, and more financial modeling and work are needed to deal with volatility like that. A bank that operates on the kind of narrow margins that ING Direct does must get very good at forecasting, and avoid rolling the dice.

Breaking Even

That's the fifth temptation. Sooner or later, for this business to last and have some control over its destiny, the financial numbers have to add up. For ING Direct's financial model, the question was, what profit can or should it make? Where is the missing 1 percent? The ING Direct business model, like any other, sets out revenue and expense assumptions and a pricing and cost strategy. Given that ING Direct was built to be a high-volume, low-margin business, the revenue was designed into the model to be a very low 150 basis points (100 basis points or bps equals 1 percent, as consumers think of it), compared to the industry average of 450 bps. It gives us a good pricing advantage for attracting deposits and selling mortgages to retail customers. With the expenses associated with high volume and standard, commodity-type products (and, yes, as few of them as necessary), the costs with good automation would run at 50 bps. Traditional banks operate on 250 bps. The industry, on average, therefore makes 200 bps; ING Direct makes 100 bps. Now or sometime in the future, the difference between those two numbers needs to be found. The 100 bps difference has to come from revenue, since you cannot drive the 50 bps cost base much lower no matter how automated you get. Again, in the short term you can justify the 100 bps difference as a growth investment, but eventually the people who put the capital into this will expect a return in line with the market and begin demanding that 100 bps. The temptation is to pretend that's not going to happen, but it's inevitable. Somehow, without betraying the mission or the model, you have to find it.

Forgetting It's Called ING Direct for a Reason

The sixth temptation is to fall into channel-oriented thinking. Bankers love to talk about channels. I do not know if this came from farming and irrigation imprinted in their genes or from watching too much television, but they are obsessed with them. In any case, for bankers channels mean all the variations in how consumers do business: through branches, the telephone, the Internet, and the mail. Banks are available any way and any time for every customer who, of course, is always right. That costs money. The trouble is, most customers take this accessibility for granted and do not want to pay extra for this great and convenient set of options.

ING Direct was organized to be direct only: no advice, no branches, and no brokers or advisers to worry about. The operating margin is very small, so to build any extra costs by adding other delivery options will not work. Splitting any revenue with any brokers or advisers would need to be priced into the product. The result would then be lower margins or less volume. Since the direct concept is rooted in high volumes to make the scale of business work, channel initiatives are counterproductive and send the whole enterprise down the wrong path. You cannot reduce costs by going direct with your left hand and work toward adding margin by selling advice with your right hand. The bank also will not grow, since you will end up looking and operating like everyone else. And the bank will therefore make too little profit to survive. At this point, most large financial groups begin to abandon direct models, saying that they cannot make the required returns. However, banks are notorious for not understanding cost accounting and for getting trapped in the business of transfer pricing, which always tends to allocate profit and expenses in the wrong places and covers up the real issues. Never mind that banks are not innovative and don't understand how to reengineer product processes and reengineer customer behavior to match. Managing for value, embedded value, and risk-adjusted return on capital (RAROC) all play a role, of course, but they do not solve the fundamental issue. For a traditional bank, it is about the cost-income ratio and the interest income margin over the long term.

Losing Your Way

The seventh and last temptation to defeat comes in failing to understand the spirit of the Orange Code itself. It is not rule based or prescriptive. It's inspirational and encourages one to do good: to be on the side of the angels; to be judged by our customers in the court of popular opinion, not in a court of law or in front of regulators and accountants. There are lots of ways to make money and lots of ways to build a viable retail bank. We have 9,600 of them in the United States to prove it. There are also lots of ways to design products and operate in the marketplace to provide financial services. Who doesn't need services that help you with your money? It's natural to assume that all businesses want to do good and make money. The trade-off as to how much of each is a tough one, but it's not impossible to solve. In a sense, if you provide too little value to customers, they will simply leave. And if you make too little money, then the capital behind you will leave (one way or the other). The challenge is that you don't know you've blown it until the price has been paid. The only way to steer a course between these two fates is to stay firmly focused on your mission.

In many industries, the struggle to create value and market products and services that people want results in more failures than successes. For the basics of living, the challenges are very different than for the wants in life. Needs can be readily defined and organized and, with resources, provided for. The only trouble, here, is that most people want them for the least amount of money. Food, shelter, medicine, schooling, and transportation are priorities for living, but people wish to pay as little as possible for them. Needs have become entitlements. Building a business to provide for people's wants is more uncertain. Wants include things like entertainment, sports, music, movies, and travel, for which people are willing to pay a lot more since they're a lot more fun and stimulating. Now, of course, this is all relative, but would you rather shell out $50 for a sports ticket or $50 for dry-cleaning? You can see the dilemma. And this is the central challenge of ING Direct's business: We have a foot in both worlds. A safe place to put your money, security for the future, these are needs; the things that money means and that it can buy, those are wants. There's no other business like it.

And Seven Deadly Sins That Can Sink Our Brand

BP: Just about every ignominious fate I've seen a brand come to began with a failure to recognize a couple of truths about them: The first is that they matter at all. Because brands are so intangible and they smell like marketing, many leaders see them as not worthy of their attention. The power of a brand as an instrument of leadership is difficult to measure and therefore may as well not exist, in their minds. And the second is that every enterprise has a brand, all the time, whether it means to or not. A brand isn't just what you say when you choose to say it; it's a product of everything you do, and the implied motive behind it. As Arkadi likes to put it, "a brand is whatever people are saying when the company isn't in the room."

If these two truths don't take root in the culture of a company, then a brand becomes vulnerable to some perils of its own, each as capable of destroying value as any of the ones that face the business itself. The difference is that the intricacies of a business model can, on their own, be explained rationally. If a leader chooses to listen, he or she can grasp them and work with them. But the intricacies of a brand are more elusive and easier for leaders and their people to ignore in the heat of day-to-day business. Slowly, imperceptibly, a cause is crushed not by one disastrous misstep, but by a million little moments of inattention and short-term thinking. This, more than almost anything, is the reason the Orange Code exists. And these are the seven deadliest temptations to betraying it.

New People

You grow, you hire. Time passes, people turn over. One way or another, new faces will regularly walk through the front door and, without an ounce of malice, every one of them is ready, willing, and able to undermine your brand. Why? Simply because they want to make their mark. They want to contribute, and they want to accomplish something during their tenure that will enhance their market value and give them something to talk about at class reunions. It's human enough, and the energy behind it is valuable to an organization. But showing up for work with that energy, undirected, ought to be about as welcome to the team as coming to work with the flu.

Here's the thing: Remember that last off-site brainstorming session you attended? Where the earnest moderator said that everybody can contribute, and there are no bad ideas? He was wrong on both counts. Contributing is a privilege earned, not a right. And there are, indeed, bad ideas, most of which are answers to questions the contributors didn't really understand in the first place. There is a reason why some of the world's finest jazz musicians were classically trained: You have to understand the rules before you can intelligently improvise on them.

The best defense against this peril is to thoroughly indoctrinate new people and actively manage your culture. ING Direct has been religious about this from the start. To this day, new employees go through an indoctrination, training, and personal development program that begins on day one, and continues throughout their time there. In it, not only are skills and attitudes developed that will help them support the brand's cause, but the culture of that cause is offered to them as a context for personal growth. Stay or go, people who work at ING Direct learn in the most direct way what makes it tick and, mostly, leave more evolved as a result.

Boredom

To illustrate the peril of boredom, consider the example of a television commercial: 30 seconds of persuasion, if you're lucky, designed to encourage some kind of commercially valuable consumer behavior. A company can spend many millions of dollars running one on television, and in doing so expect that an average member of the target audience will see that message maybe three times before the campaign is over. Three. And the executive who approved that television commercial for production? Well, between storyboards, creative testing, filming, and postproduction, he or she will easily see that commercial 20 times before it is even released to a television network. Meanwhile, the consumers who saw it only three times were likely exposed to thousands of other commercial messages on each of the days they saw this one, and, believe it or not, might actually have had other things to think about besides ads.

It's an easy, relatable example of a dynamic that applies to every kind of brand experience a company creates. Whether it's how the phone is answered in a call center, or the community charities it supports, or how its trucks are painted, or how its customer correspondence looks, the people who steward brands get bored with their choices long, long before the consumer does. Far too often, restless marketers make changes to brand experiences before the consumer has even had a chance to discern the pattern in them and decide what it means. Likewise far too often, leaders look to this seemingly ephemeral stuff as a low-risk way to exercise their authority or wake up an organization. Change for the sake of change, at its most benign, deprives people of the chance to figure you out. At its most dangerous, it tells them what they see can't be trusted, and this applies whether they work for you or buy your product.

Assume that any change of strategic importance to your brand is going to cost you something and, at least temporarily, set you back somehow. Then ask yourself if it's still worth it.

Impatience

In nature, things that happen suddenly usually either are very bad or don't last. Leaders should assume the same thing when they're tempted to make tactical moves to solve short-term problems, especially when they know those moves are in conflict with their brand's cause. And they should assume the same thing when tempted to try to beat whatever law of nature governs growth in their industry in an effort to get more than they should, sooner than they should.

If one thing characterizes most of the gone and forgotten start-ups of the first Internet boom, it is impatience and its benign disguise, optimism. Start-up after start-up built their models, raised their capital, and blew it all in the early going so they could achieve scale *right now* and those servers in the corner could start printing money. You could recognize these enterprises at the time by their lavishly obtuse Super Bowl ads and their briefly ludicrous price-earnings ratios. The predictable result was the same as it might be for an inebriated first-time gambler who bets it all on the first turn of the wheel: He's very popular with the casino for about 15 minutes, but then ends up being escorted from the premises, penniless and with a lot of explaining to do when he gets home.

ING Direct has generally avoided this peril by adopting a kind of pay-as-you-play approach to going to market. Simply put, it never seri-ously contemplated grossly overinvesting in marketing on the assumption that at some point in the future the ratio between marketing costs and customers acquired would magically invert and create a lasting, profitable franchise. Or on the assumption that the consumers were so foolish as to be hypnotized by a loud, shiny new brand and forget that their savings were at stake. ING Direct grew its business one community market at a time across North America, accepting the risk that the enemy would see them coming. And they held themselves to pretty strict standards for customer acquisition costs, deviations from which usually resulted in cranky meetings before the quarter in question had even ended. Why? Because you can never trust the motives or the staying power of a customer who had to be bribed or dazzled to join, whereas one who came at a reasonable cost probably did so as the result of genuine desire and is therefore more likely to remain.

Trust and faith not only are built over time, but they actually need the passage of time to validate them.

Not Enough Information

Years ago, when I was younger and feistier, a client of mine was a big car company. As with most of those, the relationship between this company and its dealer network was of the love/hate variety. They needed each other, but there was an assumed moral superiority among the dealers because they were self-made entrepreneurs, and another among the marketing team at the car company because they were educated head-office professionals. One year, I found myself drawing the short straw to address a dealer convention and present to them our strategy for the year to come. The strategy was built on a solid platform of market research, which I made the mistake of presenting in some detail so as to bolster our credibility. At the conclusion of the presentation, the dealers were offered microphones so they could ask us questions about what they'd heard. One grizzled veteran instead had an editorial comment to offer: "I've been selling these things for 30 years," he grumped. "I don't need expensive research to tell me how to do it. I know everything there is to know about the people who come through my door."

To this I rather intemperately replied, "Yes, but you don't know a damn thing about the people who *don't* come through your door." (There may also be a lesson in here about how being right isn't the same thing as being popular, but I digress . . .)

Snarky though it may have been, there was and remains truth in it. You have to invest in information about what works and what doesn't, and you have to invest in information about the customers you don't have yet. It's time-consuming and it's expensive, and it feels like a tax sometimes. But it's essential. Without it, you can't see mistakes coming before they show up in your quarterly results. Without it, you can't see opportunities coming, either. And without it, you deny yourself the chance to perfect what you're doing—to make it better and better.

There is another dividend to investing in information, too, one that is a bit more subversive: Good people welcome it, while people who are in over their heads in their jobs often fear it. Without information, decisions that affect your brand can be subjective matters of opinion. With it, decisions are more objective and the people who make them are more accountable.

For ING Direct, cutting off the flow of marketplace information would be crippling for three reasons. First, ING Direct exists to be a disruptive innovator, a rebel. If its only feedback came from existing clients, who are extraordinarily happy with their experience here, there would be no incentive or inspiration to innovate. We would become instantly complacent. Second, ING Direct's business model, as Arkadi has discussed, depends on razor-thin margins and tremendous efficiency. If the bank attempted to grow without learning and optimizing, it would never realize that efficiency. And third, although what ING Direct offers consumers isn't shockingly new anymore, in the scheme of things its proposition is still radically different from the way most people think about banking. New things take time to be adopted by the population, and the people who jump first are not the same kind of people as those who wait a year, five years, ten years. By definition, tomorrow's customer is not going to be much like yesterday's, not for ING Direct.

Too Much Information

And yet.

Like any of life's good things, information's value diminishes rapidly if it is all you subsist on. A steady diet of data would be bad for our or any brand's health for a few reasons. First and maybe most obvious is that information is available to anyone willing to pay for it. That means your competitors can get the same inputs as you get, which in turn means there's no advantage in it. Second, information is generally a pretty objective thing, purely functional in nature. That means that making decisions solely on the basis of data is like designing a car using only a wind tunnel: The wind wants every car to look the same, and doesn't tolerate differentiation very well. It commoditizes, which is hardly the kind of nourishment a brand needs. And third, the more information there is lying around, the less room there is to create, innovate, invent. Facts are cold, rational, rooted in the past; a rebel with a cause is passionate, creative, and focused on the future. Real progress in business depends not on the former, or even on the latter, but on the solid platform information gives you upon which to create.

There's even a human corollary to my earlier point about weaker people fearing information: Some, rather than avoid it, will hide behind it, or even use it as a stick with which to beat status quo–threatening ideas to a pulp.

In the first decade of its life, ING Direct went through periods in which decisions were being made largely on gut feeling and raw inspiration—which wasn't sustainable—and it went through the occasional spell when, in certain quarters, data seemed to be king. I would have to say that, overall, more expensive lessons were learned as a result of the misapplication of cold, hard facts than of the opposite. During those times, parts of ING Direct were being managed, not created. Based on data alone, there would have been no Electric Orange. There would have been no Orange Mortgage, and ING Direct would have been swept up in the maelstrom banks faced in the aftermath of the subprime crisis. Much of our most effective advertising would never have seen the light of day. There would be no Independence Ride, no ING Direct cafés, no free gas and subway ride promotions when ING Direct came to a new city. Based on data alone, in fact, ING Direct might never have launched at all.

As with so much of this story, the difference comes down to leadership. Information is, of course, essential. But so is inspiration. An enterprise like ING Direct can't live without either, nor can it afford to swing back and forth between the two. They are yin and yang. They are an alloy. The balance between them is struck by leadership, which keeps it there by never flinching in the face of an idea, and never shrinking from the accountability that information brings. Leadership sets this example. It might be one of the most important parts of the job.

Lack of Courage under Fire

They say there are no atheists in foxholes, but the reverse sometimes seems to be true when the cannonballs are flying in a war of brands.

One of the things an enterprise has to accept when it chooses the road less traveled is that if it succeeds in charting new territory, it won't be alone for long. Any worthwhile innovation will be copied with blinding speed by aggressive competitors. And to make matters worse, that kind of competitive response often comes with aggressive pricing to boot. You invent it, then they copy it and sell it for less. And when that happens, the temptation to fire back is almost unbearable. People who are, in more peaceful times, ardent believers in the principles for which a brand stands can suddenly be turned into bloodthirsty mercenaries in the face of an opponent who has so little regard for their own brand that they're willing to make money by imitating someone else's.

In the history of ING Direct, this kind of competitive sniping has happened plenty. And it hasn't only been where you would expect it, with our interest rates. In competitive marketing, we've seen enemy brands help themselves to the color orange, and even to our orange ball icon. We've seen them borrow our rhetoric, word for word. Even the suffix "direct," a term ING Direct brought to North American banking, was shamelessly assumed by competitive brands who wanted to be sure that consumers knew who to compare them to.

Most of the time, when this happens, it's wise to stand your ground and maintain the courage of your convictions. For one thing, competitors who will do this, by definition, lack conviction. So, they are just as likely to give up and move on to something else before they've done any real damage. For another, competitive skirmishes like this tend to alienate consumers and turn the features they are fighting over into unprofitable commodities, in which case nobody wins. And for another, it is actually quite rare that a brand that is truly committed to its cause—a brand with its own pixie dust—ever really gets confused with anyone else no matter how superficially close the resemblance may be. It's the pretenders that almost always end up paying the price in the end.

Fabulous Opportunities

There are some consequences of success that they don't warn you about in brand school. This is the thought that is going through my mind as I watch the animated young man sitting across from me, proudly presenting an opportunity that a brand like ING Direct, he insists, cannot pass up. From what I can tell, it's a media opportunity. It apparently involves teams of people in one-piece spandex suits, wearing an apparatus that suspends a flat-screen television over their heads. Thus equipped, they can wander a city's streets and sidewalks randomly confronting citizens and playing television commercials at them. They're offering it to us for a song. The price is so low, and it will make so many impressions on people, that the program will be, he gushes, practically, like, free, dude.

Success is a magnet for temptations of every kind. Fame attracts suitors who want to make you famous; profit attracts suitors who want to help you make money; and growth attracts suitors who want to sell, buy, or merge with you. In other words, once you start succeeding, people who want to help you succeed come out of the woodwork. Nothing good comes of this. Remember, they called because they need you, not because they're on a philanthropic rescue mission and believe in your organization's cause. And remember that saying yes means dividing your resources in a way for which you did not plan. And remember that being opportunistic means, by definition, compromising your agenda to accommodate that of whoever it is waiting for you in the lobby with a PowerPoint presentation and a free stress ball with their phone number on it.

A great price doesn't make changing your path a great idea. And neither does the putative awesomeness of other brands that have decided to do it. As moms everywhere might put it, "If Microsoft jumped off a bridge, would you jump off a bridge?" Staying in control of your destiny sometimes means saying no.

Three Ways to Keep the Cats Together

BP: Sooner or later, entropy has its way with everything. Companies rise, mature, and eventually decay somehow, either compromised by their own success or hoist by their own petard. They are always growing or declining; there really is no stasis, no equilibrium. To watch ING Direct being led is a study in how to stay on this tightrope. It begins, of course, with the realization that it *is* a tightrope. After that, from observing Arkadi's own herding techniques, there seem to be three secrets to keeping those cats together and pointed more or less in the same direction.

Make a List, Check it Twice

Revolutions aren't comfortable. Far from being the sort of blind optimist you would expect the "CEO of Savings" to be, Arkadi maintains and cultivates a precise list of the threats to ING Direct's business as he sees them, and draws energy from it. It's a shockingly eye-opening exercise that leaves you different afterward than you were before you started. After Arkadi proposed the idea for this chapter, I tried it myself and found it cleansing, sobering, and, in the end, galvanizing. This perverse little exercise told me where to direct my energy, and it discouraged me from the dangerous delusion that you can win just by not making mistakes. Close your door, take a deep breath, and make a list of what could do your organization in. It might just be the difference between being a manager and truly being a leader.

Short-Term Thinking is Almost Always Wrong

This isn't the same as never making short-term decisions, of course; these are inevitable and essential in many aspects of a leader's job. But when you think about it, every calamity facing humanity, from global warming to the careers of certain pop stars, has its roots in someone not thinking far enough ahead. Viewed in the grand context of history, it's generally true that a pattern of short-term thinking bodes badly, and one of long-term thinking leads to sustainability.

Few would disagree that long-term thinking is a leader's job, at least in principle (helming a publicly traded company has its own particular short-term imperatives, of course, though it seems to be here more than anywhere else that short-term thinking is calamitous). ING Direct's leadership, when it has been at its best, has taken this further by reversing the usual dynamics between a company's near and far horizons: While what's right for the cause in the long term is seldom debated, there is a reflexive aversion to any decision that seems to promise immediate convenience or easy money.

It's All about Karma

You. Are. Not. Perfect.

Leaders of all stripes need to remember that if you focus on never making mistakes, you'll never get anything done. Flawlessness is not a worthy objective, nor does it have anything to do with motivating an organization around a cause. If you're moving forward, you're going to screw things up now and then, and it's in the context of this fundamental truth that the idea of being a cause has the most power: As long as you keep your eye on that ball, you will get it mostly right most of the time, which is all any of us can hope for in business, or in life.

This has another important dimension, and that's your bank of goodwill. Have you ever noticed how some enterprises suffer for their blunders more than others do—suffer in terms of reputation, of share price, of market share, of profit? The reason that some get away with mistakes and others are pilloried for them is simple, if easily forgotten: What you do is judged in the context of everything else you've done. This is true for employees, for customers, for capital markets, even for regulators sometimes. The balance in your goodwill account will determine how much you have to pay when you try something and it fails. It's like a credit rating.

That means two things: You have to keep an eye on that balance. Using whatever measurement tools suit your business, you need to know how much forgiveness is available to you. And you have to keep topping it up. Just like putting a few dollars away every month for a rainy day, every inspired and appreciated employee, every delighted customer, every board member who feels listened to, and every regulator who feels respected is insurance against how wet you're going to get when that inevitable rainy day comes.

AK: At this point, you might be wondering, what does the subtitle of this chapter have to do with these temptations? The danger that we might snatch defeat from the jaws of victory at ING Direct is not unlike what it is for any other venture into a new frontier of any industry. There are lots of people in the mix: customers, staff, suppliers, accountants, regulators, board members, shareholders, not to mention the analysts and the media. All are customers by night and stakeholders by day. Their intentions and opinions matter. They shape the conversation and determine the basis for building on the business. Progress is the art of herding cats. And it's important to remember that the cats aren't just the people around you.

They are also the divergent agendas of your stakeholders, of your customers, and even in the principles of the Code itself. You have to draw energy from that diversity, not ignore it or fight it. The views and needs of all of them are seldom aligned, but you must constantly try to align them at least to the point that it works. How many times have you heard that such and such a business has lost the confidence of its board, its backers, or even its customers? Too often.

Most leaders try to meet the needs of each specific stakeholder. These contortionist acts do work at times. I believe that most CEOs think five years is the right length of time to serve as leader. It is directly proportional to the length of time you can either be or pretend to be a pretzel. Many times you can be offside with one or more stakeholders, but you can get away with that only for a while. "Low profits this year," you might say, "but things are looking up next year, so be patient. Bonuses will be back, profits will be back, or volumes will be back, and the second shift will be back in place."

The needs of customers versus those of shareholders are a subject everybody comments on, and it's easy to understand why. Customers want things their way and with the best value at the lowest price. The shareholders, meanwhile, want the highest return on capital with the least amount of risk. Each side thinks they are reasonable, and each operates on a principle of optimization. In other words, we all want to have our cake and eat it, too! But it's the needs of the people joining our company's journey as associates, working to make the company function, that are the most complex. They are the most difficult cats to herd. There is a famous story about a Swiss government official who was quoted on the topic of foreign guest workers there, saying, "We needed workers and now human beings showed up!" I know the feeling. It is our greatest strength and our greatest challenge.

Town hall meetings are a pretty common thing, and I have used them regularly at ING Direct. It's a great forum in which to explain the state of the company's affairs and thank everyone for their hard work and good progress. Staff tell me in the hall afterward that they appreciate the words and all the commitments to good results. During the end of each town hall meeting, the inevitable question-and-answer time is carved out. The questions are sometimes a little disappointing. "Will we have a day care facility built for those of us with small children? On which holidays do we get off early this year? Can we get closer parking?" It's hard to shake the feeling that if this is what is on everyone's mind, then where is the real battle? How connected is everyone in the company to the vision and mission? Winning their hearts and minds is a tall order. Most leaders are not conscious of the work needed or are simply not willing to make this happen. But you can never stop trying.

Aside from the complexity of dealing with the sheer number of our staff and their lives, the engagement, learning, and creative energy that are required to lead a business like this is daunting. In society today, we are becoming less homogeneous. We are split into endless divisions on a wide range of topics. Everyone is an individual. The ability of any leader to have broad appeal, let alone represent a consensus, is melting away like the arctic glaciers. Work has become, for many, less a simple responsibility and more of a calling and a search for meaning. It's personal, now, and there is no way to manage around it.

The Orange Code is an example of a platform on which a leader can create a vision that people can make intensely personal and meaningful. That's its power, and the invitation it offers. You can work for money, you can work to do your time, or you can work to change the world. You choose.

Epilogue

Peeling the Orange

A Guided Tour of the Orange Code, and What It Means to Us

BP: The Orange Code is real. It's not marketing, even though it is our brand; until now, nobody outside of ING Direct had ever heard of it, even though everyone can feel it in everything the company sells, does, and says. For ING Direct, the Orange Code is a constitution. And although this constitution doesn't frame anything as grand as a nation, for this company, it performs the same deeply important roles: It reminds everyone where ING Direct comes from, and it reminds everyone not only what the company's purpose is, but the principles by which that purpose should be lived. It is reassurance in the face of uncertainty. It's ballast for stormy seas. It's the energy of ING Direct's beginning, distilled and preserved for the benefit of anyone who might ever have to take the helm and ask themselves, "Okay, what now?"

The Orange Code was written for everyone who works at ING Direct, and its genesis might surprise you. Although nobody openly put it into these words at the time, the Orange Code's first job was really to keep marketing from taking over the organization. Imagine the temptation in those first days: We had a world-beating product to sell, one with a measurable advantage. And we had a novel distribution system to make it interesting. In the absence of a bigger, more enterprise-wide cause, it wouldn't have taken long before the cultural influence of marketing became overwhelming and the rest of the organization was reduced to serving it. From that would have followed, we believed, only brief success. ING Direct would have been an attractive shell, brittle in its dependency on a product feature. And inside it would have been an organization that was generic, cynical, and disengaged. The Orange Code did two crucial things for ING Direct. First, it collectivized the brand, made it everyone's business and responsibility. And second, it connected leadership to the operation of the company on a spiritual level. Instead of quietly assuming ING Direct will make money, the Orange Code loudly declares how we'll do it. Without this sturdy bridge between the idea of ING Direct and the practical realities of the enterprise, it very likely would not have survived.

This is our code.

1. We Are New Here

Every day is a new beginning, a new set of challenges, a chance to reinvent ourselves.

AK: Whether you are the first employee we ever hired or the one who just joined this morning, we are all new here. It's a mind-set that says we've got to earn it each day, and we need to feel that we have new challenges that can make us or break us every day. If we are to see our brand as a journey we take with our customers, then we need to make it feel *as if it's alive.* Building a reputation and a brand, much like any journey, is never the same process from one day to the next. Each day's work will last only as long as it's relevant. The nature of business is that it's always evolving— for better or worse—but we tend not to think of it in those terms. For the ING Direct brand, this was a key idea to keep the energy high and to make our success belong to all employees and, most important, to all customers. Convincing us on the inside that many consumers have still not heard of us after 10 years sounds crazy, but it's true. Our work is far from done. For you and me, we are new here. It's a new day!

Still, the challenge of keeping everyone in a start-up frame of mind never ends. Conversations like the following happen every day: It's 11:30 AM, and I'm in our Wilmington offices, speaking to an orientation class. There are 31 new faces in the room. As I get to the Orange Code section, I'm seeing blank stares and it feels like no one is home. "Okay," I say, "let's stop."

John, a new IT hire, says straight out, "How can it be new? You have built it and there are tons of rules, policies, and the like. It's a success. Give it a rest." I'm thinking, how did this guy get in here, and who told him it's a success? Well, John, we did okay in each of the last seven years, but we are only ever as good as our last year, our last day, our last transaction. We still have a lot to do, since our competition is not resting.

To get better is an ever-increasing challenge. Heck, two years ago no one bothered to think we could stay the course. As each year goes by, we are drawing more attention and more heat. Other players are copying everything we do and saying the same things we say. So my challenge to employees is: How do we keep ahead if we don't find new ways of expressing the brand and building our reputation for savings? We are inventing and redefining and we need a lot of new ideas from *you*. Everything you see in this brand and this business has been thought up by new-hire classes like this one. The thing is, they understood the challenge. You, John, have a major hurdle still to get across. The truth is, no matter what we do, 10 percent of the staff is going to be passive-aggressive and not buy into any code. They're hard to identify, and hard to move out. One of the biggest risks any brand has to deal with is new people joining.

Few times in one's professional journey do we get a chance at a blank piece of paper like this: to start fresh and get it right, unburdened by our yesterdays. When we started ING Direct in the United States in the cold winter of 2000, Y2K was the talk of the day and we all wondered what a new century would mean. Jim Kelly was up for it. So was Hudson White, having finished his walk in the wilderness of finance in Canada. Tom Hugh was there, ready for a new adventure. He was already deciding what kind of car to drive! Ironically, as we signed up for the new challenge, our personal lives were also ready for new loves, marriages, and, yes, children. Everything was new. With so many things happening at once, it is noteworthy that we focused on the values and principles that should define our enterprise. Many would and still do think of the Orange Code as a matter of labels and cultural cues, but what is a uniform without the values behind it? Putting ideas and feelings into words that communicate the principles of the Orange Code was tough. They are not just one-word labels or logos or clever designs. We have to focus on the code and the talk that goes with it. It starts to explain why we are new here.

"We are new here" is a state of mind and a point of view. You have to have an attitude that says we will take nothing for granted and we will not be tied to past practices and ideas. It's not a principle to live by for most people. It is for us.

2. Our Mission Is to Help People Take Care of the Wealth They Make

Money is the fruit of work, and saving it is fundamental to freedom. Few missions could be more important to the lives of our customers than this one.

AK: If you live on Main Street and you have an average income, you are focused on two issues: One, you want to improve your standard of living, and, two, you want to keep making progress. The threat of losing it all or of things going wrong is always there, because these things are happening around us every day, acting as a constant reminder. There are also endless distractions tempting us to spend. The good life portrayed in the media is seductive and we are bombarded by the idea of living for today. It's real, man, the here and now. In a practical sense, our cause is to help reinforce a balance of saving for things that meaningfully improve people's standard of living. Making choices that are realistic, having resources for a rainy day, and understanding that life has ups and downs and that you have to work them through are challenges. In times past, the value of independence and self-reliance was a bigger part of our way of life. Today, we are surrounded by help from our government and society at large, help that is not up to the task that most people have drifted into expecting.

A voice is needed to support the efforts of those that want to make real progress and balance their money with the reality of everyday living. ING Direct helps reinforce that voice, and gives emotional support to the idea that saving is good. It could even be cool. You can be special or unique by not having something—part of a reverse elite. "I don't need platinum. I'll take bronze. And I know, and my confidence tells you, that I could afford platinum, but I *choose* not to."

Carolyn Imparato works at ING Direct and is by any measure an independent woman. With a head of curls and a great smile, she prides herself on making commonsense choices. Having a son to take care of and wanting to build a life that is fulfilled, she balances her budget and saves.

With no debt except for a mortgage, she has control of her finances and is focused on the long term. When I asked her once, "Don't you want to treat yourself to something special?" she replied, "Buying something won't last."

"What will?"

"My house, my son's education, and my savings."

"The ads you see encouraging you to buy things?"

"They're just ads!" She has two savings accounts.

3. We Will Be Fair

Everyone has value. Everyone deserves a chance at independence.
So, everyone will be treated equally here.

AK: One of the most telling signs about the nature of the retail financial services business is that everyone is treated differently. More wealth means better deals. Larger loans get a better negotiated rate. We as consumers are surrounded with platinum, gold, silver, and prestige classes. There are lines for VIPs and special customers. The special needs and the unique needs are all sorted, and each customer who has a need sees it as important. Of course, everyone is important, but the way we deal with this has gotten out of hand. There are needs that require advice and custom services, but, for most of us most of the time, we just need simple standardized products that save time and money. Providing them is a straightforward way to create value. There are other ways, of course, but this is one way that we knew would help the most consumers. The banks and financial firms structure and sell their offerings with full service in mind. A customer can make any request, and the bank can solve it at a price. The challenge then is that fees and complexity become standard-issue. Even if you don't need anything, you still have to accept the fees and lots of paperwork. The customer with simple needs gets handed a disproportionate burden in terms of the process and the time and the cost associated with the purchase. The split between the advice and complexity banks sell and the straightforwardness and simplicity people need is widening, though, and will benefit the consumers on Main Street. ING Direct is helping to make this divergence a reality.

Still, you can't please everybody. Sitting listening to one particular new customer call a few years ago, for example, it became obvious that the conversation was not going to go well.

"Is this ING Direct?"

"Yes, how can I help you save your money?"

"I want to invest $1 million in one of your accounts. Got that? $1 million."

"Yes, I can open an account for you."

"So, what is your rate?"

"It's 5.25 percent."

"Yes, I saw that in the ad online. But what is *my* rate?"

"That's the rate, sir."

"No, look, I think a higher rate is in order. It's $1 million."

"No, I don't think so."

"Put me through to your manager."

"No, I don't think that's necessary."

"I want to talk to someone else."

"Look, everyone gets the same rate, no matter the amount or who you are."

"You're kidding, right?"

"No. It's a savings account."

"I need a name I can call, and my money needs to be looked after."

"Yes, sir, and the best place to do that is at a traditional big bank."

"I really don't like your attitude."

"I understand that. You're not used to being treated like everyone else." *Click.* Democracy for money! It made my day!

4. We Will Constantly Learn

Every experience we have will make us wiser and better at what we do.
That will always be true.

AK: A reality of building a business is that new staff is always joining and experienced staff is leaving. Turnover is a fact of life. Striving for the right, natural amount of turnover is a good objective, but even that outcome has consequences that are hard to foresee and manage. It's never fully in your control. A growth-oriented company gets used to its success and wants to keep it going. The right type and speed of change becomes a discussion point. It's also a barrier to new staff understanding their relationship to the business's ongoing success. The key is to celebrate each step of success, and then leave it behind, emotionally and psychologically. Every day is a new challenge, and everyone shares in the success of tomorrow. We need to learn and make all of our theories and our knowledge about markets and consumers relevant to today, because today is all that matters. The commitment to constantly learn is the only fair way to bring everyone in the company under the same umbrella. It is a leveler.

Being a learning organization inevitably affects the customer's experience, too. They teach us, but they also provide a mirror that confirms our learning culture is alive. We get thousands of e-mails and letters from customers on the theme of learning to save, to use money better, and to improve lives. Life is a journey of learning, and helping one another is rooted in our collective DNA the way the discovery of fire and shaping the first wheel are. From the front lines, here's a random e-mail I recently received that makes the point:

Dear Sir,

I compliment you on your article "A Saving Revolution" in the January edition of *Bright Spots* [ING Direct's customer newsletter]. Folks who don't have ING Direct accounts should read your message. I will be sharing your article and the paragraph about "Your Credit Score" with my Boy Scouts. Did you know they are required to earn the personal finance merit badge? By the way, when was the last time we heard news about double-digit mortgage rates in . . . 1980?!

J.W., Kennett Square, PA

5. We Will Change and Adapt and Dwell Only in the Present and in the Future

The world does not stand still. Neither will we. We will not resist change. We will be exhilarated by it. The value of the past lies only in what it has taught us. Our greatest treasure is our potential. We are nourished by thinking about what can be done.

AK: Everyone talks about change, but change is hard to see. When we revisit something after an absence, we can see what has changed. Likewise, we can perceive change over a long period of time. But seldom, when we are immersed in day-to-day business, do we see change as it's happening. There are a number of ways to make the spirit of change more present in any endeavor, though. Constantly focusing on new ideas and executing them is one way. Focusing routine meetings and discussions on how to improve things and make them more valuable is another. Always looking forward with a focus on executing against goals forces a change-driven attitude, and it makes people welcome it.

The readiness for change is a state of mind, and human nature naturally resists it. Here's an example of what I mean: Two new associates are riding in the elevator with me. Both look preoccupied, and had obviously been in a conversation before I stepped in, "So, how's it going?"

"Okay . . ."

"Anything new?" I ask.

"Well, not really. But I have a question."

"Shoot."

"So, how come we have this clean desk policy? Why no titles and why no offices?"

"Does that seem like an obstacle to you?" I ask.

"Well, I need quiet, and I like to have a few things around me to remind me of why I'm busting my butt. I also like to have a title on my card, because people always ask me what I do, and I am proud of my work."

"That seems logical to me," I reply.

"Well, then?"

"Okay: We are all about change. We live in the here and now, in it together. So, we are all 'Associates.' We all have an equal stake in the company. No one is above the Orange Code. That's why there's no nesting in workstations. We want one another to focus on the business, and to move around, psychologically. We are also not a library; there are distractions, but after a while they'll become white noise and just a hum. Not convinced?" I add. Blank stare. Good. They are thinking it over.

You need to feel different, organize differently, so that we project creative energy to the outside world. The focus is on hammering away at the next wave of challenges that are coming at us today, and winning.

Once the idea of change became inspirational, it became relevant. Don't sweat the small stuff, but don't ignore it, either.

6. We Will Listen; We Will Invent; We Will Simplify

Our customers can make us better if we let them. But we must first understand them. We can find a solution or create one, but if our invention does not make our customers' lives better, it will not make our business better.

AK: The best example of how this idea works might just come from our partnership with GWP. Working with them, it's ING Direct who's the customer, and it's interesting to see how they balance the need to satisfy us with the need to add value and remain true to themselves. The three partners at GWP always had the type of interpersonal dynamics going on that we, the posse at ING Direct, could identify with. Unique and eccentric, they wanted to keep digging into ideas and issues. Their willingness to look deeper had a great silver lining seldom found in advertising agencies and creative types: willingness to change their minds and look for more, without the usual "compromise for the client relationship" stuff. Philippe Garneau acts out and feels the customer reaction and interpretation of words and images. Bruce uses a big mental whiteboard and searches for the psychology of the customer and the marketplace. In the early days, Michael would drop pebbles and sometimes rocks into the lake of conversations. The interaction with us was creative and moving. We never let familiarity get in the way of this process. Innovating, listening, and creating: the hallmarks of a true team. It was a two-way conversation, and we were all the better for it. It was also the sign of a healthy relationship. I like to think this is how ING Direct's customers experience our brand, too: as a conversation, not a negotiation.

Whether you're an ad agency or a bank, the key is to balance when you should listen to your customers and when you should ignore them. Any customer will agree that saving money and saving time are attractive ideas. But how this gets interpreted and how it gets accomplished have a large perception component in the thought process. We and our customers have to be aligned on what we want. The key is not to listen to every customer, just the ones who want what we are trying to build.

7. We Will Never Stop Asking Why or Why Not

Nothing can be sacred here except for our mission. To be challenged is not to be criticized. It is to be invited into the process of invention.

AK: From a personal standpoint, asking "why?" is a pain. You have to constantly defend yourself and justify why you are "holding up the show." There is a lot of pressure to "not fix what's not broken." Obviously, just asking why and wanting to dig into everything for the sake of doing it is not the objective. You are building a business. But a willingness to change and hunt for the new idea and the next breakthrough is as applicable in financial services as it is in any other business.

Take technology, for example. There have obviously been lots of new developments in how computing and communications can be used. How best to use these things in financial services requires a unique filter that sorts out products and services from the perspective of the customer's experience. The traditional product manager looks to market research and uses it to design a feature or service. Meanwhile, the IT staff wants to use and adapt the latest state-of-the-art tools. The two points of view do not overlap easily, so we did the unthinkable at ING Direct. We blended the marketing team and the IT team to work as one unit and it performs in a very effective way if you can pull it off: no more "IT can't deliver" or "marketing got the specifications wrong"; no more finger-pointing battles over budgets and who's on first. A unified approach to asking why and why not raises the bar and challenges everyone to be more knowledgeable. Many will think we do this already, but I would suggest that the right mix of personalities and a deeper understanding of the value of this approach is a big win.

8. We Will Create Wealth for Ourselves, Too, but We Will Do This by Creating Value

Our customers want us to succeed. Profit is the proof that we are fulfilling our mission, and it is only rewarding when it is earned.

AK: A lot of comments get made regarding the success of ING Direct. Can it be profitable? Can it make good returns? The answer lies in the order of what happens when. Building a business from scratch requires a plan and a time frame. The plan is to build a new type of bank based on a new enterprise model. Using new ideas and doing things in a different order are part of this approach. Attracting customers with high-yield savings accounts was a new way to start. Traditional banks start by gathering assets—loans—and then funding them cheaply. If you do it in reverse, as we did, and if it works, then you need to gather assets at a price that allows you to make a margin. It does not sound that hard, but in practice the devil is in the details. The point is, in the end, you still need to make a profit and the customer still needs to get a good deal. We still have to create value, build and manage a balance sheet, and build business. The capital behind us demands it.

The market value in a bank is the franchise of the customer base and the value of future revenue streams. The premium over the book, or equity, is the measure used when you buy or sell a bank. If you buy a bank, you have to pay the premium based on that future value and write it off over a period of time. But if you build a bank, then you have fewer profits as you grow the customer base. The rewards come later, but you didn't pay a premium for them. In the end, it's a question of which is better for the investor, financially and economically over time, between the two methods.

Customers understand the need to make a profit, too; they just want it to be fair and transparent. This is both a perception and a realistic measure. Typically, we as consumers want the best value, but then, when we own shares of a company, we also want the best returns. These two wants are not easily reconciled. Fear and greed do play their part in all of this. My confession is that the Orange Code explains how we want to change the world, but it's not a guarantee that it will be easy. It just won't happen without kicking and screaming. Nothing worthwhile, including giving birth, ever has.

9. We Will Tell the Truth

We cannot succeed without the trust of our customers and of society.

AK: Trust is earned, not assumed. It cannot be taken for granted. A brand that has earned trust is a brand that has consistently and truthfully represented what a company sells and how it behaves. Telling the truth is not easy. The best way, of course, is to say the truth easily and quickly when the first opportunity arises. Don't say you will call back when you may not be able to. Don't say you will send this e-mail when you are not sure you can. Telling it like it is takes practice, because in our society, as in most, there are conventions for how to manage a conversation and there are conventions for what certain statements really mean. If someone says "See you later!" you know it's not meant literally. It's a figure of speech, and it means they will see you eventually. But if you are doing a direct business by Internet, telephone, and mail, you are blind to many interpersonal clues and subtleties. The key is to be human, be clear, and tell the truth. Convention also has it that each point of contact with a customer is a moment of truth, but it is a selling opportunity, not a convincing opportunity. Honesty and being authentic require telling the truth. All the time.

Being truthful often comes at a cost in the short term, and you have to have faith that it will come out right in the end. The best example of this has been ING Direct's approach to selling mortgages. Suitability and affordability are the key criteria when we're talking to a potential Orange Mortgage customer. If the customer has the down payment and the financial strength for a mortgage that will get them the house they want and let them keep it, then that's a win. But if they don't, nobody benefits if we let them think otherwise just so we can sell another mortgage. These conversations can be hard, but being straight and truthful with them is the right thing. If we are going to bet on them by lending them money, they have to be able to bet on themselves, too. Not everybody goes away from these discussions happy, but both our business and our customers are stronger for it.

Telling the truth is maybe also why GWP stays a small boutique agency in Toronto. It does work with all the challenges of any agency: keeping the payables coming in, finding new worthwhile business, staying ahead of industry trends. But watching Bruce biting his tongue and trying to be very corporate with a client is like watching a conductor practice patience with a struggling violinist. He knows the right answer but finds a way to have the paying client discover the answer for himself. What he can't accept, though, is the wrong answer, and I'm sure this has cost GWP something. No wonder he teaches at a university on the side, explaining ideas, which he loves, and leading students to the water of knowledge. With more at stake, the hemlock cup would not be far away for this philosopher.

10. We Will Be for Everyone

*To be our customer, people need only a dollar and the will to be
independent. Though we welcome everyone, we will have the courage
to accept that not everyone will hear the call, and we will remain
true to ourselves.*

AK: To us, "We will be for everyone" means everyone who wants to do
business direct. If we are to do large volumes and create value with
better pricing—the essentials of our business model—it can be done
only if products and services are streamlined and standardized. In banking, the typical approach is to please the customer, and the mandate
is that the customer is always right (again, at a price). In other retail
businesses, customers have become used to a standardized approach in
exchange for great value. There's a way to do this in banking, too. Money
matters, and people who have a lot of it are demanding and want things
done in a way that suits them. It's hard to tell them that there is only
one way and that they need to get in line like everyone else. They get
very, yes, very annoyed. The staff, the leadership, and the customers all
get the same rate and the same service. There is also an emotional tone to
this. Customers can see it for what it is or they can interpret it as a slight
against them personally. The attitude going in is a big part of the expectation. At ING Direct, a lot of communication is focused on attempting to
set this expectation, and on applauding the resulting value and the fact
that it's there for everyone.

11. We Aren't Conquerors—We Are Pioneers; We Are Not Here to Destroy—We Are Here to Create

*We have competitors, not enemies. We will respect them.
We came here to offer people a choice. It is for them, not us, to decide
who will prevail.*

AK: ING Direct has never become combative with individual competitors.
While many talk about ING Direct, the thrust of our advertising and messaging is how to get better value when compared to the industry as a
whole. The industry is fair game. The practices in the industry are fair

game. The brand's mission is to create something better for consumers by offering them a choice. The mission never was, nor is it today, to bring down other players or even to speak poorly of them. We're ready to let the consumers decide by voting with their money.

12. We Will Never Be Finished

Every generation will have its own hunger for independence, and its own challenges in achieving it. We will be there for them, as new then as we are today.

AK: The world is different. We hear it all the time and we see evidence every day that the marketplace's values are shifting and consumers are changing. The journey through life brings with it a complexity that allows us to learn from the past, yet also to make many of the same mistakes twice. A brand, to stay relevant, must adapt and change without end. It's best thought of as something that is constantly evolving, and it requires energy and constant management to keep it pointed toward its mission.

You might ask what happens to the founders and early leaders like Bruce and myself. When do we leave? How long should someone stay on a journey that is never finished? Passion either dies or is killed. If you start to talk about or begin to question yourself about leaving, you already have your answer. As a leader, you have to look at being forced out as an inevitable part of the evolution and renewal process. Sure, it's personal, but the best we can all hope for is to make our mark for others to read, and then let history judge.

ING Direct is a success story. Why not leave it alone? Creative destruction is a process that I believe is critical to building a vibrant and healthy business. Is a painting an image frozen in time, or does a painting have power because it communicates a message and stirs a story within you? In the nature of a brand, you have a choice between either constantly renewing and embracing change or staying with what works and waiting for external forces to signal you to move. The pioneer always has a better view of the horizon, always has more control. More doors will open up if the balance is driven from within. As with everything in nature, renewal is based in creative destruction. For a brand, constant renewal is the heart that pumps the energy. This should not be confused with constant change for change's sake. The vision needs to stay consistent and act as the core of the brand.

To live the Orange Code, you need to see it as a journey, not as a static way of being. The best people are aggressive about this idea of a moving horizon, and the results they can achieve over time give testimony to this. The key to success isn't really the business model. It's people. In any business, the right selection and the right mix of talents is the true heart of its success. When a brand or a business succeeds, the world usually credits strategy or timing or innovative products.

The truth is that it's the people you bring to the vision.

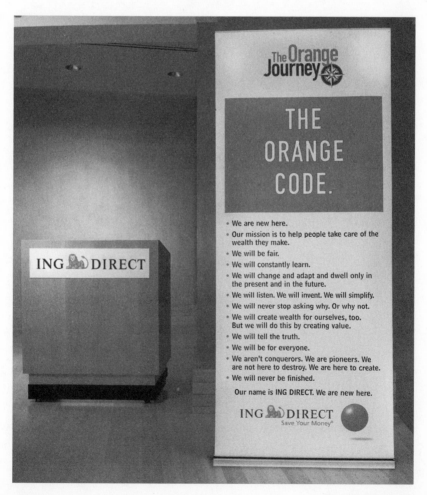

Photo by Steve Lewis

Appendix A

Orange Milestones—An ING Direct Time Line

1996

August
- ING Direct and GWP Brand Engineering meet for the first time in an empty surplus office space in downtown Toronto. ING Direct has an idea for a new kind of bank. GWP has an idea for a new kind of branding agency. Sparks fly.

October
- GWP pitches the ING Direct business—twice—and wins. The core team is in place for a launch that is now only months away.

1997

April
- Sunday, April 27: ING Direct officially opens for business and its first commercial airs during *60 Minutes.* A new kind of bank is launched with just one product (the Investment Savings Account), no branches, and an advertising spokesperson with a Dutch accent. As the launch team sits in the bank's new boardroom eating take-out food and nervously sipping champagne from paper cups, a pixel board display

counts inbound telephone calls from prospective customers. Within minutes, the call center exceeds its capacity. This might just work.

December
- ING Direct finishes its first year with 28,498 accounts, $487 million in deposits, and $564 million in assets.

1998

- ING Direct adds two one-of-a-kind products: the U.S. Dollar Investment Savings Account, which pays high interest on deposits in that currency, and the Loan Account, an innovative personal line of credit product that puts ING Direct in the lending business for the first time.
- On April 27, the bank celebrates its first birthday with a bash for its team. Meanwhile, GWP charters an airplane to circle the bank towers in Toronto's financial district towing a banner that reads, "Happy Birthday ING Direct!"
- ING Direct debuts as a corporate citizen with its first sponsorship, an exhibit of lions at the Metro Toronto Zoo.
- In November, ING Direct surpasses $1 billion in deposits.
- As the year ends, ING Direct has 96,010 clients, $1.1 billion on deposit, and $1.3 billion in assets in Canada.

1999

- ING Direct customers bank online for the first time.
- In February, ING Direct opens its 100,000th account.
- Mutual funds are added to the product offering, along with another one-of-a-kind product: the Business Investment Savings Account. Now, businesses can be savers, too.
- ING Direct opens its second café, in Vancouver.
- GWP Brand Engineering is engaged to assist in a feasibility study for a new market ING Direct is thinking of entering: the United States.
- The year ends with 215,473 clients, $2 billion in deposits, $2.3 billion in assets, and some news: ING Direct is coming to the United States, and Arkadi Kuhlmann and Jim Kelly will lead the charge.

ING Direct Canada prepares to pass the torch to a new team, while all eyes in the ING world turn to the world's biggest and most competitive retail banking market.

2000

June
- Wilmington, Delaware: The orange ball icon is created, and the brand is born in the United States.
- The ING Direct web site, at www.ingdirect.com, is launched.
- ING Direct Kids Foundation holds its first fund-raising event.

August
- ING Bank fsb is chartered.
- The Orange Savings Account is launched.
- A "friends and family" marketing campaign yields more than 10,000 accounts.

September
- ING Direct USA is officially launched with its first advertising campaign, supporting markets in Delaware, Pennsylvania, New York, and Minnesota.

October
- ING Direct moves into its Wilmington, Delaware, headquarters, dubbed "The Pakhuis," the first facility in what will become an expansive riverfront campus.

November
- Online enrollment and funds transfer are launched for the Orange Savings Account, pioneering technology that reduces costs and makes joining easy for customers.

December
- Online enrollment and funds transfer are enabled for the Orange CD, too.
- By month's end, ING Direct USA has more than 50,000 customers, $650 million in deposits, and $914 million in assets. ING Direct Canada, meanwhile, maintains its momentum, surpassing 350,000 customers and $2.5 billion in deposits.

2001

January
- "Bright Spots," ING Direct's customer newsletter, publishes its first issue.

February
- The "Direct Us" opt-in privacy policy is launched, taking customer advocacy to a new level for the industry.

March
- ING Direct passes the 100,000-customer milestone.
- "Touchless" account opening is launched, making ING Direct even more efficient.
- The *Delaware News Journal* names ING Direct "Best Up & Coming Business" in the banking and finance category, the first of many such honors that will follow.

April
- The first ING Direct Café in the United States is opened in New York City.
- ING Direct becomes a charter member of the American Savings Education Council.

June
- ING Direct holds the official grand opening of its Wilmington riverfront campus.

August
- ING Direct launches its store, selling savings tools and branded merchandise to an increasingly loyal and enthusiastic clientele online and in its cafés.

September
- The 200,000-customer milestone is surpassed.
- ING Direct airs its first television commercial.
- *Online Banking Report* names the ING Direct web site, at www.ingdirect.com, "Best of the Web."

October
- The first Orange Mortgage is launched, along with the Orange Home Equity Line of Credit.

- ING Direct's second café, in Philadelphia, is opened.
- The ING Direct Kids Foundation holds its first annual golf tournament to raise funds for children's charities.
- The American Bankers Association Marketing Network honors ING Direct with its Penny Award.

November

- The e-Statement is launched, saving money, paper, and time for customers.
- Sanchez International recognizes the "Touchless" account opening technology with its Innovation Award.

December

- The Orange Investment Account is launched.
- ING Direct finishes 2001 with 282,253 accounts, $2.9 billion in deposits, and $3.6 billion in assets in the United States. ING Direct Canada closes in on 500,000 accounts and $4.8 billion in deposits, launches its first mortgage product, and achieves profitability.

2002

March

- ING Direct launches its next footprint market, Boston. Beantown commuters are treated to free transit rides and high-interest savings.
- The St. Cloud, Minnesota, call center operation is opened.
- ING Direct cafés receive their 75,000th visitor.
- The brand garners its first advertising award, an *Adweek* Addy.

April

- ING Direct USA achieves profitability.
- *American Banker* names the ING Direct web site, at www.ingdirect.com, one of the "Top 10 US Financial Websites."

May

- As growth accelerates, ING Direct opens its 500,000th account.

June

- The "Security Q&A" innovation is implemented, raising the level of protection for both ING Direct and its customers.

July
- The Treasury team is moved to Los Angeles.

October
- Orange CDs are launched.
- Planet Orange, a Web environment for teaching financial literacy to children, goes live.

November
- Planet Orange is endorsed by the Jump$tart Coalition for Personal Financial Literacy.
- The national Ad:Tech digital marketing awards recognize ING Direct campaigns as "Best Direct Response" and "Best of Show."

December
- Planet Orange is recognized by *USA Today* as its "Best Bet Educational Website."
- By year-end, ING Direct in Canada has launched in the province of Quebec, complete with a new café in Montreal and French-language call center services based in Ottawa. The 700,000th customer is welcomed there.
- In the United States, ING Direct finishes 2002 with 788,611 accounts, $9.3 billion in deposits, and $11.9 billion in assets.

2003

January
- ING Direct's Los Angeles office opens.
- The Wilmington campus expands with the opening of a new building, called "The Orangerie."

February
- The next footprint market is launched, Los Angeles, and car-loving Angelenos are offered free gas and an invitation to save their money.

April
- ING Direct opens its millionth account.
- A new range of Orange Mortgages is launched.

May

- The Orange Home Equity Line of Credit is enhanced with a rate locking feature.
- Another café opens for business, in Los Angeles. ING Direct is officially bicoastal.

September
- ING Direct's marketing team is honored with the American Association of Advertising Agencies' Account Planning Award.

November
- ING Direct co-sponsors the New York Marathon.

December
- San Francisco becomes the newest footprint market. Free transit rides and high interest welcome America's newest savers to ING Direct.
- ING Direct finishes 2003 with 1,301,084 accounts, $16.2 billion in deposits, and $19.1 billion in assets. The Canadian operation signs its millionth customer, and deposits close in on the $12 billion milestone.

2004

January
- ING Direct becomes one of the 50 largest banks in the United States, measured by deposits.

February
- A customer satisfaction survey shows that an astonishing 98 percent of ING Direct customers are promoters of the brand.

March
- ING Direct surpasses 1.5 million accounts.

April
- With ING Direct less than four years old, a public relations trade group gives ING Direct a bronze award for "Company Positioning and Branding."

May
- Wilmington's third ING Direct facility is opened, and it, too, is given a Dutch name: "Spaarpot," which means piggy bank.
- Forbes.com names Planet Orange "Best of the Web."

June
- Planet Orange launches its Teachers' Resource Center.
- The Financial Communications Society honors ING Direct with gold and bronze awards for its marketing campaigns.

July
- ING Direct's 1,000th employee reports for work.
- The Independence Ride for children's charities is inaugurated in San Francisco. The Golden Gate Bridge is closed to regular traffic to allow more than 700 riders to pass over it, and a tradition is born.

September
- ING Direct donates $1 million to Habitat for Humanity.

October
- The 2 millionth ING Direct account is opened.

November
- *Advertising Age* names ING Direct one of its "Top 50 Marketers of the Year."
- ING Direct once again co-sponsors the New York Marathon.

December

- Baltimore, Maryland, and Washington, D.C., become the newest footprint markets: free gas for Baltimore, free transit rides for D.C.; high interest, no fees, and no minimums for everyone.
- ING Direct finishes 2004 with 2,206,310 accounts, $28.8 billion in deposits, and $36 billion in assets.

2005

March
- ING Direct runs an ad in the *Washington Post* opposing the Bankruptcy Reform Act. The headline: "Who will save the savers?"
- The 2,500,000-account mark is surpassed.

April

- ING Direct dips its toe in the waters of Hawaii, with a CD promotion aimed at giving consumers relief in what had been an uncompetitive market.
- The Health and Wellness program is launched for ING Direct staff in Wilmington's Spaarpot facility.

May

- Phoenix, Arizona, becomes the newest footprint market with a focus on mortgages to give consumers real choice as real estate booms there.
- An NBA playoff game in Dallas hosts a visitor: an ING Direct blimp.

June

- The "Summer of Orange" internship program is launched, giving aspiring young professionals a chance to experience the Orange Journey.

July

- The Orange Journey's "Docking" experience is introduced, giving new recruits formal recognition and welcome following their training, and inspiring them to help promote ING Direct's all-important culture.
- The 3 millionth account is opened.

August

- Orange Mortgage Customer Experience Certification is launched, giving associates critical training in helping consumers get the mortgage that is right for them.

September

- Customer account security is enhanced yet again as the innovative Pin Pad feature is launched.

October

- A new suite of Orange CDs is launched.
- ING Direct takes to the air again, this time with a balloon at the Thunderbird Balloon and Air Classics show in Phoenix, Arizona.

December

- Orange Mortgages are supported in mass marketing for the first time, as ING Direct encourages consumers to choose a mortgage that will "make them richer."

- ING Direct finishes 2005 with 3,546,187 accounts, $40 billion in deposits, and $53.1 billion in assets.

2006

January
- In the true spirit of retail, ING Direct launches a "Winter Sale" for savers.
- Another $1 million is donated to Habitat for Humanity.

March
- The *Delaware News Journal* names ING Direct "Best in Business for Community Involvement."

April
- ING Direct opens its 4 millionth account.

May
- Electric Orange, a pioneering paperless transaction account, is quietly launched to employees.

September
- Chicago joins the ING Direct family as the newest footprint market, featuring—what else?—Cash Cows.

October
- CEO Arkadi Kuhlmann is named "Innovator of the Year" by *American Banker.*

November
- ING Direct customers are invited to try something new: Electric Orange, the checking account reinvented.

December
- Another footprint market, Atlanta, Georgia, is opened for business, and free gas makes a welcome comeback for the city's commuters.
- ING Direct finishes 2006 with 4,970,228 accounts, $47.2 billion in deposits, and $62.7 billion in assets.
- Meanwhile, back in Canada, Calgary marks the fourth café opening and a new footprint market; ING Direct surpasses 2 million

customers, and celebrates a unique milestone of its own: $2 billion in interest paid to savers.

2007

January
- ING Direct becomes a national television advertiser for the first time.
- The 5 millionth account is opened.

March
- Miami joins the list of ING Direct footprint markets with a party to remember.

April
- A major milestone is achieved: ING Direct now has 5 million customers.
- The tenth anniversary of ING Direct is celebrated in Canada, where it all began. The occasion is celebrated in Toronto and attended by representatives from ING Direct operations from around the world.

May
- Miami hosts ING Direct's first "Savings Summit," a conference about saving money offered free to consumers, and hundreds attend.

June
- Orange for Business is launched, bringing the power of saving ING Direct style to businesses and organizations.
- A stylish new café is opened in Chicago.
- Another Independence Ride roars to life, raising money for America's kids.

July
- The Orange Mortgage celebrates its milestone of $1 billion in mortgages funded.
- The 6 millionth account is opened.

August
- Seattle, Washington, and Houston, Texas, become the newest footprint markets for ING Direct.
- Orange Days of Giving are inaugurated.

September
- ING Direct acquires the deposit customers of failing NetBank, adding $1.5 billion to its deposit business.

October
- *Kiplinger's* names Electric Orange "Best Checking Account" in the United States.

November
- ING Direct acquires Seattle-based ShareBuilder, an innovative online brokerage, and along with it $2.1 billion in assets under management.
- The 7 millionth account is opened.

December
- ING Direct finishes 2007 with 7,389,792 accounts, $62.1 billion in deposits, and $80 billion in assets in the United States. ING Direct in Canada marks 10 years of growth with a total of 2,312,715 accounts, $20.9 billion in deposits, and $24.3 billion in assets. In just a decade, ING Direct has become one of the biggest and most influential retail financial services brands in North America.

Appendix B

The Voice of Advocacy

ING Direct's leadership took responsibility for its brand at an almost personal level, using it to create the culture that created the enterprise. Ironically, this would place special importance on how ING Direct talked to its public, too. Advertising could not just sell. It had to advocate; it had to convey the personality of a company nobody had heard of or could touch; and it had to be a mirror for the people who worked at ING Direct, reminding them who they are and what they stand for.

This is the first billboard ING Direct ran in Canada when it launched in 1997. Though it relied on few words, its message was pretty clear.

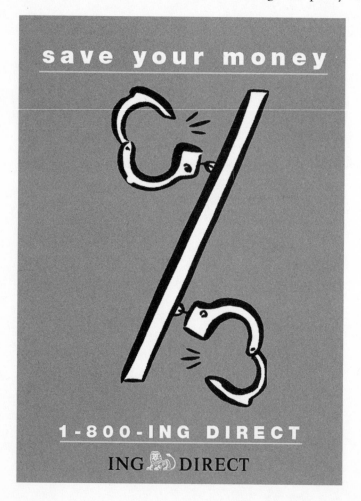

From liberating your money, ING Direct's advocacy message there broadened to deal with the injustices of the savings status quo, like bank fees and the low interest most people earned on deposits at ordinary banks. The savings account isn't dead, ING Direct said. It just needed someone to show some interest in it.

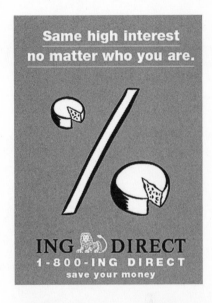

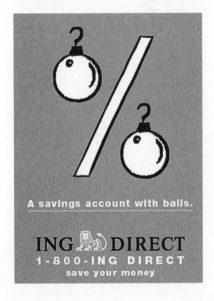

By the time ING Direct came to the United States, its tone was more brash and pointed, but the cause was as clear as ever: Lead Americans back to saving (and empower them with a simple choice in how to do it).

About the Authors

Arkadi Kuhlmann

Arkadi grew up in Toronto, Canada. After graduating from the University of Western Ontario, he stayed and taught at the Richard Ivey School of Business. His career took him from there to the Institute of Canadian Bankers in Montreal, the Royal Bank of Canada in Toronto, and then to New York as the CEO of Deak International, a foreign exchange and precious metals company. A finance professor role took him to the Thunderbird School of Global Management in Phoenix, Arizona. He later returned to Toronto as president of North American Trust, then a troubled retail bank. It was in Toronto that he met Bruce Philp and started the ING Direct journey in 1996. Arkadi is married and resides in Wilmington, Delaware, with sons Marcus and Conrad. His older children, Monika and Eric, work and live in Phoenix, Arizona. Arkadi's passions include sailing, painting, cycling, and yes, riding his Harley-Davidson motorcycle.

Photo by Bob McClain

The press has called Arkadi the "Bad Boy of Banking," but there's more to this style of leadership than being a rebel. In a cause-driven organization, just as on two wheels, leadership means independent-mindedness, guts, and absolute conviction. It also means that, when it comes to building a team, a leader needs loyalty to the cause as much as he needs an assembly of skills. A leader's image communicates expectations to his people, and somehow even becomes part of the brand they serve.

Bruce Philp

Bruce was born near Chicago, Illinois, and grew up in rural southern Ontario, Canada. A career in branding spanning nearly 30 years has seen him in creative and strategic roles at multinational advertising agencies and consumer products companies representing some of the world's most famous and loved brands. He is chairman and a working consultant at GWP Brand Engineering, the firm he co-founded in 1996, the same year he met Arkadi Kuhlmann and the ING Direct story began. Bruce also teaches at the Ontario College of Art & Design (OCAD), and writes regularly for national newspapers and trade journals as well as his blog, BrandCowboy. He divides his time between Toronto and Creemore, Ontario, and shares life with his wife, three children, and a horse named William.

Photo by Stephan Potopnyk

Consultants learn from their passions, too. Whether you're team building or brand building, no amount of force, incentive, or cleverness will ever truly be effective. It will always be about what you do, not what you say, and about the trust that transparency and consistency build over time, one experience after another. Like Bruce's 1,000-pound friend here, people ultimately have good memories, keen instincts, and the absolute power to change their minds.

Index

A

Accessibility, 118
Accountability, 64
Aceto, Peter, 54
Achievement, 26–27
Advertising, 59, 69–86, 114–115,
    235–239
  authenticity, 84
  banks, 35
  first ING Direct slogan, 44–45
  importance of consistency, 176
  and leadership, 85–86
  mistakes, 174
  television, 44, 159–160, 175–176
  what makes it good, 80–82
Advocacy, 9, 40, 42, 44, 46, 47, 83,
    235–239
AKTV, 126
Alt-A mortgage, 157
AmEX, 40
ATMs, 33
Authenticity, 29, 84, 85, 129
Awareness, 169
  brand, 80

  strategic, 183
  unaided, 159–162

B

Balance, 215
Bank of Montreal, 40, 43–44
Bankruptcy Reform Act of 2005, 122
Banks and banking:
  advertising, 35
  Canadian system, 31–32
  challenge in developing new
      system, 93
  customers, 32
  and innovation, 90–91
  Internet, 9, 43
  new business model, 87–103
  as oligopoly, 35
  telephone, 33, 43
  virtual, 33
Basis points (bps), 191–192
Belief system, 76–77
Benefits, 41
Bernbach, Bill, 61
Betrayal, 23

Bike Patrol, 106
Billboards, 114–115, 236
Bonding, 64–65
Bone, John, 56, 89–90
Boredom, 195–196
Brands and branding, 2, 3
    banks, 32
    as belief system, 76–77
    building, 17–18, 42–43, 58, 72, 176
    erosion of, 155
    extension, 166
    and GWP Brand Engineering, 60
    GWP's ideas for ING Direct, 71–72
    ING Direct's philosophy, 6–7
    internal (See Corporate culture)
    and leadership, 8, 85, 130, 144, 236
    as marketing tool, 151
    reasons for changing, 177
    sins that can mean failure, 194–201
    value, 47–48
    and vision, 164
Brossard, Johanne, 52–53
Brown bag lunches, 137
Business:
    as a cause, 10
    spiritual approach to, 21, 92
    strategy, 183
Business model:
    disruptive, 41
    new for financial services, 87–103
    revolutionizing, 100–103
Business plan, 34, 39

C
Cafés, 43, 114, 126, 128
Call center, 16–17, 33, 45, 115,
    116–119
Calling. See Mission
Canada:
    banking system, 31–32
Canadian Business magazine, 156
Canadian Imperial Bank of Commerce
    (CIBC), 43
Canadian Posse, 50

Canadian Tire, 37
Cash flow, 93
Cause, collective, 65
Certificates of deposit, 190
Change, 148–149, 213–215
Channels, 192
Chaos, 167, 170
Character, 25, 63
Charitable activities, 119–121
Checking accounts, 126, 160–163
Chicago, 114
Children, 121
Citizens Bank, 40, 44
Cognitive dissonance, 144
Collective cause, 65
Common good, 10
Communication, 137–138, 176
Community involvement, 119–121
Competence, 63
Competencies, core, 34, 64
Competition, 24, 43–44, 72, 200,
    219–220
Compound interest, 105
Compromise, strategic, 157
Confidence, 26, 42, 152, 176–177
Conflict, 173
Connectedness, 28
Conscience, 151
Consensus management, 52
Consistency, 176
Consumers:
    and advertising, 59
    advocacy for, 40, 44, 46
    and marketing, 81
    relationship with banks, 5
    research, 34–35, 92
Conversations, 116–119, 138
Cops 'n Kids Reading Room, 119, 120
Core business driver, 42
Core competencies, 34, 64, 95, 139
Corporate citizenship, 119–121
Corporate culture, 125–145
Costco, 37
Cost-income ratio, 193

Costs, operating, 37
Creative destruction, 28–29, 220
Credibility, 37–38
Credit cards, 162
Credit rating, 148
Crisis, 28, 29
Crisis of confidence, 152
Cross-selling, 155
Cultural memory, 187
Culture:
    ING Direct, 23, 64–65, 194, 195
Culture, corporate. *See* Corporate
    culture
Customers, 32, 87–88
    and advertising, 80
    advocacy for, 40, 83
    and brand, 31
    building relationships with, 59
    and Canadian banks, 31–32
    complaints of, 161
    confidence, 42–43
    conversations with, 114, 115,
        116–119
    creating value for, 94
    expectations of, 98–99
    firing, 96–98
    improving banking experience
        of, 38
    listening to, 215
    and marketing, 81
    needs, 204
    as partners, 102–103
    researching, 34–35
    satisfaction, 100
    treatment of, 219
Customer service, 33, 93
Cynicism, 138–139

D
Debit cards, 33, 162
Decision making, 52, 64, 199
Declaration of Independence, 47
de Groot, Frederik, 82–83
Democracy, 52

Derksen, Bert, 160, 164
Destruction, creative, 28–29
Differentiation, 35, 36
DIRECT Values, 132
Dirty Dozen, The, 50
Disequilibrium, 29
Docking, 136–137
Doing good, 21, 92, 119–121, 131,
    136, 193–194
Drive, 25

E
Electric Orange, 126, 161–163
Electronic processing, 38
Empathy, 118, 137
Employees, 139–143
    annual events, 65
    communication with, 137–138
    early years of ING Direct,
        52–58
    motivating, 125–145
    needs of, 204
    new, 194–195
    recruitment, 96
    turnover, 212–213
Empowerment, 121, 184
Enemy, 21–24, 219–220
Enterprise, purpose–driven, 62
Entropy, 201

F
Failure, 27–30, 132
Fairbanks, Shannon, 180
Fairness, 211–212
Fees, bank, 92, 117, 151, 161,
    188–190, 211
Financial services:
    business model, 87–103
    lack of differences among, 35
First impressions, 113–115
Focus groups, 35–36, 147
Fort Orange, 179, 182
Frost, Robert, 66
Future, confidence in, 120–121

G

Garneau, Philippe, 60–61, 70, 215
General counsel, 54
George, Bob, 126
Giving back, 20
"Good Morning Associates," 126, 137
Goodwill, 203
GRASP, 132
Greed, 150–151, 165–166
Guts, 19–20
GWP Brand Engineering, 58
    beginning of, 3, 60
    first meeting with ING Direct, 3–7,
        69–79
    ideas for ING Direct's brand, 71–72
    relationship with ING Direct,
        59–61
    and serendipity, 171–172

H

Hamburger Doctrine, 97
Harryvan, Dick, 69, 75, 78–79
Hawaii, 126
Hawthorne Effect, 127
Hegstad, Kjel, 56
Herding techniques, 185–205
Heroes, 65–67
High-interest savings account, 16,
    41, 107
Home Depot, 37
Honoring Emancipated Youth
    initiative, 120
Housing, 121
Hugh, Tom, 209
Human resources, 56–57, 128–129,
    139–143
Humility, 29

I

IKEA, 37
Imparato, Carolyn, 210–211
Impatience, 196–197
Independence Rides, 51, 120
Inertia, 35

Information, 169, 197–199
    and vision, 164
Information technology (IT), 38–39,
    42, 139, 216
ING Direct:
    advertising, 44–45, 73, 82–84,
        114–115, 236–239
    beginning of, 1–11
    Bike Patrol, 106–107
    brand, 130
    building leadership team, 50
    business model, 191–192
    business plan, 34, 39
    cafés, 43, 114, 128
    call center, 16–17, 45, 115, 116–119
    challenges faced with mortgages,
        152–154
    charitable activities, 119–121
    in Chicago, 114
    competition, 43–44
    concept as banking revolution,
        87–103
    and conflict, 173
    conversations with customers,
        116–119
    core competencies, 95, 139
    cover story in *Canadian Business*
        magazine, 156–157
    critics of, 111–112
    developing internal culture,
        125–145
    early days, 33–34
    fifth anniversary, 135
    first anniversary, 65–67
    first meeting with GWP Brand
        Engineering, 3–7, 69–79
    focus group research, 35–36
    general counsel, 54
    governance of, 178–180
    human resources, 56–57
    importance of motivating
        leadership, 15
    Independence Ride, 51, 120
    information technology (IT), 38–39

introduction of checking accounts,
160–163
Kids Foundation, 120, 121
leadership, 13–30
leadership's responsibility for
brand, 236
marketing in U.S., 17–18
mergers and acquisitions team,
180–181
mission, 210–211
mission statement, 47–48
mortgages and loans, 147–166, 218
and mutual funds, 157–158
operational mission, 94
in Philadelphia, 114
posse, 52–58
problems in Canada, 158–162
reaching out, 113–115
relationship with GWP Brand
Engineering, 59–61
as retail business, 95–96
role of marketing, 34
role of serendipity in finding
directors, 179–180
sense of purpose, 46–48, 129–130
slogan, 44–45, 83
SmartSell, 165
statistics, 9
temptations that can lead to failure,
187–194
time line, 223–234
in United States, 13–14, 50
Inner circle, 24–27
Innovation, 90–91, 94, 149, 215
Integrity, 10, 138
enemies of, 186–187
Intentions, 188
Interest, 105, 161
Interest income margin, 193
Interest rate, 40, 45, 93, 105,
147–148, 200
Orange Savings Account, 112
Interest trace, 175–176
Internal brand. See Corporate culture

Internal branding, 139
Internet, 2, 33
Internet banking, 9, 43
Invention, 216

K

Karma, 202–203
Kelly, Jim, 4, 6, 44, 69, 79, 106, 148,
166, 172, 209
and development of Orange Code,
133–134
as early member of ING team,
25–26, 53
and possibility of failure, 27–28
and trust, 130–131
Kuhlmann, Arkadi, 4, 6
and AKTV, 125–126
and Bankruptcy Reform Act of
2005, 122
conversations with customers,
114, 115
as founding CEO, 50
as leader of ING Direct, 13–30
leadership style, 20
meeting in Amsterdam, 110–111,
156
personal value system, 19–20
relationship with customers,
107–108
role as leader, 110
working in call center, 116–119
Kuhlmann's Law of Brand Value,
47–48
Kurosawa, Akira, 49

L

Leadership, 13–30
and advertising, 82, 85–86
and brand, 8, 130, 144, 151
building a team, 25, 50, 63–67
and business' culture, 64–65
challenges of, 186
and company's purpose, 48
developing, 172–174, 182–183

Leadership (*continued*)
  five fundamental requirements,
      15–30
  and mission, 46–47
  and serendipity, 184
Leadership team, 49–68
Legacy, 65
Lending products, 147
Lichter, Sebastian "Bas," 147
Listening, 215
Literacy, financial, 121
Loans, 93, 102, 147–166
Long-term thinking, 202
Los Angeles, 142
Loyalty, 22, 26, 27, 85
Lugar, Scott, 143

M
Maas, Cees, 57
Management:
  by consensus, 52
  and serendipity, 167–184
Managers:
  developing, 182–183
  professional, 186–187
ManuLife, 40
Margins, 190–191, 192
Marketing, 35, 42, 56, 111, 139, 196–197
  and brand, 151
  difference from selling, 165
  high-interest savings accounts, 41
  importance to ING Direct, 34
  main function of, 176
  and Orange Code, 207–208
  two lies of, 58–59
  what makes it good, 81
  working with IT team, 216
Market value, 217
Marlboro Friday, 1–2
Mason, John, 55–56
Mbanx, 40, 44
Memory, cultural, 187
Mission, 10, 16–19, 46–47, 210–211
  operational, 94

Mission statement, 46, 47–48
Moral authority, 14, 24
Mortgages, 117, 143, 147–166
  advertising campaign, 160
  ING Direct's challenges in
      developing, 152
  interest deductibility, 122
  selling direct, 150, 218
  subprime crisis, 121–122
  time commitments to, 190–191
  U. S. market, 180–181
Motivation, 25, 125–145
Mutual funds, 157–158, 159–160
Myres, Brian, 56
Mythmaking, 65, 135, 137

N
Needs, 193
Netbank, 40
North American Life, 23
NZI Insurance, 23

O
Oligopoly, 35
On-demand savings accounts, 190
Online banking, 9
Opportunism, 154, 155
Optimism, 196
Orange, 72
Orange Code, 130, 132–133, 172
  company values and orientation, 68
  development of, 133–136
  important business lessons linked to,
      187–188
  introduction to new employees, 142
  and marketing, 207–208
  original, 9–11
  spirit of, 193–194
  tour of, 207–221
Orange Days of Giving, 136
Orange Journey, 136, 220–221
Orange Mortgage, 218
Orange Savings Account, 112, 113,
      175–176

Organizational integrity, 186–187
Orientation class, 141–142
Outreach, 113–115
Owens, John, 56

P
Pace, 28
Peet's Coffee, 171, 177–178
Perception, 37, 42
Perles, Rick, 56–57, 128–129
Personalization, 19–21
Pets.com, 79
Philadelphia, 114
Philip Morris, 1–2
Philp, Bruce, 58, 61, 62, 70, 215
Pieterse, Jurie, 56
Pixie dust, 31–48
Positioning, 36, 38
Posse, 51–52, 59, 65
Pragmatists, corporate, 23
Pressure, psychological, 24
Pricing, 40, 200
Pride, 39–40
Productivity, 38
Product managers, 160
Profit, 95, 98, 191–192, 216
Psychological pressure, 24
Purpose, sense of, 8, 10, 31–48, 52,
        129–130, 162, 170
    and leaders, 14–15
Purpose-driven enterprise, 62

Q
Quality, 95

R
Real Estate Settlement Procedures
        Act, 122
Recession, 2–3
Relevance, 28, 174
Renewal, 220–221
Reputation, 86
Research, consumer, 34–35
Resiliency, 8

Resistance, 170
Respect, 130, 138, 219–220
Responsiveness, 118
Retail business, 37, 94, 95–96, 100, 141
Revolution, 83–84, 87–103
Risk, 148–149, 153, 182, 187
"Road Less Traveled," 66–67
Rose, Margaret, 140
Rowley, Shaun, 114
Royal Bank of Canada, 23, 43
Rueda, Marie, 55

S
Sanchez, Mike, 170–171
Sandler, Todd, 56
Savers, 105–123
    defending, 121–123
    who they are, 108
Savings
    confidence in the future, 120–121
    high-interest accounts, 16, 41, 107
    as one part of ING Direct, 188–189
    time commitments to, 190–191
Savings bank, 9
Security First Network Bank, 40
Self-empowerment, 121
Selling, 165
Serendipity, 75, 167–184
Service charges, 92, 151, 161, 188–190
Shareholders, 23, 204
Short-term thinking, 202
Simplification, 18, 94, 115–116, 215
Slogan, 44–45, 83
Sock puppet, 79
St. Cloud, MN, 56
Staffing. See Employees
Standardization, 38, 95
Starting over, 101–102
Start-ups, 150, 196
Status quo, 22, 23–24
Stewart, Deneen, 54
Storytelling, 137
Strategic awareness, 183–184
Strategic compromise, 157